Playing Companies and Commerce in Shakespeare's Time examines the nature of commercial relations among the theatre companies in London during the time of Shakespeare. Roslyn Knutson argues that the companies cooperated in the adoption of business practices that would enable the theatrical enterprise to flourish. Suggesting the guild as a model of economic cooperation, Knutson considers the networks of fellowship among players, the marketing strategies of the repertory, and company relationships with playwrights and members of the book trade. The book challenges two entrenched views about theatrical commerce: that companies engaged in cut-throat rivalry to drive one another out of business, and that companies based business decisions on the personal and professional quarrels of the players and dramatists with whom they worked. This important contribution to theatre history will be of interest to scholars as well as historians.

ROSLYN KNUTSON is Professor of English at the University of Arkansas at Little Rock. She has published in *Shakespeare Quarterly, English Literary Renaissance, Theatre Research International, Shakespeare Survey,* and *Medieval and Renaissance Drama in England* and is the author of *The Repertory of Shakespeare's Company, 1594–1613* (1991).

PLAYING COMPANIES AND COMMERCE IN SHAKESPEARE'S TIME

by

ROSLYN LANDER KNUTSON

CAMBRIDGE
UNIVERSITY PRESS

PUBLISHED BY THE PRESS SYNDICATE OF THE UNIVERSITY OF CAMBRIDGE
The Pitt Building, Trumpington Street, Cambridge, United Kingdom

CAMBRIDGE UNIVERSITY PRESS
The Edinburgh Building, Cambridge CB2 2RU, UK
40 West 20th Street, New York, NY 10011–4211, USA
10 Stamford Road, Oakleigh, Melbourne 3166, Australia
Ruiz de Alarcón 13, 28014 Madrid, Spain
Dock House, The Waterfront, Cape Town 8001, South Africa

http://www.cambridge.org

First published 2001

Printed in the United Kingdom at the University Press, Cambridge

Typeset in Baskerville 11/12.5pt   System 3b2   [CE]

A catalogue record for this book is available from the British Library

Library of Congress Cataloging in Publication data
Knutson, Roslyn Lander, 1939–
Playing companies and commerce in Shakespeare's time / Roslyn Lander Knutson.
p.   cm.
Includes bibliographical references and index.
ISBN 0 521 77242 7
1. Shakespeare, William, 1564–1616 – Stage history – To 1625.
2. Shakespeare, William, 1564–1616 – Stage history – England – London.
3. Theatrical companies – England – London – History – 16th century.
4. Theatrical companies – England – London – History – 17th century.
5. Theater – England – London – History – 16th century.
6. Theater – England – London – History – 17th century.
7. Theater – Economic aspects – England – London.
8. London (England) – Commerce.   I. Title.
PR3095.K59   2001
792.9'5'0942109031 – dc21   00–067441

ISBN 0 521 77242 7 hardback

In Memoriam:
For my sister, Sheffield
  Beloved rival of my watch
  Daily, deeply missed

Contents

vii

Map

Tables

Acknowledgements

I want to thank members of the seminars in theatre history at meetings of the Shakespeare Association of America, who have encouraged and challenged my scholarship over the years; I owe them a far greater debt than my bibliography suggests. Also, friends in the SAA beyond the immediate circle of theatre historians allowed me to believe that the subject of commerce among the playing companies might be of general interest. A longer version of chapter five was published in 1995 by *Shakespeare Quarterly* under the title "Falconer to the Little Eyases," and I thank the journal for permission to use that argument again, as well as editor Barbara Mowat and readers Paul Werstine and David Bevington for helping me make the argument coherent. A longer version of the argument on style in chapter four appears in *Studies in Philology* in 2001 as "*Histrio-Mastix*: Not by John Marston," and I thank Alan Dessen for his advice as reader, as well as editor E. D. Kennedy for permission to use it again. My readers for Cambridge University Press, Richard Dutton and William Ingram, provided valuable suggestions at every stage of this project; indeed, by their ready electronic availability, they have been my virtual officemates. The weakest parts of my argument are a result of my not asking their opinion or willfully disregarding it.

I also want to thank the many institutions and librarians who have facilitated my research. Major among these are the Folger Shakespeare Library and Laetitia Yeandle, Curator of Manuscripts. The Family History Library at the Little Rock branch of the Church of Jesus Christ of Latter Day Saints was the first site where I was able to practice what Laetitia taught me about reading Elizabethan documents, and I appreciate all the help given me there. I am also indebted to the Guildhall Library, the Public Record Office, and Duke Humphrey Library of the Bodleian. Here, in citing original documents, I expand scribal contractions in italics unless I am citing a transcription already in print. Year in and year out, the Interlibrary Loan department at the University of Arkansas at Little Rock and the library faculty have enabled me to do much of this research without having to travel more than I could afford.

Friends at UALR – colleagues and students – have added to my pleasure in doing this work by their interest and help. Byrd Gibbens let me talk out much of this while we walked. The late Andy Covington found travel money for me where none existed. Craig Parker checked parts of the manuscript and documentation for errors; Jack Jackson created the illustrative map of London parishes and playhouses. This map is based on one of London produced by the Institute of Heraldic and Genealogical Studies, 79–82 Northgate, Canterbury, Kent, CTI IBA, from their series of genealogical aids, which includes *The Phillimore Atlas and Index of Parish Registers*; it is reproduced (with modifications) by kind permission of C. R. Humphery-Smith and the Trustees of the Institute. The cover illustration is a drawing by C. Walter Hodges; I am indebted to the Shakespeare Centre Library for permission to use it.

My family gives me space, time, and understanding when I need it most. These gifts and more I always received from my sister without having to ask.

CHAPTER I

Theatre history as personality

Be not scurrulous in conue*r*sation nor Satiricall in thy iest*es*,
thone will make thee vnwelcome to all company,
thother pull on quarrells & gett thee hatred of thy best freinds,
for Sulphrous iest*es* when they savour too much of truth
leave a bytternes in the myndes of those that be toucht.
A Jacobean Commonplace Book[1]

John Alleyn, an innholder and stage player, who might have been best known even in his own day as the brother of the stage player, Edward Alleyn, deposed in a 1589–90 lawsuit in the Court of Chancery on behalf of Margaret Brayne, widow of John Brayne, a financier of the Theatre and brother-in-law of James Burbage, against whom the suit was filed. Alleyn was one of four deponents who answered interrogatories for both parties. Speaking to the widow's questions on 6 February 1592, Alleyn acknowledged knowing that the suit concerned the division of profits from the playhouse and contiguous buildings and that an arbitration had formerly been sought. Alleyn did not know details of the payments related to the arbitrated award, but he had witnessed encounters on divers occasions when the widow and an ally, Robert Myles, came to the Theatre to claim the Braynes' share. On one occasion in particular, Alleyn arrived just after Richard Burbage had chased them away with a broomstick. According to Alleyn, James Burbage bragged that he feared no retaliation from Myles and the widow because "my sones/ yf they wilbe Rueled by me/ shall at ther next comi*n*g provyde charged Pistolles w^t powder and hempsede/ to shoote them in the legg*es*."[2] Alleyn claimed that he appealed to Burbage to "haue A conscience in the matter" and pay his widowed sister-in-law her due, to which Burbage answered, "hang her ho^r . . . she getteth nothing here/ lett her wyn it at the Com*m*en lawe/ and bring the Shiref w^t her to put her in possession."[3]

Alleyn deposed further that eight days after the broomstick episode he asked Burbage for the money that had been withheld from him and his fellow players, money due them for performances at the Theatre. When Burbage refused payment, Alleyn chided him "that belike he ment to deale w^t them/ as he did w^t the po^r wydowe" and that, if he did, Alleyn "wold compleyne to ther lorde & M^r the lord Admyrall"; Burbage "in A Rage" countered "that he cared not for iij of the best lord*es* of them all."[4] Deposing for the Burbage faction three months later (6 May 1592), Alleyn stood by his account of the broomstick episode; further, he refused to confirm the charge invited by the phrasing of the Burbage interrogatories that he had reported Myles's threat to "pull the defend^{tes} Burbag*es*" out of the Theatre "by the eares."[5] Alleyn added three key details to the matter before the court: that James Burbage had paid Henry Laneman half the profits of the Theatre in exchange for half the profits of the nearby Curtain playhouse; that Burbage had disparaged Alleyn's lord and lords generally "in the Attyring housse/ or place where the players make them readye . . . in the hearing of one James Tunstall . . . and others"; and that Burbage's boasts following the broomstick episode had happened "about A yere past."[6]

In 1913 Charles W. Wallace, who found the interrogatories in the Chancery lawsuit and collated them in *The First London Theatre* with already published materials, deduced solely on the basis of the angry exchange between John Alleyn and James Burbage that Alleyn's "interference" in the confrontation between Margaret Brayne and the Burbages "led to the withdrawal of the Admiral's company from the Theatre."[7] Wallace deduced further that Tunstall and the rest of the Admiral's Men, when they heard Alleyn request their pay and receive nothing but verbal abuse, left the Theatre to rejoin Alleyn at Philip Henslowe's Rose playhouse (which Wallace believed Alleyn had leased when he left the Burbages at the Theatre). By commenting subsequently that "the Burbages and the Alleyns belonged to rival companies" after the incident at the Theatre, Wallace implied a link between personal quarrels (the Alleyn-Burbage encounter at the Theatre in 1590) and commerce (the Admiral's Men versus the Chamberlain's Men, 1594–1603).[8] E. K. Chambers, in *The Elizabethan Stage* (1923), and W. W. Greg, in *Dramatic Documents from the Elizabethan Playhouses* (1931), accepted Wallace's inference of polarized relations between the Alleyns and the Burbages. Robert B. Sharpe was therefore in the mainstream in 1935 when he constructed a narrative of commercial rivalry on the hypothesis of a "bitter personal enmity between the Burbadges and the Alleyns and their violent quarrel at the Theatre in 1591."[9] In a recent commentary on playhouse commerce, Andrew Gurr does not mention the feud but accepts its corollary that "between 1594 and 1600 . . . only two companies were competing for the London playgoing crowds"; he describes business between the Admiral's Men and the Chamberlain's Men as a "settled rivalry at opposite ends of the City."[10]

The narrative of an Alleyn-Burbage feud might have been new in 1913, but the telling of theatre history by way of personal quarrels was not. It was at least as old as the conversations in 1619 between Ben Jonson and William Drummond of Hawthornden. Jonson, in addition to taking pot-shots at fellow poets such as the jibe that Shakespeare "wanted Arte," told Drummond at least one story germane to issues of theatrical rivalry: that "he had many quarrells with Marston beat him & took his Pistol from him, wrote his Poetaster on him the beginning of y^m were that Marston represented him jn the stage."[11] These conversations did not become public until 1711, when *The Works of William Drummond of Hawthornden* appeared in print. Already, however, the perception of Jonson as choleric had influenced literary criticism. The complementary pairing in Thomas Fuller's *Worthies* of Jonson, the Spanish galleon, in contests of wit with Shakespeare, the English man-of-war, as well as the measured comparison in John Dryden's "Essay on Dramatic Poesy" (1668), were supplanted by Dryden himself in "Discourse Concerning the Original and Progress of Satire" (1693). There he criticized Jonson's poem, "To the Memory of my Beloved, the Author Mr. William Shakespeare," which appeared among the dedicatory verses in the First Folio in 1623. Dryden called the poem an "An Insolent, Sparing, and Invidious Panegyrick," and he labeled Jonson *"the worst-Natur'd Muse"* for offering the "most God-like Commendation" of Shakespeare-the-personality while denying that praise to Shakespeare-the-playwright.

In "Some Account of the Life, &c. of Mr. William Shakespear," the biographical essay accompanying an edition of Shakespeare's plays in 1709, Nicholas Rowe added to the impression that Jonson was jealous by telling a story of his ingratitude. According to Rowe, Jonson took a play to the Chamberlain's Men, some of whom "turn'd it carelessly and superciliously over," and were to reject it "with an ill-natur'd Answer" when *"Shakespear* luckily cast his Eye upon it, and found something so well in it as to engage him first to read it through, and afterwards to recommend Mr. *Johnson* and his Writings to the Publick."[12] Rowe, observing that afterward the two men "were profess'd Friends," implied that Jonson might not have given Shakespeare "an equal return of Gentleness and Sincerity" for the good turn of recommending his playscript.[13] Rowe's tone, which disparaged Jonson and praised Shakespeare, was perpetuated in the commentary that accompanied editions of Shakespeare's works at the end of the eighteenth century.

By 1808 Jonson's supporters had had enough. In *An Examination of the Charges Maintained by Messrs. Malone, Chalmers, and Others of Ben Jonson's Enmity, etc. towards Shakspeare*, Octavius Gilchrist railed at Shakespeare's recent editors, George Steevens in particular, claiming that the "fair fame" of Jonson had "been blackened, his memory traduced, and his writings perverted, for the unworthy purpose of raising a rival poet [Shakespeare] on the ruins of his reputation."[14] In 1816 William Gifford replaced Gilchrist as Jonson's apologist. In *The Works of Ben Jonson*, in an essay called "Proofs of Ben Jonson's Malignity, From the Commentators on Shakspeare," Gifford insisted that the relations between Jonson and Shakespeare had been all sweetness and light: "It is my fixed persuasion . . . that Jonson never received either patronage, favour, or assistance of any kind from Shakspeare. I am further persuaded that they were friends and associates till the latter finally retired – that no feud, no jealousy ever disturbed their connection – that Shakspeare was pleased with Jonson, and that Jonson loved and admired Shakspeare."[15] In an accompanying biography, "Memoirs of Ben Jonson," Gifford absolved Jonson and blamed everything on his critics: "Having gratuitously supposed a quarrel, the next step is to make it up."[16]

Gifford blamed not only Shakespeare's editors for maligning Jonson but also a group of Jonson's fellow playwrights. In the biographical essay that accompanied his edition of the plays ("Memoirs of Ben Jonson"), Gifford claimed that John Marston and Thomas Dekker "viewed his success with peculiar mortification, and . . . lent themselves to the cabal already raised against him."[17] Dekker had been charged with enmity toward Jonson for some time, but the naming of Marston was new. The charge against Dekker was that he resented being satirized in the figure of Crispinus in *Poetaster* and retaliated in *Satiromastix* by mocking Jonson in the character of Horace (Jonson's admiring self-portrait in *Poetaster*). The resulting face-off, *Satiromastix* vs. *Poetaster*, took the name of "Poetomachia," a term coined by Dekker to describe the wits-combat in an address "To the World" published with the quarto of *Satiromastix* in 1602. In *An Account of the English Dramatick Poets* (1691), Gerard Langbaine dismissed Dekker and his play with a shrug of critical disdain, declaring that they "were no ways comparable" to Jonson and his.[18] However Gifford, perhaps influenced by Jonson's remarks about Marston in the Drummond conversations (information unavailable to Langbaine), named Marston as the butt of Jonson's scorn in the character of Crispinus. In a note on *Poetaster*, Gifford exclaimed enthusiastically "that the CRISPINUS of Jonson is MARSTON" and "Decker. . . the Demetrius of the present play."[19]

Gifford failed to convince Shakespeareans of Jonson's innocence, but he succeeded in promoting a scholarly industry based on satirical pointings in the plays of 1599–1601 that came to be called the "War of the Theatres," or "Stage Quarrel." Dr. Robert Cartwright, in an 1864 essay that otherwise pitted Jonson against Shakespeare, found characters in *Cynthia's Revels* that satirized Marston, Dekker, John Lyly, and Shakespeare.[20] Richard Simpson opened a new line of research in 1878 when he proclaimed in *The School of Shakspere* that Marston was part-author of *Histrio-Mastix*.[21] Scholars rushed to detail the dramatists' rivalry by way of additional satirical pointings both in dramatic and non-dramatic literature. Josiah H. Penniman took the phrase, "War of the Theatres," as the title of his monograph in 1897, which used material developed by F. G. Fleay in *A Chronicle History of the London Stage* (1890) and *A Biographical Chronicle of the English Drama* (1891). Coincident with Penniman's work, James T. Foard published "The Dramatic Dissentions of Jonson, Marston, and Dekker" in *The Manchester Quarterly* (1897). Building on Penniman, Roscoe A. Small published *The Stage Quarrel Between Ben Jonson and the So-Called Poetasters* (1899). Fleay thus spoke for his generation by calling the War of the Theatres the defining event in the history of relations among the Elizabethan companies: "any criticism of any play bearing as date of production one of the three years 1599 to 1601 which does not take account of this, for the time, stage-absorbing matter must be imperfect and of small utility."[22]

Fleay, by characterizing the War of the Theatres as "stage-absorbing matter," invited scholars to assume that quarrels among dramatists had commercial ramifications, specifically, an equivalency in quarrels among the playhouses. Small asserted the complicity of company commerce in professional quarrels explicitly by claiming that the rivalry among the dramatists "and the theatrical companies represented by them must necessarily have grown very strong, and given rise to many petty feuds."[23] In *The Elizabethan Stage*, E. K. Chambers declared that the War of the Theatres was an issue "for literature and biography," yet he did not reject the concept of company rivalry in which personality was treated as theatre history.[24] In *The Real War of the Theaters* (1935), R. B. Sharpe merged the players' and dramatists' quarrels into an explicit theory of commerce; appropriating Penniman's title and Wallace's feud among players, he constructed an argument about commercial rancor between companies and playhouses: the Admiral's Men at the Rose and Fortune vs. the Chamberlain's Men at the Theatre and Globe. In *Shakespeare and the Rival Traditions* (1952), Alfred Harbage transformed Sharpe's war between the two men's companies into a class war between the public and private playhouses. Harbage identified the rival companies as "the 'common players' with their repertories, and the 'little eyases' who cried out on top of question," that is, the men's companies versus the boys'.[25] There, in effect, the perception of playhouse commerce rests: typified in 1594–1599 as a rivalry between the Admiral's and Chamberlain's Men and in 1599–1603 (or 1609) as a rivalry between the men's and boys' companies.

In making the argument for the Admiral's Men vs. the Chamberlain's Men, Sharpe gave the competition a political spin. He argued that playhouse rivalry mirrored the rivalry of the two powerful factions in Elizabethan politics, the Cecil party (Admiral's Men) and Essex party (Chamberlain's Men); for, as he noted, the men's companies "were of course in politics, whether they wished to be or not; they were attached to the persons of the great place-holding nobles."[26] The ways in which government and patronage affected the business relationships among companies has received more attention in recent years. In *The Business of Playing* (1992) William Ingram notes the influence of a decree in 1550 by the Court of Aldermen that prohibited players without a license from playing in London; according to Ingram, this decree hastened not only the affiliation of players into companies with a patron but also the disappearance of "loose and informal associations of players in the City of London."[27] It seems also to have led some players to think of their business in terms more specifically managerial. As Ingram puts it: "The licensing regulations and the increased governmental assertion of control impelled the players . . . to take into their own hands . . . the terms and circumstances under which they played."[28] For some players, as Ingram shows, one such circumstance was the erection of buildings to be used exclusively for playing. Another, as I argue in subsequent chapters, was the development of a business protocol and repertory practices that enabled individual companies to flourish and the industry itself to expand. The model for these relationships, as I also argue, was the guild.

Several recent studies have explored the ways in which specific politicians and patrons affected the formation and success of individual companies. In *The Queen's Men and their Plays* (1998), Scott McMillin and Sally-Beth MacLean consider the role of Sir Francis Walsingham in the creation of the Queen's Men in 1583 and the circumstances of their playing. McMillin and MacLean see Walsingham as having had two basic intentions for the Queen's Men: they were to travel, and thus "carry the name and influence of the monarch through the country"; and they were to perform plays that promoted Walsingham's agenda of moderate Protestantism and Tudor allegiance.[29] As a politically protected company, as well as explicitly the Queen's Men, the company had significant advantages commercially: the players received rewards for performances in the provinces that were "double or triple the amount usually given to visiting troupes";[30] also they were guaranteed performances at Court (eleven of fourteen performances by adult professional companies, winter 1583 – spring 1586). Otherwise, the Queen's Men were on their own to develop strategies by which their company might flourish. As McMillin and MacLean tell the story, their decisions were successful for a while. Perhaps their most important repertorial decision was to take the mandate of presenting Tudor history and turn it into the English history play. This strategy proved to be commercially sound as long as the presentation in the plays of the "substantial truth and plain speech" of history was a novelty to audiences,[31] but the Queen's Men did not foresee that their dramaturgical style would soon look old-fashioned and that a new generation of dramatists would work magic with blank verse and characterization. Perhaps their most important decision about location was to continue being primarily a touring company. Initially, too, this was smart, for the company split up and multiplied its profits. But by the 1590s other companies were established in

London in their own playhouses where they attracted crowds six and seven days a week without paying for horses, a wagon, and lodging for twelve men and some boys.

Andrew Gurr and Richard Dutton consider the influence in the 1590s of the Privy Council and a pair of its members who were also the patrons of players. In *The Shakespearian Playing Companies* (1996), Gurr describes the years of 1583–1594 as ones of cooperation between Charles Howard, briefly Lord Chamberlain and later Lord Admiral and Earl of Nottingham, and Henry Carey, Lord Hunsdon and Howard's father-in-law as well as his successor as Lord Chamberlain. After 1592–3 when plague disrupted playing, Hunsdon, by then Lord Chamberlain, thought it was "essential to set up a new regime with strong companies."[32] His model was the monopoly of the Queen's Men established by Walsingham, and the result was a duopoly of the Admiral's Men and Chamberlain's Men, who divided up the best players and settled comfortably across town from one another. And, according to Gurr, this arrangement was understood by the respective companies who "knew themselves to be based in London as part of the government's policy, with accompanying privileges."[33] Dutton, extending an argument in his *Mastering the Revels* (1991), considers the pivotal order of 22 June 1600 by the Privy Council in the licensing and control of playing companies. In that order the Privy Council allowed "two howses and noe more" to be used for stage playing,[34] specifying their addresses in Middlesex and Surrey. In this allowance, the order named the servants of the Lord Admiral and the Lord Chamberlain as the authorized companies; it further specified that "the two howses allowed maie play each of them in there seuerall howse twice a weeke and noe oftener."[35] In Dutton's opinion, this order "reinforced the prerogatives of the status quo," that is, it reinforced the Privy Council's endorsement of the cartel, or duopoly, established by the lords Howard and Hunsdon in 1594.[36]

And yet, as Dutton himself observes, the order of 22 June 1600 – clear and categorical though it was – did not prevent the expansion of the playhouse industry. The Curtain was in business after 1600, as it had been since 1576. The Swan, built in 1595, might have been closed in 1598, but William Ingram finds "no clear evidence" that it was and some evidence that Francis Langley, owner of the playhouse, "was not yet finished as an entrepreneur at the Swan."[37] The Boar's Head was built in 1598 and expanded in 1599; Herbert Berry determines that it served alternately as the London venue for Derby's Men (1599 to 1601, 1602 to 1603) and Worcester's/Queen Anne's Men (1601 to 1602, 1603 to 1605 or 1606). The boys' playhouses were arguably exempt from the Privy Council's order; nonetheless, their business contributed to the spread of the theatrical industry: the playhouse at Paul's opened in 1599; Blackfriars opened in 1600. And more playhouses were to come, including the Red Bull and Whitefriars. Neither did the June 1600 order stop the lord mayor and aldermen from complaining about "the great abuse and disorder within and about the Cittie of London by reason of the multitude of Playhowses,"[38] as they did some time before 31 December 1601, as they had for years, and as they were to continue to do. Neither did the order succeed in limiting the days of playing to two. In fact, regulations by the Privy Council and apparent favoritism by powerful lords seem to have had no more effect in the 1590s than had the lord mayors' and aldermen's regulations on "the continuing expansion and prosperity of the enterprise" in the 1550s and 1560s.[39]

Scholars interested in a "material theatre" have directed attention to the Elizabethan marketplace, in both its real and metaphoric senses, as a stimulant in the economic success of the playhouses. For Steven Mullaney the theatrical industry succeeded in that market by "dislocating itself from the strict confines of the existing social order and taking up a place on the margins" of civic, governmental, and economic life in London; outside the City, the companies could develop "a new and ideologically mobile drama" that, presumably, might subvert political hegemonies but draw in customers (*The Place of the Stage*, 1988).[40] Paul Yachnin modifies this argument by claiming that the players won "a privileged, profitable, and powerless marginality" and appealed "to a large and heterogeneous audience" by promoting the idea that drama, as play, was "separate from real life . . . [and therefore] separate from power" (*Stage-Wrights*, 1997).[41] Douglas Bruster takes a less political and more sociological approach to the theatrical marketplace by pursuing the thesis that "[p]roviding dramatic commodities for public consumption, the Renaissance theater functioned as an institutionalized, profitable market" (*Drama and the Market in the Age of Shakespeare*, 1992).[42]

By perceiving theatres as markets and plays as commodities, scholars loosen the hold on playhouse competition of the tightly scripted narrative about quarreling dramatists. In the following chapters, I separate further the commercial policies of the companies from the personal or ideological quarrels of players and poets. I argue in chapter two that commerce among the playing companies was built on patterns of fraternity, the roots of which were feudal hierarchies such as kinship, service, and the guild. In doing so, I build on Ingram's observation that there was a transition of companies from loosely organized groups of common players to relatively stable companies under the banner of a lord, a transition that (I suggest) coincided with a shift from troupes with discrete economic existences to companies with a shared commercial agenda. Governmental pressures might have actually, if unintentionally, facilitated the economic cooperation of the companies. By a combination of sanctions and limitations, various political powers – e. g., lords, Privy Council, aldermen, lord mayor, Bishop of London – defined a space wherein the companies could do as they pleased commercially. That the companies quickly recognized this safe zone is suggested in the response of the Corporation of London to the Queen's Men's petition in November 1584. The Queen's Men asked the Privy Council for permission, now that winter was coming on, to play in the City; the Corporation objected, giving as one reason that the toleration granted the previous year had been abused, and "all the places of playeing were filled with men calling themselues the Quenes players."[43] Viewed from this angle, the protection given one company in 1583, and two companies in 1594, made it possible for all companies to operate within limits somewhat protected from the collective disapproval of civic officials and churchmen.

Also, the official expectation that the Queen's Men would travel appears significant to several developments in company business. For one, touring was further institutionalized as normal commerce. Scholars in the Records of Early English Drama project (REED) have found by mapping the provincial visits of companies that touring was neither an act of economic desperation nor the refuge of bad companies. Companies traveled, even after playhouses were built in London; thus, when those playhouses were closed, the companies had a familiar and routine business practice to fall back on. For another, the continued habit of touring meant that there was some fluidity in the London theatrical marketplace. The Admiral's Men might have had an exclusive lease at the Rose and Fortune, and the Chamberlain's Men at the Theatre and Globe, but companies came and went at the Swan, Curtain, and Boar's Head. New versions of old companies opened at the playhouses at Paul's and Blackfriars, reclaiming many from their former clientele and attracting *nouveaux* gallants. To Gurr, the stability of two companies in settled rivalry looks like a commercial duopoly, but to the London playgoer the runs of different companies at stages around London might have given the marketplace a variety and vitality that profited every organization. A necessary feature of that variety was the company repertory. As more companies had extended runs at London playhouses, they needed a diverse battery of offerings continuously supplied with new plays to attract playgoers. In chapter three I explore the contributions of playwrights, repertory offerings, and the market for plays in print to a company's business and its commercial relations with other companies.

Tucca, the braggart captain in *Satiromastix*, makes explicit the companies' competitive repertorial strategy in the epilogue when he asks the audience to applaud the play and thus prod Jonson into a retaliatory sequel. For the most part, however, scholars have heard only bravado in Tucca's invitation. Their perception has been reinforced by the belief that satirical pointing is the most significant commercial feature of *Satiromastix* and *Poetaster*. Similarly, a confidence that the "little eyases" passage belonged to the "essential" Shakespearean *Hamlet* in 1600 has stifled consideration of an interpretation less dependent on a rivalry between the men's and boys' playhouses. Further, if Marston wrote part or all of *Histrio-Mastix*, it must also be that the antagonism of Jonson and Marston absorbed the commercial energy of the playhouse industry for three years or more. In chapter four, I argue that *Histrio-Mastix* had no significant role in any commerce stemming from a Jonson-Marston quarrel because it was not written by Marston and not played at a commercial playhouse at any time including 1599. In chapter five, I argue that the "little eyases" passage of *Hamlet*, traditionally credited with articulating the commercial anxiety of Shakespeare and the Chamberlain's Men at the reopening of Paul's or Blackfriars, belongs not to 1600–1 but to 1606 (or thereabouts); it therefore articulates Shakespeare's company's fear that the willfulness of the Children of Blackfriars to satirize well-connected noblemen could bring about prolonged, even permanent, playhouse closures. In chapter six, I consider *Poetaster* and *Satiromastix* as companion offerings that promoted the business of playing in similar ways. By removing these four plays as evidence of a cut-throat rivalry among the companies, I open discussion to alternative strategies of competition such as imitation and cooperation.

Instead of focusing on quarreling dramatists, I turn attention to the behavior of companies and theatrical entrepreneurs who faced, on the one hand, a political environment that imposed limitations on their business but, on the other, a customer base that encouraged expansion. From the viewpoint of the company, I evaluate the engagement of playwrights, acquisition of diverse repertories, and a targeted use of the book trade as commercial strategies. By situating plays such as *Histrio-Mastix, Poetaster,* and *Satiromastix* in a broader theatrical environment than personal and professional anger, and by reassigning the "little eyases" passage in *Hamlet* to different date and theatrical agenda from that of the reopening of the boys' playhouses in 1599–1600, I expose the assumptions that led nineteenth-century scholars to construct a model of commerce for the playing companies based on the personalities of players and dramatists. Setting aside the construct of theatrical wars, I explore relationships among companies that indicate a commercial predisposition toward cooperation grounded in the patterns of hierarchy and fraternity in the patronage and guild systems.

But first I would like to be more specific about why I find a theory of commerce based on personalities, often called the War of the Theatres or Stage Quarrel, unsatisfactory both as theatre history and narrative. Its primary weakness for me as theatre history is exclusivity. The story of quarreling dramatists calls attention to the commerce generated by three companies, three playhouses, and seven plays to explain the dynamics of competition, 1599–1601: *Every Man Out of his Humour* and *Hamlet* in the repertory of the Chamberlain's Men at the Globe; *Histrio-Mastix, Jack Drum's Entertainment,* and *What You Will* in the repertory of the Children of Paul's at Paul's; and *Cynthia's Revels* and *Poetaster* in the repertory of the Children of the Chapel at Blackfriars. Yet more companies, playhouses, and repertories were involved in the commercial life of the Elizabethan theatre than these. According to Herbert Berry in *The Boar's Head Playhouse* (1986), at least three companies played at the Boar's Head from 1598 to 1616. The company that launched the playhouse in 1598 was successful enough to encourage the investors to renovate it completely, and Derby's Men and Worcester's Men played there from 1599–1602. In 1600 there was a flashy new playhouse, the Fortune, in Golding Lane in Middlesex. The purchases of playtexts and playing gear in the diary kept by Philip Henslowe testify to the viability of the Fortune as a commercial entity, and the return of Edward Alleyn to the stage in revivals of Christopher Marlowe's plays (among others) testifies to its ability to draw an audience. As S. P. Cerasano observes, the Fortune "was a chief contributor to Henslowe and Alleyn's wealth."[44] Also, the Curtain playhouse was certainly in business during this time, and the Swan in use occasionally, as illustrated by Richard Vennar's venue for his promised "England's Joy."[45] The Curtain, sanctioned by the Privy Council in May 1601 for political satire, was nonetheless authorized along with the Globe and Fortune in April 1604. John Underwood, a player with the King's Men, owned shares not only in the Globe and Blackfriars when he died in 1624 but also in the Curtain, and the inference is that the building was still worth something.

In addition to providing only a partial map of London playhouse enterprises, the narrative of theatrical wars gives a one-sided view of touring. Three plays in the Matter of the War of the Theatres have references to touring companies: Sir Oliver Owlet's Men in *Histrio-Mastix*, the Elsinore company in *Hamlet* (with the accompanying "little eyases" passage), and the allusion in *Poetaster* to the players' song from *Histrio-Mastix*. All three depict touring as the desperate act of failing companies. However, touring was a significant aspect of company life, profitable in more ways than gate receipts. As McMillin and MacLean have established, touring was part of the charge of the Queen's Men from their inception. Their political connections in the 1580s neutralized powerful critics at a time when companies were beginning to recognize the commercial potential of such aspects of London business as a large repertory. And, even though they did not make one of the London playhouses their home, they were a factor in commerce among the companies in the 1590s. Their repertory continued to participate in the popularity of theatrical genres such as the chronicle play, at bookstalls if not on stage, as evidenced by the publication in 1598 of *James IV* and *The Famous Victories of Henry V*. As the new data in REED volumes on the experience of provincial troupes and London companies make clear, even companies located primarily in London spent considerable time on the road. And, contrary to old opinion, provincial towns welcomed the players more frequently than they sent them away. J. A. B. Somerset finds that companies on tour had "3,119 successful visits out of a total of 3,279 records, giving an actual success rate of

95.12 per cent" during the years of Shakespeare's lifetime, 1563/4 – 1616/17.[46]

The War of the Theatres focuses on four dramatists: Jonson, Marston, Dekker, and Shakespeare. It does not include men in other categories whose theatrical motives were less likely to be ideological and literary. One such group was playhouse investors. Philip Henslowe was a playhouse investor and entrepreneur as well as banker and manager of a playing company. Despised for the wrong reasons by John Payne Collier's generation of theatre historians, he has been rehabilitated by Bernard Beckerman, who argued that Henslowe was a relatively benign participant in company business.[47] Francis Langley *was* a bad theatrical entrepreneur, in that he managed the Swan very poorly. But he believed that playhouses were money-makers when he built the Swan in the summer of 1595, and he had not lost that faith when he became an investor in November 1599 in the Boar's Head enterprise started by Oliver Woodliffe and Richard Samwell.[48] Henry Evans also knew what a successful playhouse venture might bring when he leased Blackfriars from Richard Burbage in 1600, or he should have, for he had led a boys' company there previously. Burbage, like his father before him, was immersed in playhouse commerce at many levels. As player, sharer, house-holder, and playhouse landlord, he provides a broader perspective on the influence of individuals in company commerce than do dramatists and their quarrels. Other players similarly were entrepreneurs or expected to be: Edward Alleyn at the Rose and Fortune, Robert Browne at the Boar's Head, and Christopher Beeston at the Red Bull and Cockpit.

Five plays associated with the War of the Theatres were published in quarto within a year or two of their stage runs: *Every Man Out of his Humour* (1600), *Jack Drum's Entertainment* (1601), *Cynthia's Revels* (1601), *Poetaster* (1602), and *Satiromastix* (1602). The proximity of the registrations at Stationers' Hall of *Satiromastix* (S. R. 11 November 1601) and *Poetaster* (S. R. 21 December 1601) might suggest that the playwrights or companies sought publication in order to extend the life of the wits-combat after the plays themselves were retired from the stage. The fact that Dekker advertised the Poetomachia in the address, "To the World," published with the 1602 quarto of *Satiromastix* is evidence that he wanted readers on his side; the fact that Jonson hinted at the Apologetical Dialogue even though he was unable to publish it with *Poetaster* in 1602 suggests that he had the same motive. However, from the perspective of company commerce, the two periods of significant trade with stationers were 1593–4 and 1600–1. Peter W. M. Blayney notes that twenty-seven plays were registered at Stationers' Hall during each of these periods, [49] and, while advertising was a common denominator in both events, dramatists' quarrels were not. Also concerning texts and publication, the War of the Theatres calls attention to the "little eyases" passage in the folio *Hamlet*, but it excludes the one about "the humour of children" in the quarto published in 1603. Due to recent scholarship on texts, particularly that on "bad" quartos, discussions of company commerce need to consider the kinds of texts that might become available, the reasons why a company might sell and a stationer might buy playtexts, and the effect that the publication of its offerings might have had on a company's commerce.

The War of the Theatres, by focusing on playwrights and their quarrels, does not encourage inquiry into the politics of company commerce. It does not take into account the Privy Council, which might order playhouses to be torn down, or plays to be taken off the stage, or certain companies to be authorized, or the number of days of playing per week to be limited. It does not include performances at Court such as those in the winter of 1600–1 when two companies shared the date of 1 January (Children of Paul's and Derby's Men) and four companies shared the date of 6 January (the Chamberlain's Men, Admiral's Men, Derby's Men, and Children of the Chapel). Further, the Stage Quarrel puts great emphasis on the personal barbs exchanged by Jonson, Marston, and Dekker; however, political satire was potentially the more serious threat to company commerce. The plays by Jonson, Marston, and Dekker in 1599–1601 did not attract the attention of the Privy Council, but a play shown at the Curtain in 1601 did. On 10 May, the Privy Council advised the justices of Middlesex that a company of players at the Curtain were satirizing "some gentlemen of good desert and quallity"; councilors instructed the justices to "forbidd" the playing of such a play, to interrogate the dramatist, and, if the judges found the play as objectionable as rumored, to bring their leader before the Council to account for the company's "rashe and indiscreete dealing."[50] Jonson faced some sort of injunction when he tried to publish the Apologetical Dialogue with the quarto of *Poetaster* in 1602, but he was not jeopardizing the business at Blackfriars. The risk in satirical pointing was in presenting prominent figures; for, as Richard Dutton points

out, even complimentary political impersonations "might be par-
tisan."[51] An example of an apparently safe representation of current
notables is the play described by Rowland Whyte in a letter to Sir
Robert Sidney dated 26 October 1599. According to Whyte, in a
play called "The Overthrow of Turnholt," the dramatist used
characters from the historical event, with costumes to identify the
participants: Sir Frances Vere was presented by "a Beard resembling
his, and a Watchet Sattin Doublett, with Hose trimd with Siluer
Lace"; Sir Robert was presented by "Killing, Slaying, and Over-
throwing the *Spaniards.*"[52] But a year or two later that same play or
one representing the same politicians might have created a firestorm,
for Sir Francis Vere and Sir Robert Sidney were supporters of the
Earl of Essex. The Chamberlain's Men found out the peril of an
association with that circle in February 1601 when they agreed to a
command performance of *Richard II.*

As a way of telling theatre history, the narrative of the War of the
Theatres evokes the narratological innocence of Samuel Johnson,
who mused that the historian "has no other labour than of gathering
what tradition pours down before him, or records treasure for his
use."[53] Johnson opined that the writing of history must be a simple
task, "for what should make him that knows the whole order and
progress of an affair unable to relate it?"[54] Hayden White finds the
construction of historical narrative more complex. In "The Value of
Narrativity in the Representation of Reality," he examines alternative forms of writing history in order to study "the cultural
function of narrativizing discourse."[55] Curious about what historical
reality would "look like" if configured in a non-narrative form such
as annals, White observes that the emphasis on a chronology and a
principle of selectivity remain, but the "history proper" (his term for
the Johnsonian historical narrative) loses its moral structure, or
"order of meaning." [56] Some theatre historians have experimented
with the annals form for certain kinds of information: J. P. Collier
designated a section of *The History of English Dramatic Poetry* (1837) as
an "Annals of the Stage," and F. G. Fleay made lists of court
performances, outbreaks of plague, and bad weather. The narrative
of the War of the Theatres, however, does not lend itself to a
reconfiguration as annals, and the reasons why suggest additional
limitations of that story-complex as a representation of historical
reality.

Annals require a fixed chronology of occurrences; in the narrative of the War of the Theatres, events are ordered in different sequences, depending on which scholar is telling the story. The chronological relationship of *Histrio-Mastix* and *Every Man Out of his Humour* is an example. In the announcement that John Marston had written certain inflammatory passages in an old play called *Histrio-Mastix*, Richard Simpson dated *Histrio-Mastix* by way of *Every Man Out of his Humour*, which he believed contained allusions to Marston's additions. He settled on a time before Christmas of 1599 for the debut of *Histrio-Mastix*, because he thought that to be the date of the stage run of Jonson's play.[57] F. G. Fleay and R. A. Small moved the debut of *Histrio-Mastix* to August or September 1599, virtually coincident with the debut of *Every Man Out of his Humour* (which they thought to be September 1599).[58] In "John Marston's *Histrio-Mastix* as an Inns of Court Play," Philip J. Finkelpearl moved the debut of *Histrio-Mastix* back to Christmas 1598–9 to accommodate the venue of Middle Temple. James P. Bednarz resists Finkelpearl's solution, arguing that *Histrio-Mastix* appeared after *Every Man Out of his Humour* and that Jonson added Clove's belittling allusion in fustian-speak to *Histrio-Mastix* when *Every Man Out of his Humour* was already in performance.[59]

Perhaps a greater problem for a compiler of annals than the variable chronology of the War of the Theatres is the high incidence of undatable occurrences. It is not clear when the beating occurred that Jonson claimed in conversations with William Drummond to have given Marston. It is not clear when the three-year period began that Jonson claimed in the Apologetical Dialogue to be the provocation for his satire against poetasters ("three yeers/ . . . On euery stage," ll. 96–98). If the period concluded with his writing of *Poetaster* in midsummer 1601 (if, indeed, he started the play that late), the provocation must have occurred in mid-1598. But only Finkelpearl's date of Christmas 1598 as the debut of *Histrio-Mastix* comes close. Also undatable are the putative exchanges of satirical pointings between plays. It cannot be proved that *Satiromastix* immediately followed *Poetaster* to the stage, but the proximity of their registration at Stationers' Hall makes such a claim plausible. In comparison, the alleged sparring between *Cynthia's Revels* and *What You Will* is entirely dependent on conjectural dates for the respective stage runs. *Cynthia's Revels* can be dated by its registration at Stationers' Hall and subsequent publication in 1601, but *What You Will* was not published until 1607 and the title page of its quarto gives no information on its theatrical venue. It is also impossible to determine when annals of the War of the Theatres should end. The selection of events might continue into 1602 (the publication of *Satiromastix* and *Poetaster*), or 1605 (the collaboration of Jonson and Marston with George Chapman on *Eastward Ho!*), or 1606 (the publication of *The Second Part of the Return from Parnassus*), or 1610 (the publication of *Histrio-Mastix*), or 1616 (the publication of the Apologetical Dialogue in Jonson's *Works*), or 1619 (Jonson's conversations with Drummond). R. A. Small's annals-like "Chronological Table of Literary Works and Identifications" in the appendix to *The Stage Quarrel* is even longer; it begins with entries in 1590–2 and terminates, after a stupefying list of nearly sixty entries, with Jonson's *Staple of News* in 1625.

Annals of the War of the Theatres would be stripped of essential features such as character and motive unless the names of Jonson, Marston, Dekker, and Shakespeare were included. But the names alone are inadequate. The narrative needs to include the personality, literary style, and theatrical ideology of the dramatists, for the significance of each battle depends on the opinions they supposedly had of one another and their eagerness to parade those opinions on the stage.[60] Jonson left enough evidence of his vanity, jealousy, and violent encounters to support stories based on personal grievance. But John Marston, who quarreled in print with Joseph Hall, left no evidence of a quarrel with dramatists beyond that fashioned by scholars from interpretations of his canonical and attributed play-texts. When Marston spoke openly and publicly of Jonson, as in the dedication of *The Malcontent*, he was all praise and friendship. Likewise Thomas Dekker left nothing of his opinions of fellow dramatists except the withering portrait of Horace-Jonson in *Satiromastix*.

The difficulties of the War of the Theatres as a representation of reality and as sufficient context for company commerce in Shakespeare's time come together in assumptions about audiences. Alfred Harbage, like scholars before and after him, believed that the children's companies drew off the better class of playgoers, who had formerly patronized the men's houses. However, Ann Jennalie Cook argues that after the opening of the boys' playhouses, "gentlemen continued to attend both kinds of troupes and playhouses."[61] The play-scraps in the commonplace book of Edward Pudsey identify at least one gentleman who did. Pudsey copied quotations from plays performed at the Globe, the Rose or Fortune, Paul's, and Blackfriars.

By any measure, audience taste is difficult to verify, being not necessarily as tied to class as scholars of a former time liked to assume. Even if fuller repertory lists and more scripts from the boys' companies survived, scholars would argue over the appeal in this or that play. Also an issue of audiences is the frequency of performances at the men's and boys' playhouses. If the Privy Council order of 22 June 1600 was enforced, the men's companies were limited to two performances a week; however, there is no evidence that this part of the order was observed. The boys' companies, in contrast, gave fewer performances in smaller playhouses for a shorter season (from Michaelmas into Trinity Term).[62] Under these conditions, even with higher prices, the boys' companies did not represent a sustained financial challenge to the men.

Hayden White, musing on the principles of selection and privilege in the annals form, observes that the "absence of any consciousness of a social center . . . prohibits the annalist from ranking the events he treats as elements of a historical field of occurrence."[63] The narrative of the War of the Theatres, in contrast, is a closed field of privileged occurrences. Initiates know to include the intertextualities of *Cynthia's Revels* at Blackfriars and *What You Will* at Paul's but to exclude the competition for patronage implied by the plays named "Oldcastle" in the repertories of the Admiral's Men and Chamberlain's Men, 1599–1600.[64] They know to include the debut of Jonson's *Poetaster* at Blackfriars but not the revival of *The Spanish Tragedy* at the Fortune, with additions by Jonson for which he was paid by the Admiral's Men in September 1601 and June 1602. They know to exclude companies, playhouses, dramatists, and players tagged as second-rate, whatever their contribution to the commercial dynamics of the London theatre. They know to include epigrams by Everard Guilpin in *Skialetheia* (1598); they know to exclude the epigrams in William Rankins's *Seauen Satyres* (1598), Thomas Bastard's *Chrestoleros* (1598), and Samuel Rowlands's *The Letting of Humours Blood in the Head-Vaine* (1600). They know to exclude *Dyets Dry Dinner* (1599) by Henry Buttes because it does not address the issue of the poet's role as defined by academic humanism or carry epigrams lampooning poet-apes; yet one subject of Buttes's treatise – tobacco – is frequently satirized in the plays of 1599–1603, particularly those by Jonson and Marston.

To Samuel Johnson, the historical narrative was not a site for invention; the historian had simply "to employ all his powers in arranging and displaying . . . [the] materials . . . provided and put into his hands."[65] The materials of company commerce in the eighteenth and nineteenth centuries were displayed as a cult of personality: a worship of William Shakespeare and everything made golden by his touch, balanced by a contempt for Ben Jonson and everything poisoned by his spleen. But company business was a larger enterprise than the temperament of its practitioners. As John Alleyn's interrogatories reveal, there were incidents of conflict, yet the business of playing continued. The guild offers a model for commerce among similarly skilled entrepreneurs who occasionally needed internal regulation but always needed a hospitable public environment for their craft or trade. Never sufficiently organized to form such an alliance in fact, the companies nevertheless developed commercial relations that gave them some of its benefits. Operating within the limits defined by various governmental pressures, the companies developed protocols and marketing strategies by which their industry might expand and prosper. Players learned strategies of cooperation from the networks of patronage in which they had grown up. They learned strategies of growth and productivity from the guild structures where newly authorized members were absorbed into the commercial life of the profession. They shared the need to market their skills against competing recreations such as bear-baiting and games of hazard. They shared the need to minimize the effect of common enemies such as the plague, civic authorities, and anti-theatrical clergymen. In a political environment where an innocuous passage in one play might be taken on a Tuesday as welcome praise of an adored public figure and on a Saturday as treason, they shared the need to exercise as much control as possible over long-established protocols of pointing at topical events and persons. In short, the companies stood to gain much from cooperation and little from rivalry.

CHAPTER 2

Players and company commerce

True men can differ vigorously and be friends.

Henry Morley[1]

According to Charles W. Wallace in *The First London Theatre* (1913), John Alleyn and the Admiral's Men left the Theatre for the Rose in November 1590 because of a quarrel over money owed to Alleyn and his company by James Burbage. Wallace's evidence was Alleyn's depositions in the lawsuit, in which Alleyn testified to an angry exchange between himself and Burbage about the playhouse receipts. Wallace implied that this quarrel became a commercial rivalry between the Admiral's Men and the Chamberlain's Men.[2] The alleged Alleyn-Burbage feud was soon regarded as fact. W. W. Greg in *Dramatic Documents from the Elizabethan Playhouses* (1931) explained the provenance of playhouse documents by way of it,[3] and R. B. Sharpe in *The Real War of the Theaters* (1935) based a theory of commerce on it. Current narratives of company histories continue to show residual effects of the belief that a players' feud became company rivalry. In *The Shakespearian Playing Companies* (1996) Andrew Gurr, who elsewhere argues for the cooperation of the Lord Admiral and the Lord Chamberlain in the establishment of their respective companies in 1594, depicts the Admiral's Men as losing "no time in moving" to the Fortune when the Chamberlain's Men moved into the Globe, across the street from the Rose; he adds that Philip Henslowe brought the company of Worcester's Men into the Rose "as a reprisal of sorts, putting it in direct competition with its new rivals and neighbours at the Globe."[4]

For the Alleyns and Burbages, the most familiar model of commerce was the guild. John Alleyn was for a time an innholder, like his father before him; James Burbage initially earned a living as a joiner. Scholars have known for a long time that many playhouse investors and stage players had their commercial origins in the guilds, but it has taken the research of theatre historians such as Herbert Berry, S. P. Cerasano, Mark Eccles, and William Ingram to suggest that this business environment was significant to the entrepreneurial endeavors of members of the playhouse world.[5] One such entrepreneur was Francis Langley, owner of the Swan playhouse in 1594. Langley entered a life of business apprenticed to a draper; as a youth in the London home of his uncle John, Francis witnessed a family version of the Great Twelve Companies, in that his uncle was a goldsmith, his aunt's brothers were a clothworker and a grocer, and his brother was apprenticed to a haberdasher.[6] Another entrepreneur, John Brayne, grocer, applied his business acumen to the construction of the Red Lion playhouse in 1567; not sufficiently discouraged by the collapse of this venture, he accepted the offer of his brother-in-law (Burbage, the joiner) to collaborate in the building of the Theatre and profit-taking from it.[7] Another, Philip Henslowe, a dyer, turned his business skills to the construction and operation of the Rose playhouse. And yet another, Oliver Woodliffe, a haberdasher, put together the partnership that resulted in the construction of the Boar's Head playhouse in 1598.[8]

A list of players who were freemen of their respective guilds would include not only John Alleyn (innholder) and James Burbage (joiner) but also Robert Armin, goldsmith; Andrew Cane, goldsmith; Thomas Downton, vintner; John and Lawrence Dutton, weavers; Thomas Goodale, mercer; John Heminges, grocer; Ben Jonson, bricklayer; John Shanks, weaver; Martin Slater, ironmonger; Richard Tarlton, vintner; and James Tunstall, sadler.[9] This list, though incomplete, illustrates both the variety of guilds represented by players and the ubiquity of freemen in the men's companies from the 1570s to the 1590s when commercial relationships among the London-based companies were being developed. The company affiliations of these men include Warwick's Men, 1575, the Duttons; Oxford's Men, 1580, the Duttons; Queen's Men, 1583, the Duttons and Tarlton; Worcester's Men, 1583, Tunstall; Admiral's/ Strange's Men, 1589, Alleyn, Tunstall, and Goodale; Admiral's Men, 1594, Slater and Tunstall; Chamberlain's Men, 1594, Burbage, Heminges, and Armin; Pembroke's Men, 1597, Downton, Jonson, and Shanks; the Queen Anne's Men, 1603, Slater (dates of company affiliation are approximate).

Knowing the background in business of members of the playhouse

world, nineteenth-century scholars might have considered the influence of the guild as players organized themselves into functional
units, secured places to perform, and avoided constraints from the
lord mayor and Privy Council. As a rule, however, they seem to have
been more aware of the lines of power in a hierarchical model that
views the companies vertically, either looking down from the perspective of the patron on the men he has chosen as his players or
looking up from the players to a powerful and attentive patron. A
newer version of this hierarchy seems to lie behind Andrew Gurr's
hypothesis that the Lord Chamberlain and the Lord Admiral
conspired in 1594 to set up a duopoly of companies that would
replace the Queen's Men as the allowed organizations. Gurr,
uncertain whether the players would have "had much say" in the
selection of their fellows, assigns considerable power to the company's patron, whom he sees as having "deliberately left room in his
new grouping" for qualified extras such as Richard Burbage and
William Shakespeare.[10] Paradoxically, nineteenth-century theatre
historians developed a horizontal model for the years between 1594
and 1603 based on scenarios of feuding that produced the Fleay-
Penniman-Small version of the War of the Theatres. This horizontal
model is perpetuated by Sharpe's thesis of war between the Admiral's Men and Chamberlain's Men and by Alfred Harbage's rivalry
between the men's and boys' companies. In the received wisdom
from E. K. Chambers and others, the hierarchical ranking of
companies returns after 1603, when the Chamberlain's (now King's)
Men supposedly triumphed in the alleged War of the Theatres and
all of the companies acquired royal patronage. In this restructuring,
the King's Men occupied the privileged position, the Prince's Men
and Queen Anne's Men took a poor second, the boys' companies
were increasingly marginalized, and the rest of the men's companies
fought for place at the bottom.

As a commercial paradigm, the guild does not preclude hierarchical lines of power between a company and its patron; indeed, the
guild is itself a hierarchical structure. Yet its design offers stability for
the company when beset by misfortunes such as changes in membership, changes in patronage, playhouse closures, and personal quarrels. Although "[i]t is important not to sentimentalize these kin
networks as emblems of preindustrial harmony," as Kathleen
McLuskie and Felicity Dunsworth caution,[11] the model of the guild
invites a collegiality regardless of company affiliation. Indeed,

players might not have recognized the divisions among companies as sharply as have scholars who narrate company histories. Because of their social class and economic history, players who were born into guild families or who took up guild membership would have perceived others in their trade as fellows, inviting friendships across company lines, the union of families through marriage, and executorial care in the disposition of worldly goods. Also, like stationers or butchers or fishmongers, players often lived in neighborhoods associated with their places of business. They would have seen the value of "cluster marketing," that is, the value of having areas where one playhouse could take advantage of the ability of another to attract customers. They would have learned to regulate themselves – their personal disputes, the legitimacy of their membership – in an expansionist economy. It would have been natural in a guild for some members to become wealthier and more powerful than others, and to assert authority thereby, but it would have been unnatural to drive a member out of business unless his behavior became so unruly and intransigent that his continuation in business jeopardized the profession itself.

The names of players in two playhouse documents, plus one set of texts, offer the opportunity to explore the networks of friendship, kinship, and parish residence that form a community larger than the unit of the Elizabethan playing company. The first of the documents, the manuscript Plot of "The secound parte of the Seven Deadly Sins" ("Sins"), was discovered among papers at Dulwich College and published in Edmond Malone's two-volume *Supplement* to the 1778 *Plays of William Shakespeare*, edited by Samuel Johnson and George Steevens.[12] The Plot carries no date or author's name, but it provides the names of twenty players and their parts in its outline of the dramatic action. The second document is a license issued by the Privy Council on 6 May 1593; it authorizes a company of players to tour until such time as the restraints against playing in London during an epidemic of plague are lifted.[13] The texts, which contain names of players associated with Pembroke's Men in 1592–3, are *The Taming of A Shrew, The First Part of the Contention Betwixt the . . . Houses of York and Lancaster* (*1 Contention*), *2 Henry VI* (the First Folio version of *1 Contention*), and *3 Henry VI*.[14] The players' names, coordinated as theatre historians generally agree, are listed in Table 1.

Scott McMillin, focusing on the known company affiliations of players in the cast list of "Sins," finds that ten of the twenty players

Table 1. *Players' names in playhouse documents and texts*

Names in the Plot of "2 Seven Deadly Sins"	Names in the license issued to Strange's Men, May 1593	Names in texts played by Pembroke's Men, 1592–3
1. Mr Brian (George)	1. George Bryan	
2. Mr Phillips (Augustine)	2. Augustine Phillips	
3. Mr Pope (Thomas)	3. Thomas Pope	
4. R Burbag (Richard)		
5. W Sly (William)		5. Slie (William Sly)
6. R Cowley (Richard)		
7. Jo Duke (John)		
8. R Pallant (Robert)		8. Robin (Robert Pallant)
9. J Sincler (John)		9. Sinklo (John Sincler)
10. Th Goodale (Thomas)		10. Tom (Thomas Goodale)
11. J Holland (John)		11. John Holland
12. T. Belt		
13. Harry (Henry Condell)		13. Harry (Henry Condell)
14. Kitt (Christopher Beeston)		
15. Vincent		
16. Saunder (Alexander Cooke)		16. Sander (Alexander Cooke)
17. Nick (Nicholas Tooley?)		17. Nick (Nicholas Tooley?)
18. R Go (Robert Gough)		
19. Ned		
20. Will		20. Will
	21. Edward Alleyn	
	22. William Kempe	
	23. John Heminges	
		24. George (Bevis?)
		25. Humphrey (Jeffes)
		26. Gabriel (Spencer)

named in the Plot were members of the Chamberlain's Men at some time between 1594 and 1601: George Bryan, Augustine Phillips, Thomas Pope, Richard Burbage, William Sly, Richard Cowley, John Duke, Henry Condell, Christopher Beeston, and Thomas Vincent.[15] Judging from the names in the license issued by the Privy Council on 6 May 1593, three of these men – Bryan, Phillips, and Pope – were fellows in Strange's Men with William Kempe, John Heminges, and Edward Alleyn (who identified himself with the Lord Admiral). Another eight players from the Plot plus William Sly – Robert Pallant, John Sincler, Thomas Goodale, John Holland, Henry Condell, Alexander Cooke, Nicholas Tooley, and "Will" – turn up in marginalia and stage directions of the texts associated with Pembroke's Men,

1592–3. McMillin draws the conclusion from this distribution of names across the documents that an unusually large company (that which performed "Sins") split into the groups represented by the Pembroke texts and the May 1593 license for Strange's Men.[16]

Whether these men were playing together or were separated by the exigencies of business, their connections over time in families and parish neighborhoods illustrate the fraternal bonds that linked many players. Augustine Phillips, who moved with a cadre of players in the "Sins" company to Strange's Men in 1593 and to the Chamberlain's Men in 1594, is an exemplar. Near death in the spring of 1605, Phillips made a will that specified bequests to a number of his fellows: William Shakespeare, Henry Condell, Richard Cowley, Alexander Cooke, and Nicholas Tooley.[17] He also appointed three of his long-time fellows to be executors of his will: John Heminges, Richard Burbage, and William Sly. These acknowledgements of friendship are not surprising; Phillips played with these men daily for perhaps fifteen years, and he had taken responsibility for actions of company members (as in his having been their witness in examinations resulting from the performance of *Richard II* at the Globe on 7 February 1601). But in addition, by bequests to Robert Armin, who had joined the company around 1600, and Lawrence Fletcher, who had joined in 1603, Phillips's will shows the apparently cordial absorption of new members into a company; the bequests to Armin and Fletcher were as generous as those given by Phillips to his oldest friends.

Further, Phillips included Christopher Beeston among his legatees. Beeston had left the Chamberlain's Men to join Worcester's Men by 1602 (as had John Duke and William Kempe, though the men might not have left together); in 1605 his company had become Queen Anne's Men. Much old scholarship on players implies that changes in affiliation were accompanied by hard feelings, an attitude consistent with an interpretation of commerce among the playing companies as a rivalry based on feuds. Yet there is no evidence to support it. Certainly Beeston himself provided none, nor does Phillips's will. Phillips left Beeston the same bequest – 30 shillings in gold – that he left to Shakespeare and Condell. Evidently, therefore, Phillips remained friends with his former colleague (whom he calls "servaunte" rather than "fellow"), even though by 1605 Beeston as a Worcester's/Queen Anne's Man had played at three playhouses – the Rose, the Curtain, and the Boar's Head – supposedly rival to the

Globe, in which Phillips had invested. Beeston obviously returned Phillips's affection. Long after leaving the fellowship of Phillips's company, he christened a son, Augustine, in the parish of St. Leonard Shoreditch on 16 November 1604. Given the custom of naming children for their godparents, Beeston had probably asked Phillips to be godfather to the infant Augustine.

Phillips also remembered his apprentices in the will. To his former apprentice, Samuel Gilborne, he left 40s., his sword and dagger, a musical instrument (bass viol), and apparel (including "mouse Colloured veluit hose"). To his current apprentice, James Sands, he left 40s. and three instruments ("a Citterne a Bandore and a Lute"). Phillips's care to specify that Sands was not to receive his legacy until he had served the "yeares of his Ind*entur* or Aprenticehood" suggests that players who took apprentices perceived the terms of that contract in the context of the Statute of Artificers of 1573, which regulated apprenticeships in the livery companies.[18] Unlike lists of apprentice bindings for guilds such as the Carpenters, Haberdashers, and Ironmongers, lists of theatrical apprentices have not survived. Fortunately, other documents provide a few pairings. In his will Alexander Cooke asked that his "master hennings" be one of the men to oversee the deposit of funds at Grocers' Hall for his unborn child, thus implying his former position as Heminges's apprentice.[19] Nicholas Tooley bequeathed £29 13s. to Sara Burbage, daughter of his "late Mr Richard Burbadge." From bequests of "wering aparrell and . . . arms" in the will of Thomas Pope to Robert Gough and John Edmonds, it appears that they were formerly Pope's apprentices. In the Sharers Papers (1635), John Shanks claimed to have "supplied . . . [the King's Men] with boys," naming Thomas Pollard, John Thompson, John Honyman, and Thomas Holcome specifically.[20] Cast lists in surviving Plots show that Richard Jones, Edward Dutton, Edward Alleyn, and Thomas Towne had boys.[21] Thomas Downton had a boy for whom he bought a costume for "Cupid and Psyche" (*HD* 135), a "little boy" who played in "Tamar Cham," part one (*HD* 332), and a "biger boy" who witnessed a loan to William Bird and delivered the money to him (*HD* 77, 75).[22] Philip Henslowe also acquired at least one apprentice in December 1597: "Bowght my boye Jeames brystow of william agusten player the . . . for viij[li]" (*HD* 241).

In addition to fellow players and apprentices, Augustine Phillips left bequests to family members. The identities of the legatees illustrate a joining of professional and personal lives that was common among (but not exclusive to) members of guilds. One connection was marriage. Phillips left £10 to his sister, Elizabeth Gough, whose marriage to Robert Gough was entered in the parish register of St. Saviour's, Southwark, on 2 February 1602/3. This Robert Gough, probably the "R Go" who played Aspasia and Philomel in the second and third playlets of "Sins," was therefore a fellow with Phillips in 1592 or earlier. Gough disappears from records of players until 1603 when he is named in the royal patent of the King's Men (19 May), but he probably belonged to Strange's Men in 1593 and the Chamberlain's Men in 1594, as did Thomas Pope, his master (however, another of Pope's apprentices, John Edmonds, resurfaces eventually in Worcester's/Queen Anne's Men). Whatever his company affiliation from 1592 to 1603, Gough, by the marriage to Elizabeth, was tied personally as well as professionally to the Chamberlain's/King's Men.

Another marriage reminiscent of the pattern of spousal choices among guildsmen is that of John Heminges and Rebecca Knell on 10 March 1588. Presumably Rebecca was the widow of William Knell, who joined the Queen's Men in 1583 and was therefore a fellow of Richard Tarlton and the Dutton brothers; on the evidence of the marriage to Knell's widow, theatre historians have posited that Heminges also was a Queen's Man. The Hemingeses lived in the parish of St. Mary Aldermanbury, where Rebecca had married Knell in 1586; christenings and burials of thirteen Heminges children are recorded starting in 1590. Fitting this pattern also is the marriage of Thomas Greene and Susan Browne. Formerly Susan was the wife of Robert Browne, who according to Herbert Berry "owned much of the Boar's Head" and was most likely the leader of Derby's Men.[23] Greene, a member of Worcester's Men, would have met Susan and Robert Browne by 1601 at the latest, when Derby's Men subleased the Boar's Head to Worcester's Men. Browne died of plague in 1603. Greene's marriage to Browne's widow was the predictable result of professional opportunity.

Augustine Phillips's bequest of £10 at their majority to Myles Borne and Phillips Borne, sons of a second sister, Margery Borne, illustrates another connection among players' families: children who were namesakes of their father's professional associates.[24] As in the Bornes' choice of "Phillips" as Christian name, players showed respect and affection for their fellows in naming children. For example, Richard Cowley, a member of the "Sins" company and subsequently the Chamberlain's Men, christened a son "Cuthbert" on 8 May 1597. The fact that Cuthbert Burbage was one witness at Cowley's deathbed in 1618 makes reasonable the assumption that Cuthbert Cowley was Burbage's namesake and godchild. Likewise it seems obvious that Burbage Underwood, son of John Underwood, was so named in acknowledgement of the father's professional association with the Burbage family, initially as a child player in the Children of the Chapel at Blackfriars and subsequently as an adult with the King's Men. The name Rebecca is too common to enable a reliable tracing of fellowships; however, the coincidence of the names of Rebecca Phillips and Rebecca Cooke, given the company affiliations of their fathers, Augustine Phillips and Alexander Cooke, makes it hard not to see the choice as a gesture of respect toward Rebecca Knell Heminges. The name William is certainly too common, yet I cannot resist one connection: William, son of Richard Burbage and his wife, was christened on 7 November 1616, a mere seven months after the death of Burbage's long-time fellow, William Shakespeare.

If the clerk of a parish provided details of christenings, marriages, and burials, his entries in the parish books are likely to specify the professions of the parishioners. This information often also indicates that the businesses of the parishioners lay within the parish. Clerks of St. Leonard Eastcheap, for example, noted that various parishioners were butchers. One burial in 1604 indicates that St. Leonard Eastcheap also had butcher shops: "A poor famished boy seeming to be about 13 y. old was found dead in the hole vnder Robert Clement*es* stall."[25] The registers of St. Gregory by St. Paul, St. Dunstan in the West, and St. Martin Ludgate show the residences of stationers whose shops were in Paul's Cross Churchyard or to the west of Ludgate Hill. Players also lived as neighbors in parishes near playhouses. In essays discussing the diversity and stability of the neighborhoods of the Swan and Globe, William Ingram comes close to drawing a map, lane by lane, of players' residences in the districts of St. Saviour's (the "boroughside" to the east, Paris Garden to the west, and the "Bankside" or Clink Liberty in the center).[26] Here it must suffice merely to enumerate the players who might have been Phillips's neighbors in the years between 1592 and 1603. A number of men either in the "Sins" company, Strange's Men in 1593, or subsequently in the Chamberlain's Men with Phillips lived in Southwark during these years: Alexander Cooke, William Kempe, Robert

Gough, Thomas Pope, and William Sly. Phillips and Sly were literally neighbors in 1593, both living in Horse-shoe Court. The initial draw to the Bankside might have been the location of the Rose; certainly, a number of players in the Admiral's Men lived in St. Saviour's in the 1590s: Edward Alleyn, Richard Alleyn, William Bird, Thomas Downton, Edward Dutton, Anthony Jeffes, Humphrey Jeffes, Richard Jones, Edward Juby, Thomas Marbeck, Robert Shaa, John Singer, Martin Slater, and Thomas Towne. Robert Pallant, who moved from the "Sins" company (where he was a fellow of Phillips) to Pembroke's Men (where he was a fellow of Sly and Humphrey Jeffes) to Worcester's Men (where he was a fellow of Beeston and Duke), was living in St. Saviour's when Worcester's company was playing at the Rose, 1602–3. Thomas Heywood, who sold plays to the Admiral's Men and who wrote part or all of seven plays for Worcester's Men in 1602–3, appears in entries in the register of St. Saviour's, 1600–5.

When the Swan first opened in 1595, two players possibly associated with the Queen's Men lived in the neighborhood: George Attewell and Francis Henslowe (who, like Thomas Pope of the Chamberlain's Men, lived in Francis Langley's "new rents").[27] Four of the players in the list of Admiral's Men – Bird, Downton, Jones, and Shaa – played with Pembroke's Men at the Swan in 1596–7. Jones was already living in St. Saviour's when the playhouse was built; the other men might have moved into the parish at that time, though they do not appear in the register of St. Saviour's until 1600 (Bird) and 1603 (Shaa). There were, in addition, players about whom little is known. The Robert Browne in the register cannot be differentiated from one, maybe two, players of the same name. John Hill (or Hull) may be the player who toured in Germany, 1600–1. Harry Tottnell, whom the clerk called a barber in 1585 and a player in 1591, does not appear elsewhere in theatrical records. Some years later there is an entry in the register of St. Saviour's of the burial of Edmund Shakespeare, a player, for whom someone paid 20s. for a tolling of the great bell in the forenoon (31 December 1607). Like Tottnell, Edmund has not been identified with a company, although he has been given a brother, William. Edmund's residence in the parish, documented only in the termination of that residence in death, is a reminder that these records are a feeble measure of players' personal lives. Even so, they are valuable counterweights to stories of quarrels and the theories of commerce constructed on

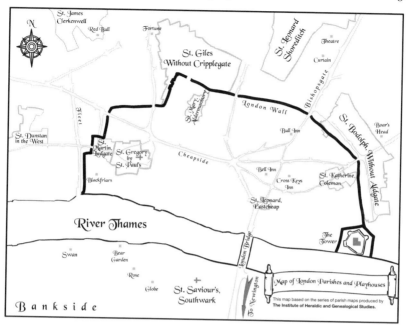

Map of London parishes and playhouses

those quarrels because they suggest that players might have developed a sense of professional community as neighbors regardless of company affiliation.

In 1597, Augustine Phillips lived in Mr. Spynola's rents in the parish of St. Botolph Aldgate for a month or two before moving to Mr. Hammond's rents in September. The records kept by Thomas Harridance, the clerk of St. Botolph Aldgate in the 1590s, show that other players lived in the parish at this time. E. M. Denkinger explained the appeal of the neighborhood: it was convenient to the Theatre and Curtain playhouses as well as to inns such as the Bull, Bell, and Cross Keys, which had been sites for playing since the 1560s; it was immediate to the Boar's Head playhouse built in 1598; and its area of Houndsditch, "tenanted by pawn-brokers and dealers in cast-off clothing, . . . might attract the patronage of indigent players who were called upon to supply their own wardrobes."[28] Whatever Phillips's reason for moving from St. Saviour's in 1596 to St. Botolph Aldgate in 1597, he would have found himself in a neighborhood with several men whom he probably knew from his days as a member of the "Sins" company but who had not gone with him to Strange's Men or the Chamberlain's Men. Chief among these players was James Tunstall.[29] If the "Sins" Plot belongs to 1590–2, Phillips is most likely to have known Tunstall, even played with him, in some configuration of the Admiral's/Strange's Men at that time. Tunstall was certainly playing at the Theatre, 1590–1, when he and other players in the tiring house heard James Burbage refuse to pay John Alleyn for services rendered.

Tunstall moved to the parish of St. Katherine Coleman Street before his death in 1599, but he was buried in the church in St. Botolph Aldgate. Thomas Harridance recorded his age (forty-four years), the fact that he had been "long sick," his burial place "in the new Vault lately made in the Northesyd alley or Ile in the Church," and the acknowledgement of his death by a "knell with the greate bell" in the forenoon.[30] William Ingram fancies that among the bereaved might have been "fellow players William Augustine, Richard Darloe, Thomas Goodale, John Hill, and Robert Lee, all near neighbors of Tunstall's when he lived among them."[31] This collection of players, plus Phillips, plus John Read and Robert Armin (both of whom lived in St. Botolph by 1600), is another instance of players with different company affiliations as neighbors. John Hill might not have had lodgings in St. Botolph Aldgate, but his daughter Isabell was baptised there in November 1595. Harridance phrased the entry of Isabell's christening in such a way as to raise doubt both about the player's residence and the legitimacy of the child's birth: "Isabell Hill dawghter to Ihon Hill a player of Enterlude*es* who is said to be beyond the seas this said Chyld was borne of the bodie of Elizabeth hill als shelton his Reputed wyfe Lyeng at the howse of one henry Cotes a Clothworker."[32] Harridance's uncertainty about the residence of Hill and his whereabouts "beyond the seas" suggests that this John Hill was the same man whose daughter Alyce was christened at St. Saviour's in 1601 and who toured in Germany, 1600–1. The company memberships of Augustine and Read are unknown (Augustine was the player from whom Henslowe bought an apprentice).

Augustine Phillips, James Tunstall, Robert Armin, Thomas Goodale, Richard Darloe, and Robert Lee can be located in London during the 1590s, busily playing in allegedly rival companies. Phillips of the Chamberlain's Men and Tunstall of the Admiral's Men represent Gurr's duopoly. Armin, having come from Chandos's Men, joined Phillips in the Chamberlain's Men around 1600. Goodale, Darloe, and Lee turn up in playhouse records initially in the Plot of "2 Seven Deadly Sins" or "The Dead Man's Fortune." None of the three men can be identified with a specific company while they were living in St. Botolph Aldgate, yet all were active in some organization if Harridance is right in his designation of each in his daybooks as "a player of Enterludes." From 1593 to 1600 Harridance recorded events in the family lives of the three players. Two Goodale children were christened in the parish, and three were buried. During this time, the Goodale family lived in Mr. Gaskins's rents "neare the signe of the flower de Luce in hownsdich."[33] Three Darloe children were christened and buried between 19 September 1595 and 29 August 1602 while the family lived at the southern end of the parish "in garden alley being in the precinct neare the Tower hill."[34] Lee, like Goodale a resident of Gaskins's rents, was married in the parish in 1595; he and his wife christened two children there. Goodale, like Phillips, is named in the Plot of "Sins," but unlike Phillips, Goodale joined the segment of the "Sins" company that became Pembroke's Men and played *The Taming of A Shrew* and *1 Contention*. Darloe and Lee were fellows in a production preserved through the Plot of "The Dead Man's Fortune," which also names Richard Burbage and (apparently) a boy named Sam.[35] Darloe and Lee are therefore linked in theatre history to Phillips and Goodale, and all four are further linked by the provenance of the Plot of "The Dead Man's Fortune" and the Plot of "2 Seven Deadly Sins."

Predictably, because of the location of the Theatre, Curtain, Fortune and Red Bull playhouses in Middlesex, there is evidence of players and their families in the parish registers of St. Leonard Shoreditch, St. James Clerkenwell, and St. Giles Cripplegate. However, unlike the parishes of St. Saviour's and St. Botolph Aldgate, in which players with different company affiliations shared neighborhoods, the player-residents in the Middlesex parishes are more exclusively identified with the companies at the local playhouse (if surviving records give an accurate picture). The primary theatrical family in St. Leonard Shoreditch was the Burbages – James, Richard, and Cuthbert – who lived on Halliwell Street (after 1576) and who did not move to the neighborhood of the Globe when the Theatre, near Halliwell, was dismantled. The parish register shows traces of players whose companies might have performed at the

Theatre before 1593: for example, Richard Tarlton, a member of the Queen's Men, who was buried in the parish in September 1588; and Simon Jewell, who was buried there on 21 August 1592.[36] The Red Bull was built in 1605, and Robert Lee of Queen Anne's Men lived in St. James Clerkenwell in the following years (when his company was playing at the Boar's Head, Lee lived in St. Botolph Aldgate).

The register of St. Leonard Shoreditch after 1594 contains one exception to the rule that players in that neighborhood were by and large members of companies playing at the Theatre and Curtain. The exception is Gabriel Spencer, who was a member of Pembroke's Men (1592–3, 1597) and the Admiral's Men thereafter, until Ben Jonson killed him in a duel in Hogsden Fields on 22 September 1598. The parish record of his burial on the 24th states that Spencer "was slayne."[37] Theatre historians usually gauge the reaction of players to this death by the words of Philip Henslowe, who wrote to his son-in-law, Edward Alleyn, on 26 September with this news: "I haue lost one of my company wch hurteth me greatley that is gabrell for he is slayen in hoges den fylldes by the hands of benge Jonson bricklayer" (*HD* 286). But Spencer was a fellow parishioner of the Burbages, and the Chamberlain's Men were currently playing Jonson's *Every Man In his Humour*. It is reasonable to assume that the Burbages and their players, as well as Henslowe and Alleyn, felt emotional aftershocks from this violent encounter, but neither group held this personal loss against business with Jonson. The Chamberlain's Men followed his *Every Man In his Humour* with his *Every Man Out of his Humour* for their opening season at the Globe in 1599. The Admiral's Men paid Jonson in August and September of 1599 for collaborations on "Page of Plymouth" and "Robert II, King of Scots" and paid him for additions to *The Spanish Tragedy* and "Richard Crookback" in 1601 and 1602.

The Fortune playhouse was built in 1600. The parish register of St. Giles Cripplegate does not show an influx of players as soon as the Fortune opens, but there is a steady increase in subsequent years. Predictably, the player-residents of St. Giles Cripplegate were members of the Admiral's/Prince's Men. The most familiar names in the register in the early 1600s are of players whose names had turned up previously in Henslowe's diary, for example, Thomas Downton, who was a member of Strange's Men in 1593 along with Augustine Phillips, George Bryan, Thomas Pope, and John Heminges.[38] In 1594 Downton joined the Admiral's Men, along with

Edward Alleyn, who had been touring with Strange's Men, and James Tunstall, who probably had. After a shift in company affiliation to Pembroke's Men at the Swan, Downton returned to the Admiral's Men where he became increasingly valuable to the entrepreneurial activities of the company, buying playbooks and authorizing payments for goods and services. While he was playing at the Rose and Swan, Downton lived in St. Saviour's, Southwark, but sometime after July 1601 he moved to St. Giles Cripplegate, where a son was christened on 22 June 1606. Preceding Downton into the parish were Anthony Jeffes and perhaps also Humphrey Jeffes, both specified in Henslowe's book of accounts as members of the Admiral's Men in the list of October 1597 ("the ij geffes," *HD* 84). Anthony, who was born in St. Saviour's in 1578 and married there in 1601, apparently moved immediately to St. Giles, where his first child was christened in June 1602.[39] Humphrey Jeffes's daughter was christened in St. Saviour's in January 1601. Perhaps he, like Anthony, moved immediately thereafter to St. Giles; however, the register of the parish does not indicate his presence until 21 August 1618, at his burial. An exception among these resident members of the Admiral's/Prince's Men is Nicholas Tooley (perhaps the Nick of the Plot of "Sins" and the marginalia of the Pembroke texts), who began his playing career as the apprentice of Richard Burbage. Tooley was buried in St. Giles Cripplegate in June 1623.[40]

In telling the story of commercial relations among companies, many theatre historians have distrusted two features of the theatrical business in the 1590s that indicate cooperation rather than a bitter rivalry. One is the phenomenon economists now call "cluster marketing," the other the instances of companies playing together. The manifestations of cluster marketing today include food courts in suburban malls, car dealerships on arterial highways between urban centers and bedroom communities, and the motel-restaurant-gas-station complexes at highway interchanges. An example in Shakespeare's London of such marketing is the cluster of bookshops in Paul's Cross Churchyard. Similarly, playhouses benefited from nearby playhouses, as the builder of the Curtain playhouse near the Theatre understood. James Burbage, seeing opportunity for himself in 1585, negotiated a deal with Henry Laneman, owner of the Curtain, that enabled "the proffitt*es* of the said ij° Playe howses might for vij yeres space be in Dyvydent betwene them."[41]

From a commercial point of view, some theatre historians have

disdained the Curtain, assuming that it was small, poorly constructed, leased by second-rate companies, and capable only of
meager revenues. Part of the reason may be the odd phrase in
Laneman's testimony that Burbage and Brayne were interested in
the Curtain as "an Esore to their playe housse." The meaning of
"Esore" (easer?) is not clear, but at the least the word implies a
commercial reciprocity between the playhouses: performances at the
Theatre and Curtain were meant to be good for each other's
commerce.[42] At some moments in its history, the Curtain was more
than an esore. In 1597–8 when Giles Allen, owner of the property on
which the Theatre stood, refused to renew the lease, the Chamberlain's Men moved next door to the Curtain and offered plays as
usual. The Curtain was included in the Privy Council order of 28
July 1597 that all playhouses be plucked down, but like the others it
remained standing. It served in a cluster of markets with the Boar's
Head after the latter's construction in 1598. It was singled out for
examination and perhaps restraint on 10 May 1601. Thus, however
good or poor its architecture for playing, the Curtain was a
functional commercial establishment for many years. At their
deaths, men who had formerly been players there – Thomas Pope,
Thomas Greene, and John Underwood – considered their shares in
the building to be assets.

Perhaps because the Burbages stood to make money from both,
the pairing of the Theatre and Curtain has not produced narratives
of rival playhouses as have the Rose and Globe. In the Shakespeare-
centered story (the teleology of which is the commercial and artistic
triumph of the Chamberlain's Men), the Burbages' choice of the
property on Maid Lane as the site of the Globe ratcheted upward
the level of competition with the Admiral's Men, and as a result the
Admiral's Men were soon "put to flight."[43] Even though the
Admiral's Men said themselves in a letter dated 12 January 1600 to
the justices of Middlesex and others that their reasons for moving to
the Fortune were "the dangerous decaye" of the Rose and the "verie
noysome . . . resort of people in the wynter tyme" to Southwark,[44] a
narrative of rivalry requires that the company's claim be considered
disingenuous; the real reason for the move must have been the need
to relocate beyond the reach of the Chamberlain's Men, against
whom the company could not compete at close range. S. P. Cerasano
dismisses the motive of rivalry and takes the Admiral's Men at their
word. She points out that Philip Henslowe and Edward Alleyn were

"knowledgeable, shrewd entrepreneurs" who realized "by the late 1590s" that the Rose should be remodeled or replaced; their description of the playhouse in 1600 as "'thirteen years old and in poor repair'" indicates that they did not want to upgrade the Rose (as Henslowe had done in 1592) but to copy the Chamberlain's Men by building a new, grander, more functional structure.[45]

William Ingram suggests that Francis Langley saw a marketing opportunity for himself in 1594 in the "great numbers of Londoners who chose to cross the Thames by boat rather than by bridge to get to the Bankside" where the Rose had reopened in June; from Paris Garden stairs or London Bridge, the crowds had to pass by property of his own, and "a playhouse built even nearer to these landing places would intercept much of that traffic."[46] If the Swan was not as commercially successful as the Rose in the 1590s, the reasons were not duopolies or the cut-throat commercial tactics of other playhouse operations. It was bad luck that the Earl of Essex led expeditions to Cadiz in the summers of 1596 and 1597, thus drawing off scores of young men such as John Donne, who might otherwise have spent the lazy summer afternoons frequenting plays. It was bad luck (aggravated by the venomous reporting of Richard Topcliffe) that the Privy Council took notice of the play, "The Isle of Dogs," in August 1597 and called for an inhibition of playing at just that time. But it was bad judgment on Langley's part to become embroiled in a suit with the members of Pembroke's Men who had joined the Admiral's Men at the Rose when playing resumed in October 1597. Including as well the trouble with Derby's Men at the Boar's Head, Ingram comments on Langley's abysmal managerial skills: "The punitive bonds, the lawsuits, the constant harassment and threat of arrest, must have made Langley the last choice of every playing company in London for a landlord."[47] Even under these conditions, the Swan continued as a playhouse, outliving Langley.

Like the proximity of playhouses, the marketing strategy by which a playhouse owner had a stake in more than one theatrical operation suggests an expansion through cooperative ventures rather than settled rivalries and theatrical wars. The interest of Francis Langley in the Boar's Head playhouse in 1599 (alluded to above) is one instance. His offer of £400 to buy out Oliver Woodliffe, an initial investor in the playhouse, came to naught because the entire scheme was stalled by lawsuits, but at one point Langley must have thought that "a popular gallery in a good playhouse" was worth having, even when he owned the whole of an apparently rival business (the Swan).[48] Perhaps James Burbage had a similar idea when he approached Henry Laneman to share receipts at the Curtain. And in acquiring the property at Blackfriars in 1596, Burbage might have envisioned the marketing situation that eventually transpired, when the Chamberlain's/King's Men joined the Blackfriars playhouse and the Globe in partnership. When Burbage died, his son Richard inherited the Blackfriars lease. He contracted in September 1600 with Henry Evans to rent out the playhouse to a company of boys. Therefore, for the years of Harbage's supposed war between the boys' and men's companies (1600–8), Richard Burbage and all who profited from his financial ventures had an interest in the success of the Blackfriars company. Philip Henslowe, who built the Fortune with Edward Alleyn in 1600, leased the Rose to Pembroke's Men in October 1600 and to Worcester's Men in 1602–3, serving the latter company as he continued to serve the Admiral's Men by authorizing their purchase of playbooks and apparel.

The other feature of the theatrical business in the 1590s that many theatre historians treat gingerly is the evidence of companies playing together. It has troubled no one that companies played together at Court; the scheduling of two companies on New Year's night and four on Twelfth Night during the holiday season of 1600–1 appears not to be the companies' decision.[49] Yet one record suggests actual joint performances: the entry for 1611–12 in the Revels Accounts of performances the Sunday after Twelfth Night (12 January) at Greenwich by Queen's Anne's Men and the King's Men of *The Silver Age* and for the night following (13 January) of *Lucrece*. It has also troubled no one that there are many instances of companies playing together in the provinces. One set of records concerning the Admiral's Men in performance with other groups of players serves as illustration: Ipswich, 7 August 1592, with Derby's Men; York, April 1593, with Morley's players; Newcastle, May 1593, with Morley's players; Shrewsbury, sometime after 24 July 1593, with Strange's Men; and Bath, 1593–4, with Lord Norris's players.[50] Of these, only the performance at Shrewsbury with Strange's Men is expected, both because of the May 1593 license that indicates a union of Strange's Men with at least one Admiral's Man (Edward Alleyn) and because of the letter from Alleyn to his wife written in Bristol on 1 August 1593 in which he asked that she send any future letters to him with a message that they "be keptt till my lord stranges players come" (*HD* 276).

But it has been troubling that companies played together in London. Two instances have been explained away by the fact that players from one company were joining another. One is the case in which some players from the Admiral's Men and Pembroke's Men played together at the Rose in October 1597. Another is the case in which the Queen's Men and Sussex's Men played "to geather" at the Rose in April 1594 (*HD* 21).[51] In the opinion of Paul E. Bennett, the trio of companies credited with having first played *Titus Andronicus* (i.e., Derby's, Pembroke's, and Sussex's Men) was an expedient merger of fragmented player-groups.[52] These instances of fluid company affiliation suggest that the exigencies of making a living, not personal quarrels, governed players' business relationships. A different accommodation happened at the Boar's Head playhouse, 1599–1603. According to Herbert Berry, Robert Browne of Derby's Men owned the lease to the playhouse; and in 1601 Browne sublet the Boar's Head to Worcester's Men.[53] In some sense, then, Browne was sharing the profits of his playhouse with a second company. Narratives of theatrical commerce as rivalry offer no way to account for this kind of cooperation.[54]

An instance of companies playing together that may fit neither of these explanations is that of the Admiral's Men and Chamberlain's Men at the playhouse in Newington in June 1594. Henslowe recorded the performances in his typical formulaic style: "In the name of god Amen begininge at newington my Lord Admeralle men & my Lorde chamberlen men" (*HD* 21). The event is particularly noteworthy because these companies, by old narratives of theatre history, are supposed to have been feuding. Even before Wallace published John Alleyn's story about fighting with James Burbage, Fleay separated the companies by deciding that they had performed on alternate days.[55] Greg had been inclined in 1908 to interpret the Newington run as joint performances, facilitated by "some sort of juncture" between the Admiral's Men and Chamberlain's Men in the provinces earlier in the spring,[56] but he was sufficiently influenced by Wallace's report of the quarrel at the Theatre to base theories of provenance for the Plots of "2 Seven Deadly Sins" and "The Dead Man's Fortune" on feuding companies. Confident that the companies would not have played together voluntarily, some theatre historians have suggested reasons why neither would have liked doing so. Carol Rutter raises the possibility that the lead players had giant egos: "Sharing a stage may not have appealed to either" Edward Alleyn (Admiral's Men) or Richard Burbage (Chamberlain's Men).[57] Andrew Gurr implies that playing at Newington was a temporary convenience until the "duopoly" arranged by their respective patrons could be set up, each in its proper place in the balance of power.[58]

Whether Fleay was closer to the truth with his sense of alternating days of performance (and therefore discrete repertories) or Greg with his sense of a temporary merger (and therefore cooperation on issues of repertory and performance), there is a place in the discussion of commercial relations for the role of fellowship among the men who came together to play until their companies followed separate destinies. A significant number of the players temporarily joined in performances at Newington had been in Strange's Men in 1593. Alleyn and Downton, now of the Admiral's Men, had been touring in the provinces with at least six men who were now Chamberlain's Men: Bryan, Cowley, Phillips, Pope, Kempe, and Heminges (Downton and Cowley, not named in the license, are named in Alleyn's letters from the tour). Tunstall, presumed to have been with the Alleyns wherever they were, belongs on this list also. That very January, a quarto of a play in the repertory of Strange's troupe – *A Knack to Know a Knave* – had been published advertising its successful performances "by ED. ALLEN and his Companie. *VVith KEMPS applauded* Merrimentes." In correspondence with Joan, his wife, early in the tour (May), Alleyn conveyed an anxiety about his family in London, but when he spoke of his fellows, his tone is cordial: "we ar all well & in helth wch I pray god to contine<w> w^t vs in the contry" (*HD* 274). In correspondence later in the tour (August), Alleyn spoke with obvious regret that the company "shall nott com hom till allholand tyd," but his tone remained companionable as he described the receipt and post of letters by men who would allegedly be his rivals in less than a year: "I reseved yor letter att bristo by richard couley. . . I have sent yo^u this by berer Thomas popes kinsman" (*HD* 277, 276). This letter is the same in which Alleyn asks his wife to send her letters via the town ahead on their schedule and to ask that letters "be keptt till my lord stranges players come" (*HD* 276), thus identifying himself by the patron of the larger segment of the players, not his own patron, the Lord Admiral.

Philip Henslowe wrote several letters to his son-in-law, Edward, during that same summer tour of 1593. In each he sent his best wishes to Alleyn's fellows: "comend me harteley to al the Reast of your fealowes in generall" (*HD* 279). To this particular phrase, Henslowe added "for I growe poore for lacke of them," wording that appears to color his sentiment with commercial self-interest. Yet it does so no more than do the words of an Elizabethan fiancé who might speak of his bride-to-be's beauty and £100 a year in the same breath, with equal delight. Furthermore, here Henslowe couched the lament about enforced closure in a diplomatic context: because of it he had "no geaftes to sende but as good & faythfull a harte as they shall desyer to haue comen a mongeste them" (*HD* 279). There is also evidence that the father and daughter, lonely in London, were on companionable terms with the families of the company's players: Henslowe, chiding Edward for not having written Joan, nonetheless knew that the tour was going well because "the other wifes had leatters" (*HD* 278). Twice Henslowe gave Alleyn personal and professional news of fellows in other companies: "Robart brownes wife in shordech & all her chelldren & howshowld be dead & heare dores sheat vpe" ((*HD* 277); "as for my lorde a penbrockes wch you desier to knowe wheare they be they are all at home and hauffe ben t<his> v or sixe weackes for they cane not saue ther carges <w>^th trauell as I heare & weare fayne to pane the<r> parell for ther carge" (*HD* 280). Ten years later in October 1603, when another outbreak of plague had driven the companies from London, Joan Alleyn wrote to her husband that all of the companies were well and safely home, including his own; she added, sadly, that "Browne of the Boares head is dead & dyed very pore, he went not into the countrye at all" (*HD* 297). Scholars often cite the reference to Pembroke's Men to show the precariousness of touring and the failure of that company to compete, yet it and the reference to Browne of the Boar's Head show also an empathy with fellows who face the hazards common to all in the business.

It confuses psychology and commerce to build a history of the Elizabethan playing companies on the premise that Edward Alleyn and the Admiral's Men, as well as Richard Burbage and the Chamberlain's Men, made financial decisions in light of a moment in November 1590 when John Alleyn was scorched by residual fire from James Burbage's anger at the widow Brayne. Burbage was not the only member of the playhouse world who was hot tempered and violent. William Knell was killed in June 1587 in a fight with a fellow player in his company, John Towne. Christopher Marlowe was stabbed through the eye in a quarrel over the payment of a bill for the day's quantity of liquor. Ben Jonson killed Gabriel Spencer in a duel in September 1598. Spencer had already killed a man named James Feake in a duel in December 1596, but neither that experience nor his ten-inch longer sword gave him sufficient advantage against Jonson. On 6 June 1599 John Day, dramatist, assaulted Henry Porter, dramatist, "giving . . . [him] a mortal wound on the left breast of his body of the length of one inch and of the width of one inch"; Porter died the next day.[59] On 25 November 1600 Philip Henslowe recorded a loan of £3 to the wife of William Bird, the player with the Admiral's Men, "to descarge her husband owt of the kyng*es* benche when he laye vpon my lord Jeffe Justes warant for hurtinge of a felowe" (*HD* 83).

If by chance the archives of the Public Record Office had preserved the progress of this William Bird in the courts as fully as that of the Burbages, and if the reputation of Shakespeare had not focused attention on the Chamberlain's/King's Men and their play-houses, there might be narratives of commerce in which episodes of hot anger occurred, and lawsuits were filed, and the business of playing continued uninterrupted. The career of Bird in the business of playing suggests that personal and professional disputes within and across company boundaries were not the source of commercial rivalries but rather a means by which the theatrical enterprise developed protocols for regulation and expansion. Without a court system and officers of a livery company to adjudicate and enforce acceptable behaviors, players in the 1570s and 1580s developed guidelines for themselves, one of which was that a company should not acquire a script of another company and perform it as its own, even when that script had been published. When the protocol of ownership was abused, the violated company shamed the offender publicly, thus pressuring an adherence to normative practice. A familiar instance of this response is the reaction of the King's Men to the acquisition of their play, "Jeronimo," by the Children of the Chapel at Blackfriars. As the Induction to *The Malcontent* makes clear, the King's Men justified their taking of the Blackfriars play as revenge for the theft of their own.

Ian W. Archer speaks of the willingness of artisans in a livery company to endure "the shortcomings of their rulers" in order to receive benefits such as "the arbitration of disputes."[60] These disputes ranged from shouting matches to charges of corrupt business practices. Records from the Court of Assistants of the

Carpenters' Company indicate the assessment of fines for behavior such as disobeying a summons, criticizing another's work, partnership with a "forren" worker, drawing a dagger, "evell & Rebukying wordys," and quarreling.[61] In October 1581 William Loggen and George Cotton were brought before the Court of Assistants of the Grocers' Company "for certain slaunderous wordes" exchanged at Sturbridge Fair.[62] Cotton, who had called Loggen a "bankroute," repented and submitted to mediation. Before the court two months later, Cotton and his wife "did openly confesse that they had misreported" Loggen, who forgave them, as the mediator had decreed he should. Another grocer, John Palmer, committed fraud. Officers of the company who raided his house found rotten raisins, spices labeled as garbled when they were not, and counterfeit cinnamon powder, cloves, and pepper. Palmer appeared before the Court of Assistants "shewinge great disobedience with his cappe on his head" and threatened a suit in Chancery. The wardens, overlooking this additional provocation, fined Palmer five marks in hopes he would amend "suche falts as he hathe nowe bene charged with."[63] The Court of Assistants of the Pewterers' Company adjudicated a dispute concerning Richard Staple, who was accused of an intolerable self-aggrandizement. On 20 May 1590 Staple was fined 2s. 6d because "he mad bostynge of his ware to be better than an other mans."[64] On 8 October of the same year, Thomas Cowes renewed the complaint against Staple, claiming that Staple was guilty of dispraising Cowes's wares and "vaunting his ware to be better then other mens."[65] Archer's observation that "[p]aternalistic values were widespread in this society and shaped the ideal of company rule" may be applied to the theatrical industry as to the livery companies.[66] In response to disputes, the playing companies used peer pressure to discourage aberrant behavior while maintaining commercial operations at a profitable level.

William Bird first appears in playhouse records in 1597 in the context of "The Isle of Dogs" affair, a famously disruptive event in theatre history. Most discussions of the affair focus on political aspects: the relationship between the order by the Privy Council on 28 July that all playhouses be plucked down and the Council's order to Richard Topcliffe on 15 August to investigate rumors of a "lewd plaie that was plaied in one of the plaiehowses on the Bancke Side, contanynge very seditious and sclanderous matter."[67] For the players, however, the affair was a commercial disruption. Details of the event from Bird's point of view are as follows. Bird, Thomas Downton, Richard Jones, Robert Shaa, and Gabriel Spencer were members of Pembroke's Men in February 1597 when they signed a bond of £100 with Francis Langley, owner of the Swan playhouse, to play at his house as a company. In August the London playhouses were closed down; Shaa, Spencer, and Ben Jonson (part-author of the offending play, "The Isle of Dogs") were imprisoned in the Marshalsea; Bird, Downton, and Jones (for himself and Shaa) signed bonds of one hundred marks with Philip Henslowe to play at the Rose. In November Bird and his fellows filed suit against Langley.[68] They asked that he be prevented from enforcing the £100 bond, and they disclaimed responsibility for a debt of £300 that Langley claimed he had incurred in readying the Swan for their use. They argued that they would have returned to the Swan when the restraint was lifted if Langley had secured a license to play. But he had not, and they now believed that he had contrived to make their playing for him impossible, both by not securing a license and by arresting their fellows, thus causing their company to be broken up. On 29 May 1598 the court settled in favor of the players.

The maneuvers of Bird to protect himself and his livelihood suggest that the paramount concern in a time of upheaval was to stay in business. Before Topcliffe even received the order to investigate, Bird had signed a bond with Henslowe to play at the Rose (10 August, *HD* 240). Henslowe's concerns were to hire available talent and to secure a license for his playhouse to resume operations when the official ban was lifted. Langley acted first to pressure his players by claiming the bonds, but in the meantime (according to the players' replication, 6 February 1598), he brought in "oth[r] players to his great gaines" and converted the apparel he had bought "to his best p*r*ofytt by lending the same for hyre."[69] Secure at the Rose by November, Bird and his fellows appear to have tried to buy Langley off. Through April 1598 they borrowed money from Henslowe (*HD* 70, 72, 78, 82), possibly for their own living expenses but possibly also to delay Langley's action against them. The money, if paid to Langley, was not enough; Henslowe had to loan 13s. 4d to Bird on 29 March 1598 to discharge his arrest by Langley (*HD* 77). In spite of hostilities from the recent lawsuit, Bird and his fellows did business with Langley in September and October 1598, apparently in "an agrement betwext langley & them" that included the purchase of apparel (*HD* 98).[70] Langley received sums of £35 and £19 (*HD* 98,

98). Entering perhaps an additional transaction on 4 October 1598, Henslowe made clear that the loan of £3 to pay "m^r langleyes his money for the agrement & . . . the Riche clocke frome pane" was to be paid by Jones, Shaa, Downton, and Bird, not by the company of the Admiral's Men (*HD* 68).

William Bird was involved in another lawsuit, coincident with the "Isle of Dogs" affair. On 8 March 1598 Bird, Downton, and Spencer borrowed 30s. from Henslowe "abowt the sewt be twext marten & them" (*HD* 77). This "marten" is Martin Slater, who was a member of the Admiral's Men in 1594 (*HD* 8) and who left on 18 July 1597 (*HD* 60), about a month before events at the Swan attracted the attention of the Privy Council. It is unclear why Slater left, where he went, or whether there were hard feelings. However, he did not go empty handed. He took five playbooks from the Admiral's Men's stock: the two parts of "Hercules," new in May 1595; "Pythagoras" and "Phocas," new in 1596; and "Alexander and Lodowick," new in January 1597 and still in production when Slater left. On behalf of the Admiral's Men, Henslowe paid Slater £7 on 16 May to buy back the five books, plus an additional 20s. on 18 July (*HD* 89, 93).[71] Although the subject of the lawsuit with Bird, Downton, and Spencer is unknown, an obvious possibility is that the Admiral's Men sued for the return of its plays, an action Slater might have resisted if he considered himself owner by right of authorship. However, the specification of the three former Pembroke's players as the litigants ("be twext marten & them") suggests a connection to business at the Swan. Could Slater have taken the Admiral's plays to the Swan in July, joining ever so briefly with Pembroke's Men, then remained at Langley's playhouse when Bird and the others left, taking a number of Pembroke's plays with them? Whatever the nature of the suit, the significance for commercial relations among the companies is that business mattered more than personal disputes. The suit with Slater apparently came to nothing, and the Admiral's Men got back their scripts. Playing continued at the Rose and the Swan, and Slater moved on to new theatrical ventures.

William Bird spent the remaining years of his career with the Admiral's/Prince's Men, performing, witnessing agreements with additional personnel, overseeing payments for apparel and play-books, and borrowing money from the playhouse owner. He scouted new talent, purchasing "Jugurtha" with the promise to reimburse his fellows if they were displeased (*HD* 130). He became a dramatist himself, writing "Judas" as well as additions to *Doctor Faustus* with Samuel Rowley. However, other entries suggest different stories from this one of placid commercial stability; unfortunately, like the suit with Slater, the entries begin narratives for which there are no subsequent episodes. For example, on 30 August 1598 Bird borrowed 10s. from Henslowe "to folowe sewt agenste Thomas poope" (*HD* 76). Presumably, this "Thomas poope" is the Thomas Pope who was a member of the Chamberlain's Men, fellow of Burbage, Phillips, and Shakespeare (and formerly a fellow with Edward Alleyn in Strange's Men). Nothing occurred in the commercial lives of Bird's and Pope's companies at the time to suggest what business the men had together. Documents in the suit, if it was filed, have not been located, and the story ends here. A second example is a letter in 1599 from Bird to Henslowe, asking desperately for a 40s. loan: "M^r henchlowe I pray let me intreate yo^u to lend me forty shilling*es* tell the next weeke and Ile then paye it yo^u agayne by the grace of god I pray as yo^u loue me fayle me not . . . if yo^u will doe me this fauour yo^u shall comaunde me in a greater matter" (*HD* 298–9). Henslowe complied (*HD* 83). But nothing more of this episode is known. Disruptive as these events clearly were in Bird's personal life, they had no visible effect on his company's commercial activities.

William Ingram observes that "a company of players is always an ephemeral thing, no more susceptible of meaningful biographical limning than any other ongoing corporate body."[72] In this sense it is unlike a livery company about which detailed histories are written based on apprentice bindings, livery lists, charters, ordinances, Court of Assistants minutes, feast accounts, inventories, and records of charitable acts. Without documentation to show which company was at which playhouse during the years when the Brayne-Burbage suits proceeded, or to provide receipts for the Chamberlain's Men over the years when Henslowe provided daily accounts for the Admiral's Men at the Rose, or to track the course of business at Paul's playhouse and Blackfriars when the War of the Theatres presumably raged, theatre historians such as Wallace, Sharpe, and Harbage turned to the personalities of players and dramatists for insight into business practices. John Alleyn's alleged anger at James Burbage became a commercial rivalry from which the dates of playhouse documents were deduced, the personal relations among players in companies temporarily joined were inferred, and the departure of a company from its old playing site to a new one was given motive. But anger is not a reliable measure of commerce. As the career of William Bird illustrates, players became entangled in lawsuits or were provoked into brawls, but their companies did not develop a new commercial strategy as a result. Ian Archer notes that the livery companies "never made common cause" in spite of their many shared grievances because of disputes involving turf and "corporate pride."[73] The playing companies likewise shared grievances in the repeated attempts by officials of the city, church, and crown to restrict or eradicate playing but did not make common cause against these threats. Yet they were joined in the determination to continue in business, in spite of disputes among players. The fellowship of class and neighborhood, plus the very instability of the company as unit during periods of distress, meant that players formed friendships, kinships, and professional connections across company boundaries. Rather than disrupt the conduct of business, personal relationships facilitated the development of cooperative commercial strategies that accommodated change and promoted growth.

CHAPTER 3

Playwrights, repertories, the book trade, and company commerce

Mr Henshlowe we haue heard their booke and lyke yt their pryce is eight pound*es*, wch I pray pay now to m^r Wilson, according to our promysse, I would haue Come my selfe, but that I ame troubled wth a scytation.

yo^{rs} Robt Shaa

Cuthbert Burby was the elder brother of Richard Burbadge, the great actor, and his name, as Cuthbert Burbidge, is sometimes so written in the Stationers' Registers . . .

John Payne Collier[1]

William Shakespeare was unusual among fellow playwrights in that he wrote exclusively for one company for most of his career, acted in its offerings, and invested in its playhouses. He was therefore also unusual in having a direct stake in his company's commerce. His primary contribution to that commerce was to the repertory: each year he supplied the company with new plays that continued to be profitable when revived, taken to Court, and taken on tour. Many of those plays were further profitable as advertisements when they were printed with title pages naming the company. By a fortunate combination of commercial shrewdness and artistic inspiration, Shakespeare consistently chose subjects and dramatic formulas that attracted audiences. As in-house dramatist, he presumably also provided routine services such as prologues and epilogues for occasional performances, revisions for changes in venue or company personnel, and emendations to avoid censorship or facilitate a revival.[2] It is therefore not surprising that old narratives of theatrical commerce placed Shakespeare and his company at the center. F. G. Fleay asserted that the Chamberlain's Men competed successfully by staging a mere four new plays a year, most if not all by Shakespeare; R. B. Sharpe raised the number of new plays per year but nonetheless maintained that "on playwrights the Chamberlain's men

48

would . . . score with Shakespeare over all rivals."[3] Two stories linking Shakespeare and Ben Jonson have a commercial spin, and in both Shakespeare is the hero: he recommends Jonson's play to the Chamberlain's Men (without receiving Jonson's thanks), and he purges the pestilent humor of Jonson's *Poetaster.*

However, if Shakespeare and his company belong at the center of a commercial narrative, it is not for the old reasons. As Bernard Beckerman has made clear, the Chamberlain's/King's Men followed the practices of other companies in staging a large and diverse repertory supplied by a battery of playwrights.[4] Also, stories of a Jonson-Shakespeare quarrel are poor indicators of theatrical commerce. In the first place, there is no evidence that there was such a quarrel. In the second, nineteenth-century apologists for Jonson, who denied the anecdote about his ingratitude and justified his bad humor by insisting that he was provoked by John Marston and Thomas Dekker, have been replaced by scholars who perceive the issue of dramatists' quarrels either as an advertising gimmick or a controversy over literary taste. But even these new explanations for the dramatists' quarrels do not fully address several aspects of commercial relations among the playing companies. As I have argued in previous chapters, narratives of companies at war – even if revised to emphasize art or marketing over petulance – underestimate the ways in which the companies regarded one another as business partners in a manner similar to the fellowship of members of a guild. The players, having worked with one another in various organizations and lived as neighbors, might have been friends or enemies, but their personal relations did not govern company commerce. Rather, the playing companies relied on a cooperative workforce of playwrights who could readily supply scripts on popular topics in fashionable genres that were marketable on stage and, when some advantage to the companies presented itself, at the bookshop.

PLAYWRIGHTS AND COMPANY COMMERCE

The papers of Philip Henslowe and Edward Alleyn provide most of the available data on the relationships between playwrights and companies. The first epigraph above is one item of correspondence between Henslowe and Robert Shaa, a player who joined the Admiral's Men in 1597 and often conducted the company's business.

In the note Shaa asks Henslowe to pay Mr. Wilson £8 for a play that members of the company have heard and liked; on the back of the note is a sketch of opening scenes of the play. A complementary entry in Henslowe's diary, or book of accounts, provides more information about the transaction: the £8 was "full payment," the title was "the second part of Henrye Richmond," the date of the payment was 8 November 1599, and "R" Wilson signed for the dramatists (*HD* 126). The wording of Shaa's note ("their pryce") indicates that Wilson wrote the play with one or more collaborators. The entry in Henslowe's diary does not name these men, but other entries show that Wilson worked with Michael Drayton, Richard Hathaway, and Anthony Munday in October 1599 on the first part of *Sir John Oldcastle* and with the same consortium in January 1600 on "Owen Tudor" (*HD* 125, 129).[5]

Such transactions, once considered peculiar to the stable of dramatists kept by Henslowe at the Rose, are now believed to be generally representative of arrangements between playwrights and companies in the theatrical industry. As G. E. Bentley puts it, playwrights "were the employees of the acting companies."[6] The Shaa note and diary entry provide considerable information about that employment, but a number of questions remain concerning the role of playwrights in company commerce. For example, did playwrights as a rule form their own partnerships, choose their subjects and generic formulas, and design scripts for specific audiences? Did companies seek out repertory offerings that they particularly wanted for some commercial reason and also seek out the playwrights most able to comply? What exigencies of commerce encouraged companies to sign contracts with playwrights to write for them exclusively? When a playwright moved from one company to another, did he take the initiative, or was he recruited by a company representative?

Scholars have opinions on these matters, but little conclusive documentation. In *A Companion to Henslowe's Diary* (1988), Neil Carson addresses the issue of syndicates and suggests a pattern of collaboration in which playwrights who "associated with one another on several projects during a particular season will go their separate ways, disappear, or realign themselves when playing ceases."[7] Such appears the case from October through February, 1599–1600, with Wilson and his collaborators on "2 Henry Richmond" as well as the first part of *Sir John Oldcastle*, "Owen Tudor," and perhaps "2 Sir John Oldcastle." Carson notes the operation of a second syndicate during that same season: Henry Chettle, Thomas Dekker, John Day, and William Haughton. The pattern of their collaboration varied from the threesome of Chettle, Dekker, and Haughton on *Patient Grissil*, to a pairing of Day and Haughton on "Cox of Collumpton" and "The Tragedy of Thomas Merry," to a threesome of Day, Dekker, and Haughton on "The Spanish Moor's Tragedy." During this period also, men who collaborated on projects occasionally wrote solo: Chettle, for example, worked on "The Stepmother's Tragedy," "The Orphan's Tragedy," and "Damon and Pythias"; Dekker worked on *Old Fortunatus*; and William Boyle (otherwise unknown) supplied "Jugurtha."

The thrust of documents such as Shaa's note on "2 Henry Richmond" is toward an independence on the part of playwrights in regard to working relationships with their fellows and with companies. It is hard to imagine the Admiral's Men insisting to Wilson that he work with Drayton, Hathaway, and Munday; it is more plausible that the men, all of whom had supplied plays to the Admiral's Men before, made up their own teams. The fact that collaborators who had written the first part of a serial remained in partnership for the second part is further evidence of the poets' initiative. As the entries in Henslowe's diary show, the same sets of playwrights received payment from the Admiral's Men for the two parts of the Robin Hood plays (*The Downfall of Robert, Earl of Huntingdon* and *The Death of Robert, Earl of Huntingdon*), "Earl Godwin," and "Six Clothiers." This practice is consistent also for Worcester's Men, who paid the same set of collaborators for the two parts of "Black Dog of Newgate."[8] Two serials follow a different pattern of collaboration, but neither necessarily suggests the intervention of the company in the makeup of the teams. One is the collaboration of Drayton, Munday, and Wentworth Smith with Chettle on part one of "Cardinal Wolsey." Chettle had received full payment for "Cardinal Wolsey" (which apparently became the second part) in July 1601, and he received payment in earnest on part one in August. By October, however, he had acquired partners. Since he worked both solo and in syndicates, there is no reason to guess that the company directed him to acquire partners this time.[9] Another case is the second part of "The Blind Beggar of Bednal Green" and the spin-off, "Tom Strowd." Chettle and Day worked on the first part in May 1600; Day and Haughton worked on the second part from January to May 1601 and the spin-off from May to

July 1601. It appears that, in the lapse of time from May 1600 to January 1601, Day found himself a different partner to continue the "Blind Beggar" series.

In another instance of collaborative activity, a number of playwrights who had been writing for the Admiral's Men (though perhaps not exclusively) began to write also for Worcester's Men when that company leased the Rose playhouse in 1602. The partnerships of Day, Chettle, and Thomas Heywood illustrate various patterns of collaboration, but none of the patterns suggests that the companies determined the membership of the teams. Day had a relatively uncomplicated set of arrangements with his fellows in that he worked with nearly the same syndicate for both companies. For Worcester's Men he wrote the two parts of "Black Dog of Newgate" and "The Unfortunate General" with Hathaway, Smith, and another poet; and "Shore's Wife" with Chettle. For the Admiral's Men he wrote "As Merry as May Be" with Hathaway and Smith; and "The Boss of Billingsgate" with Hathaway and "felowe poetes" (*HD* 208). In comparison with Day's fairly stable collaborations, Chettle worked with a different combination of playwrights on most of his projects in 1602–3. For the Admiral's Men, he wrote "Felmelanco" with a man named Robinson and the first part of "The London Florentine" with Heywood. For Worcester's Men, he wrote "Lady Jane" with Heywood, Smith, and John Webster; "Christmas Comes but Once a Year" with Dekker, Heywood, and Webster; an unnamed play with Heywood; and "Shore's Wife" with Day. Thomas Heywood, who putatively came with Worcester's Men to the Rose (he had played with and written for the Admiral's Men previously), might have taken some responsibility as in-house dramatist for a supply of new plays, but his partnerships do not suggest direction by the company. For the four projects that he provided in collaboration, he worked in different combinations with the same four men: with Smith on "Albere Galles"; with Smith, Chettle, Dekker, and Webster on "Lady Jane"; with Chettle, Dekker, and Webster on "Christmas Comes but Once a Year"; and with Chettle on an unnamed play. In the midst of this activity, he wrote the first part of "The London Florentine" with Chettle for the Admiral's Men.

Of more significance to the commerce of the companies is the independence of the playwrights in terms of theatrical subjects and genres. Shaa's note about "2 Henry Richmond" implies that Wilson auditioned the script for members of the Admiral's Men, and they were free to purchase it or not. This sequence – the playwright wrote the play, members of the company heard some or all of it, they agreed to buy it – is indicated by another note on purchases among Henslowe's papers in which Samuel Rowley tells Henslowe that he has heard "fyue shetes of a playe of the Conqueste of the Indes" and he does "not doute but It wyll be a verye good playe" (*HD* 294). G. E. Bentley is thinking of this kind of evidence when he says that "it was normally the acting company which decided to buy the play," but in the same breath he says that the acting company might also "commission the dramatist."[10] As far as I know, there is no document in Henslowe's papers to support the claim of a company commission, and Bentley does not provide one from another source.[11]

Two desiderata appear to come into conflict on the issue of playwrights and the choice of theatrical subjects and genres. It is good if playwrights chose the matter and treatment of their plays, for their abilities as artists may then be seen to have had free rein. Such independence invites scholars to consider the works of a dramatist over time as reflecting his state of mind and creative development. Yet it is also good if companies sought out a given subject in a given genre, for it suggests that the players perceived the repertory as having a commercial design. As evidence of repertory planning and anticipation of the marketplace, however, there are only the lists of plays per season and the entry of payments to playwrights in Henslowe's diary, and playlists assembled for other companies from diverse sources such as title-page advertisements and records of performances at Court. It is possible to argue backward from these records (as indeed I do in the section below on the repertory and company commerce), but evidence for the arguments is only circumstantial.

Perhaps a middle ground is suggested by Thomas Dekker in a Star Chamber lawsuit in 1624. Dekker testified that he belonged to a team of dramatists who were "making and contriving . . . [a] play called Keep the Widow Waking and did make and contrive the same upon the instructions given them by one Ralph Savage" (Savage was apparently an agent for the Red Bull playhouse).[12] Dekker's language implies a cooperation of company and playwrights that is most plausible for an in-house dramatist. It is reasonable to suppose, for example, that Shakespeare received "instructions" from the

Chamberlain's Men in the summer of 1596 to make a play to respond to yet another revival of *The Jew of Malta* at the Rose; and he, acting on those general instructions, exercised his genius for generic experimentation to redeem Marlowe's tragedy as a comedy. It is also reasonable to suppose that a company, having promised to buy a play from the plot alone, or a few sheets, might instruct the playwrights to include some particular feature such as an advertisement of the playhouse or an allusion to the company's license to play.[13]

Perhaps it is also plausible that playwrights who worked for a company regularly were familiar enough with the abilities of company personnel and the tastes of its usual audience to choose subjects and formulas that the company would want to buy. If so, those playwrights deserve more credit than they are normally given for the prosperous economy of the playhouse world in Shakespeare's time. Henry Chettle, a regular with the Admiral's Men, is rarely evaluated from a commercial point of view; rather, he is called a hack for writing prolifically and a wastrel for spending what he earned (and more). The image of Chettle in Dekker's *A Knight's Conjuring* (1607), "sweating and blowing, by reason of his fatnes" when he joined the congregation of playwrights in the Fields of Joy, more often comes to mind than does the welcome of his fellows, who stand at his coming due to their "olde acquaintance" with him.[14] But Chettle should be judged by his contributions to the commerce of the Admiral's Men, which are measurable by the volume of his work and its diversity in subject matter and genre. Chettle worked on approximately four dozen projects between 1598 and 1603. His subjects included folklore ("Friar Rush and the Proud Woman of Antwerp"), chronicle history ("The Famous Wars of Henry I"), foreign history ("King Sebastian of Portugal"), sensational biography (the two-part "Black Bateman of the North"), classical history and myth ("Catiline's Conspiracy," "Agamemnon"), and biblical story ("Tobias"). He wrote comedies ("It's no Deceit to Deceive the Deceiver"), tragedies (*Hoffman*), tragical histories ("Robert II, King of Scots"), pastoral romances ("The Arcadian Virgin"), and moral plays ("All is not Gold that Glisters"). Chettle also worked on one or both parts of at least eight two-part plays. In addition, due to his work on *Patient Grissil* (domestic relations) and the two-part "London Florentine" (the upwardly mobile clothes horse?), he deserves credit for initiating or promoting new developments in generic formulas.

It is possible that Bentley was thinking of a contract between a playwright and a company when he suggested company commissions. Two contracts with playwrights are preserved in Henslowe's diary: Henry Porter bound himself to write exclusively for the Admiral's Men on 28 February 1599; Henry Chettle similarly bound himself on 25 March 1602. However, there seems to be no particular commercial logic behind these contracts, nor is there any specification to choose particular subjects and genres. Both Porter and Chettle had been writing for the Admiral's Men long before they signed the contracts, and they had been borrowing money from Henslowe. Perhaps the contracts were insurance that the playwrights would not shift company allegiance and sell elsewhere what the Admiral's Men had paid for already in loans. It might be argued that the timing of the Porter contract anticipated the relocation of the Chamberlain's Men from Shoreditch to Maid Lane, across the street from the Rose. If so, the Admiral's Men were prevented from profiting from the contract by a quarrel between playwrights, for Porter died on 7 June 1599 after being wounded in a duel with John Day. The date of the Chettle contract preceded the arrival of Worcester's Men at the Rose in August 1602, but the contract apparently had no force (or it implicitly included companies playing at the Rose), for Chettle worked on as many projects for Worcester's Men, 1602–3, as he did for the Admiral's Men. In April 1613 Robert Daborne signed a contract with Philip Henslowe (and thus perhaps accepted a commission) to write "Machiavel and the Devil"; he soon contracted for another new play, "The Arraignment of London" (renamed "The Bellman of London"). Daborne, seeking advances from Henslowe, hinted several times that the King's Men wanted to buy the play out from under Henslowe. The correspondence suggests that Daborne did not consider himself too tightly bound by his agreement with Henslowe.

Playwrights without contracts presumably were free to move from one company to another, but it is not clear whether they took the initiative or companies recruited them. John Marston (in 1599) and Ben Jonson (in 1600) left writing for men's companies to write for boys' companies. It is often assumed in discussions of the moves that Marston and Jonson changed affiliations because the men's companies and their audiences were too common a theatrical environment, or offered the playwrights too little artistic control, or were not as receptive to dramatic satire as the boys' companies. From the point of view of company commerce, the latter explanation is the more significant. It suggests a fortuitous match of marketing and talent: the children's companies wanted satires; Marston and Jonson could provide them. One problem with this explanation, however, is that it is based on partial repertory lists for each company *circa* 1600; another is that those lists do not reveal the "preponderance of satirical comedies" of which Alfred Harbage spoke so confidently.[15] For the Children of the Chapel, for example, a repertory list for 1600–2 includes Jonson's *Cynthia's Revels* and *Poetaster*, a few plays by Chapman, and John Lyly's *Love's Metamorphosis*. For the Children of Paul's, a repertory list for the same period includes Marston's *Antonio and Mellida*, *Antonio's Revenge*, *Jack Drum's Entertainment*, and possibly *What You Will*; the anonymous *Maid's Metamorphosis* and *The Wisdom of Doctor Dodypoll*, and Dekker's *Satiromastix* and *Blurt, Master Constable* (with Thomas Middleton?). These offerings at Paul's look very much like those at the Globe: a two-part revenge play (to compete with *Hamlet*), a couple of humors comedies (to compete with *Every Man Out of his Humour* and *Twelfth Night*), and a couple of pastorals (to compete with *As You Like It*). *Satiromastix* was played both at the Globe and at Paul's. Scott McMillin and Sally-Beth MacLean, studying the life of the Queen's Men, set forward certain characteristics as equivalent to the identity of a company: "its acting style, its staging methods, its kinds of versification, its sense of what constituted a worthwhile repertory of plays."[16] The identity of the children's companies in 1599–1600 when Marston and Jonson began to write for them had long been set by their small, indoor theatres and use of inter-act music; their acting style was a product of the players' youth; and their repertories (from the titles of surviving plays) appear to have offered audiences a variety of genres, not a specialization in one kind of comedy.

REPERTORY PRACTICE AND COMPANY COMMERCE

The repertory was a company's most potent commercial instrument. Perhaps not in 1576 when companies began to play regularly at the Theatre and Curtain, nor in 1583 when the Queen's Men began to play frequently in London, but possibly by 1587 when Philip Henslowe built the Rose, and certainly by 1595 when Francis Langley built the Swan, the men's companies at London playhouses needed a large, diverse repertory and a steady supply of new plays.

The playlists in Henslowe's diary for 1595–6 show the composition of the repertory of the Admiral's Men during a time when playing was continuous over eleven months except for a break during Lent. From 25 August 1595 through 18 July 1596 (except for 28 February through 12 April 1596), the company performed thirty-seven plays.[17] Of these thirty-seven, seventeen were new, fifteen were being continued from the offerings in 1594–5, and five were old plays being revived.[18] Because only six of the thirty-seven plays survive, it is impossible to be accurate about the subjects and genres represented by the repertory; nevertheless, some general groupings seem plausible. Seventeen, or roughly half, of the plays appear to be some kind of comedy; sixteen appear to be some kind of history; and four are tragedies.

As a group, the histories illustrate several commercial features of the repertory as a whole. One is the diversification within a genre. For example, the two-part "Hercules," "Pythagoras," "Julian the Apostate," and "Troy" represent a category of myth, ancient history, and pseudo-history. The two-part *Tamburlaine* and the two-part "Tamar Cham" were foreign histories. Part one of "Godfrey of Boulogne" and "Chinon of England" appear to have been pseudo-historical romances. "Longshanks," "The Siege of London," and "Henry V" represent the English chronicle play; "Long Meg of Westminster" and "Bellendon" belong to a sub-category of sensational biography that focused on notorious characters. One popular kind of history, the biblical play (e.g., "Samson," 29 July 1602), is missing from the 1595–6 repertory but well represented in other years.

Commercial features illustrated by the 1595–6 repertory include the duplication of popular subject matter, the extension of that matter into sequels or serials, and the expansion of a popular figure into a spin-off. "Henry V" surely looked back to *The Famous Victories of Henry V* (S. R. 14 May 1594, Q1598), and "Longshanks" to George Peele's *Edward I* (S. R. 8 October 1593, Q1593). Christopher Marlowe implied in the prologue to the second part of *Tamburlaine* that he was writing a sequel in response to audience demand, not for artistic reasons of his own. The author of the two-part "Hercules," in contrast, seems to have conceived the story in serial form, if the speed with which part two followed part one to the stage is an indication (two weeks, from 7 May to 23 May 1595). There are no examples of the spin-off in the 1595–6 repertory, but Henslowe's entry of "the welche man" on 29 November 1595 suggests the commercial logic: a popular character (the Welsh rebel, Lleuellen) from one narrative complex (the reign of Edward I) is promoted into his own play.[19] Here, though, Henslowe's "the welche man" is probably just another performance of "Longshanks."

W. W. Greg puzzled over the relationship of "Godfrey of Boulogne" to plays with apparently similar subject matter such as Thomas Heywood's *Four Prentices of London*, and in so doing he exposed several assumptions widely held in his time that have obscured the commercial significance of duplicate plays, multi-part plays, and spin-offs. One is the assumption that plays on the same general subject were the same play, or revisions of the same play. Greg considered the possibility that "Godfrey of Boulogne" was the "Jerusalem" play in the repertory of Strange's Men at the Rose in March 1592. He also noted the registration at Stationers' Hall of a "Godfrey of Boulogne" on 19 June 1594, a month before Henslowe entered the second part in the playlists of the Admiral's Men. And yet, after suggesting that these plays were versions of one another, Greg expressed doubts about the identifications because details of the story and characters did not fit; nevertheless, he decided that "[o]n the whole . . . it is perhaps probable that the present play ['Godfrey of Boulogne'] was that later published as the *Four Prentices*."[20] Greg also struggled with the issue of multiple parts. Although Henslowe clearly marked two entries of "Godfrey of Boulogne" as the second part (e. g., "2 pte of godfrey of bullen," 19 July 1594), Greg decided that "one play only appears to be meant" by the twelve entries collectively.[21]

A commentary on "Godfrey of Boulogne" written from a commercial point of view differs significantly from Greg's commentary. Instead of collapsing the plays on apparently similar subjects into a single play, or revised versions of that play, such a commentary emphasizes the theatrical popularity of the subject of the conquest of Jerusalem, a popularity that continued from 1592 and "Jerusalem" (if it was indeed about the conquest) through 1632 and the second publication of Heywood's *Four Prentices of London*. This popularity spawned at least four plays on the subject, and at least three companies profited thereby (Strange's Men, 1592; Admiral's Men, 1594–5; Worcester's/Queen Anne's Men, in the 1600s). The production of "Jerusalem" at the Rose in 1592 brought Henslowe an average of 32s. per performance; the two parts of "Godfrey of

Boulogne" brought in slightly more than 32s. per performance in 1594–5. More than one dramatist (Heywood) made money from writing the plays, and more than one stationer (John Danter, John Wright, and Nicholas Okes) expected to make money from publishing them. Whoever wrote "Godfrey of Boulogne" recognized the value of the subject matter well enough to expand the narrative into two parts, focusing on the single heroic figure of Godfrey. Heywood saw the advantage of emphasizing both the commoner background of his heroes and the theatrics of the fight, which Francis Beaumont remembered in *The Knight of the Burning Pestle* in the citizen's reference to the pikes thrust by the four apprentices.

The treatment of histories in the weekly offerings of the Admiral's Men, 1595–6, also suggests several marketing strategies of the repertory generally. When the players resumed playing at the Rose after a summer hiatus of two months, they scheduled popular favorites from the previous year to draw audiences back to the playhouse. Their opening show, *A Knack to Know an Honest Man*, had been new in October 1594, and it had already received sixteen performances; it was to continue playing into the autumn of 1596–7. The company added three more money-makers from 1594–5: "The Wise Man of West Chester," "Seven Days of the Week," and "Long Meg of Westminster."[22] The first new play, introduced in the opening week of playing, was the English chronicle history, "Longshanks." It proved to be among the most successful offerings of the year, receiving fourteen performances through 9 July 1596 with an average return to Henslowe of 31s. The Admiral's Men introduced four more new histories in 1595–6, two in the fall-winter season and two in the spring-summer. Except for "Julian the Apostate," all did well, returning on average more than 30s. per performance to Henslowe.

The Admiral's Men had three multi-part history plays in 1595–6, and their deployment of these in the calendar of offerings illustrates the marketing possibilities of serial parts and duplicate material. Both the two-part *Tamburlaine* and the two-part "Hercules" were old in 1595–6, having been introduced in 1594–5 (*Tamburlaine* was even then in revival). Part one of *Tamburlaine* was in its ninth performance (17 December 1594) when the second part was revived on 19 December to accompany it. Thereafter the plays were scheduled consecutively five times including their mutual retirement on 12 and 13 November 1595.[23] The second part of "Hercules," introduced two weeks after its first part, thereafter appeared in tandem with its mate for six of seven performances.[24] In an extraordinary demonstration of the commercial appeal of multi-part plays, the Admiral's Men anticipated the debut of part two of "Hercules" by scheduling part one on 20 May 1595, the two parts of *Tamburlaine* on 21 and 22 May, and the new second part of "Hercules" on 23 May; thus for four days straight the two parts of two plays were performed.

The appearance of the "Tamar Cham" plays in Henslowe's lists illustrates another option in scheduling. Strange's Men, who owned both parts in 1592, appear to have marketed them as substitutes. They introduced part two, played it twice, then introduced part one, and played it exclusively for four performances. The Admiral's Men played both parts of "Tamar Cham" as they did the two-part "Hercules" and two-part *Tamburlaine*, that is, as serial parts or sequels. The players introduced part one first and gave it five performances before introducing part two, which they played in tandem with part one on 10 and 11 June, 19 and 20 June, and 26 and 27 June.[25] However, in a variation of the strategy of Strange's Men, in which the two parts were perceived as substitutes, the Admiral's Men appear to have substituted the two-part "Tamar Cham" for the two-part *Tamburlaine*. The latter pair was retired in November 1595; the former pair was introduced in May 1596. As a result, from 28 August 1594 when part one of *Tamburlaine* was introduced, through 13 November 1596 when part one of "Tamar Cham" was retired, audiences at the Rose could have seen a total of thirty-six performances of plays similar in name, genre, structure, and exotic appeal.

The introduction of "Henry V" in the 1595–6 repertory suggests another variation on the complementary – as well as contrastive – commercial value of items in a company's repertory. Together with the *Tamburlaine* plays and the "Tamar Cham" plays, "Henry V" appears to represent a clustering of epic drama with larger-than-life heroic figures. I argue elsewhere that the two-part "Hercules" might have belonged to this group as well.[26] If so, the Admiral's Men had three kinds of historical drama through which to explore the stage as a site of epic action and heroic behavior: the foreign history, English chronicle, and classical play. In terms of scheduling during 1595–6, the company had advertised the complementarity of the two-part *Tamburlaine* and two-part "Hercules" plays in May 1595, when the new second part of "Hercules" led to a four-day promotion of multipart epics. The company maintained that connection in the fall of 1595 by playing either the *Tamburlaine* plays or the "Hercules" plays in eight of the fourteen weeks of August through November. On 28 November, the company introduced "Henry V." The two parts of *Tamburlaine* had just retired, and in subsequent months "Henry V" was twice scheduled in tandem with the first part of "Hercules" (16, 18 December, with no intervening play; 5, 6 January). The first part of "Tamar Cham" was not introduced until 6 May 1596 and its second part on 11 June. Once in June (17, 19, 20, with no intervening play) and once in July (8, 10 July, with "Longshanks" intervening), these plays were scheduled in the same week as "Henry V." In the months between the retirement of the two-part *Tamburlaine* and the introduction of the two-part "Tamar Cham," the play that seems to have been coordinated with "Henry V" is "Chinon of England." After its debut on 3 January, it often alternated weekly performances with "Henry V"; in the fourth week of May, it played in a three-day run with part one of "Tamar Cham" and "Henry V" (25–27 May 1596). Perhaps, then, the offerings in heroical romance attracted audiences similar to those who liked plays about Tamburlaine, Hercules, and Tamar Cham.

Companies exploited offerings not only in their own repertory but also in the repertories of their competitors. The play of "Henry V" in the repertory of the Admiral's Men, 1595–7, illustrates the proliferation across company lines of plays on similar subjects. The Chamberlain's Men, no doubt aware of the success of "Henry V" at the Rose, might have "instructed" Shakespeare to provide them with a similar play (or he might have gotten the idea himself). It is possible, however, that the Admiral's Men (or their dramatists) had themselves been prompted to produce a play on Henry V because of events at the Swan playhouse. William Ingram conjectures that the Swan was built by mid-1595 and that men including George Attewell and Francis Henslowe were players there.[27] Scott McMillin and Sally-Beth MacLean are willing to conjecture that the company was the Queen's Men but not that specific plays associated with that company were staged there.[28] And yet, at least one play owned by the Queen's Men – *The Famous Victories of Henry V* – appears to have had stage life after its registration at Stationers' Hall on 14 May 1594. The evidence is its publication in 1598, with a title-page advertisement of the Queen's Men.

If the Queen's Men did play at the Swan in the summer of 1595, and if they played *The Famous Victories of Henry V,* it is reasonable to suppose that the Admiral's Men acquired a similar play themselves because they recognized the theatrical value of Henrican story materials. It is reasonable to suppose further that the Chamberlain's Men saw the same commercial advantage and acted similarly to acquire Shakespeare's *1 Henry IV.* McMillin and MacLean, pointing out the emphasis on historical subjects in the repertory of the Queen's Men, lead me to conjecture that other such plays in the possession of the company were also played at the Swan. Perhaps, then, Shakespeare's *King John* was the Chamberlain's competitive response to the performance of *The Troublesome Reign of King John* at the Swan. Presumably, the Chamberlain's Men had Shakespeare's *Richard III* in repertory in 1594–5; the Queen's Men might then have been tempted to revive their *True Tragedy of Richard III* at the Swan in 1595. Still another history play, Peele's *Edward I*, might have participated in a cross-company repertorial competition. Published in 1593 without the name of its company owners on the title page, *Edward I* was published again in 1599; if it had been revived by some company between 1593 and 1599, it might have had a commercial influence on the appearance of "Longshanks" in the repertory of the Admiral's Men.

Surviving texts show commercial influences not obvious from the clues of similar titles and story materials. McMillin and MacLean discuss the attempts by the Queen's Men to counter the influence of Marlowe's drama in the language, themes, and characterization of *The Troublesome Reign of King John* and *Selimus*. Shakespeare responded to the revival of *The Jew of Malta* in the repertory of the Admiral's Men in 1596 with the appropriation of Barabas and Abigail as well as the parody of Barabas's speech about his daughter and his gold.[29] But the text of *Romeo and Juliet* shows that he had responded also to the performances of *The Jew of Malta* in 1594 by appropriating Marlowe's balcony scene for his own lovers; and, in case audiences missed the connection, he transformed Barabas's line about the star shining in the east into Romeo's romantic sighting of Juliet at the window. Given the popularity of *Romeo and Juliet*, and the evidence that it was in production at the Curtain in 1597, the Chamberlain's Men might have had both it and *The Merchant of Venice* in repertory in 1596–7 to capitalize on the commercial success of the Admiral's revival of *The Jew of Malta* in the spring of 1596. Another familiar instance of commercial allusions is Shakespeare's parody in *2 Henry IV* of Tamburlaine's line, "Holla, ye pamper'd jades of Asia!" (4.3.1). The second part of *Henry IV* was on stage probably in 1598–9, after

Henslowe's records for performances of the second part of *Tamburlaine* had ended. Shakespeare's line might then have been an indirect advertisement of another Tamburlaine play, one in his own repertory at about this time, "The Tartarian Cripple."[30] Costuming must also have been a dimension of commercial competition in similar plays. An instance suggested by the similarity of *Edward I* and "Longshanks" is the coronation suit for Edward. The text of *Edward I* specifies a glass suit. An inventory in Henslowe's book of accounts indicates that the Admiral's Men had had a character-specific costume, "longe-shanckes sewte," that by 1598 was "Gone and loste" (*HD* 317).

A narrative of theatrical wars or quarreling dramatists, with alterations of emphasis, could accommodate the description here of commercial uses of the repertory. Much depends upon whether the companies perceived the repertory to be a broad instrument for the attraction of playgoers or a targeted one. The playlists in Henslowe's diary suggest an attempt to appeal to all available customers; presumably the offerings at other public houses such as the Globe and Boar's Head had a similar intent. On very little evidence, however, scholars such as Harbage have supposed that the Children of Paul's in 1599 and the Children of the Chapel in 1600 targeted a small part of the theatregoing London populace, specifically the wealthy leisured class. In *The Privileged Playgoers of Shakespeare's London* (1981) Ann Cook challenges this received wisdom by suggesting that these privileged playgoers were in fact a large part of the men's theatrical market. Even if repertories were targeted at a specific audience, it behooved the boys' companies as well as the men's to increase the size of that audience further. To Londoners who had developed a taste for playgoing due to such attractions as Marlowe's action figures and mighty line, the boys' companies were a "noveltie" in 1599 and 1600, as Gilderstone wryly observed in the text of *Hamlet* published in 1603. But, as Richard Dutton suggests, as long as the boys' companies played only once a week "the commercial competition from their small houses was always finite."[31]

THE BOOK TRADE AND COMPANY COMMERCE

John Payne Collier, as part of his proof that Shakespeare must have written *Edward III*, argued that Cuthbert Burby, who registered the play at Stationers' Hall on 1 December 1595, was the brother of

Richard Burbage. Collier conjectured "that the play found its way to the press through the person [Richard] who, doubtless, had sustained the principal part in it on the stage."[32] As evidence that the Cuthberts were the same man, Collier cited an entry in the Stationers' Register on 5 May 1592, where Burby's name is rendered "Cuthbert Burbidge."[33] This confusion of identities illustrates one kind of mistake by scholars concerning the commercial relationships of stationers and playing companies. Others include a desire to read stationers' records from the point of view of Shakespeare, a misunderstanding of normative practices at Stationers' Hall, and a misrepresentation of the value of playbooks to individual stationers. However, in the last quarter-century scholars have been revising the arguments of Collier, W. W. Greg, A. W. Pollard, and their generation of editors on issues concerning the book trade.[34] Most textual scholars today assume that stationers who acquired playbooks did so legitimately. It remains unclear why a stationer might buy a given playbook because plays were merely one of his many commodities and not his best-selling wares. However, that same book had substantial commercial value in the playhouse. It is thus even less clear why a company might sell it to stationers. Scholars have conjectured, reasonably, that companies withheld their property from publication until the plays had exhausted their stage popularity, yet there might have been times when companies saw an advantage to themselves in having their plays in print. Peter W. M. Blayney points out two eighteen-month periods when an unusually large number of plays were registered at Stationers' Hall: December 1593–May 1595 and May 1600–October 1601. In the details of these transactions, there are clues to the role of the book trade in commerce among the playing companies.

Blayney identifies December 1593 through May 1595 as the first of two "peak periods" of playbook acquisition by stationers.[35] Twenty-seven plays were registered at Stationers' Hall during these months. Of these, fourteen reached print by the end of 1595; another four were printed by the end of 1599, and another two were printed eventually (1605, 1633).[36] In general, therefore, the stationers who acquired these playbooks carried their initial investment through into publication. Furthermore, six of the fourteen printed by the end of 1595 were published again, with the initial stationers again profiting. For example, *A Looking Glass for London and England*, printed in 1594 by Thomas Creede for William Barley, was reprinted by

Creede for Barley in 1598 and for Thomas Pavier in 1602. Burby backed two editions of *Orlando Furioso* (1594, 1599) and *Mother Bombie* (1594, 1598). The *Contention Between the Houses of York and Lancaster* (*1 Contention*) and *The True Tragedy of Richard Duke of York* (*True Tragedy*) were printed in 1594/5 and 1600 for Thomas Millington. Edward White sold editions of *Titus Andronicus* at the sign of the Gun at the little north door of Paul's in 1594, 1600, and 1611. Blayney excludes seven plays published in 1594 or 1595 without registration, but I include these below in discussions of company commerce with stationers because the title pages of their quartos identify their company owners.[37]

Profitable as the plays acquired in 1593–5 might have been, they were not a major source of revenue for these stationers. John Danter printed thirty-three works in the years 1593–5, only six of which were plays.[38] Danter is one of the men formerly accused of trading in pirated playbooks. A. W. Pollard revealed not only his misunderstanding of stationers' business but also the prejudices of his age against stationers who dealt primarily in ephemera by characterizing Danter as an unprincipled bottom-feeder.[39] Yet nothing in Danter's transactions during 1593–5 raises an eyebrow now. Even by Pollard's erroneous standards, Danter's treatment of five plays printed in 1594–5 was routine, with authorized entries in the Stationers' Register and uncontested subsequent publications. The fact that two of Danter's registrations apparently did not result in publications is insignificant, given that many other items registered by him were not printed. Thomas Creede also supposedly profited disproportionately from the trade in playbooks, but during the time that he was printing six of Blayney's twenty-seven plays plus *1 Contention* and *Selimus*, he was making money on the printing of twenty-six non-theatrical items.

Blayney finds plausible Pollard's supposition that this first peak period occurred because "the acting companies themselves offered an unusual number of manuscripts for publication," [40] but he is not persuaded by Pollard's explanation that the companies were willing to sell because they had been "very hard hit" by the 1593 plague.[41] Blayney observes that "the peak period happened *after* rather than during the closure and . . . the sums involved [in the sale of playbooks] would have been relatively small." [42] One company cited as the prime candidate for the liquidation of its repertory due to financial hardship is Pembroke's Men. Philip Henslowe provided evidence of the company's trouble when he told Edward Alleyn in a letter dated 28 September 1593 that Pembroke's Men had discontinued their tour and sold their apparel to cover debts (*HD* 280). Andrew Gurr includes playbooks in their sale.[43] If so, there should be entries in the Stationers' Register that mark the sales. There is one entry, but it is somewhat early for Henslowe's time frame: *Edward II*, which was registered at Stationers' Hall by William Jones on 6 July 1593. The others are somewhat late: *Titus Andronicus* was registered by John Danter on 6 February 1594 (six months later); *The Taming of A Shrew* was registered on 2 May 1594 (nine months later). Two more books might have been sold around this time, but features of their handling by stationers diminish their value as evidence: *1 Contention* was registered at Stationers' Hall on 12 March 1594 and published in 1594, but its title page does not advertise its ownership by Pembroke's Men; *The True Tragedy* does advertise the company on its 1595 title page, but because it was not registered, its acquisition cannot certainly be linked to Pembroke's alleged fire sale. Even if all five of these books were sold to stationers in the late summer and autumn of 1593, Pembroke's Men would have raised a mere £10 for their creditors.

The Queen's Men also are often thought to have sold playbooks when money was tight. McMillin and MacLean offer another explanation for the company's sales in 1590. They see a "cultural contest" triggered by the publication of the two-part *Tamburlaine* in 1590, in which the Queen's play, *Three Lords and Three Ladies* (also 1590), was unable to compete.[44] The Queen's Men tried again in 1591 with the publication of *The Troublesome Reign of King John*, marketing it in two parts with a preface that imitated the preface "To the Gentlemen Readers" published with *Tamburlaine*. G. M. Pinciss has argued that Thomas Creede was a major conduit by which Queen's plays came into print. From 1594 to 1599, Creede registered and printed ten plays, four of which have title pages that advertise the Queen's Men (*The Famous Victories of Henry V, The True Tragedy of Richard III, Selimus,* and *Clyomon and Clamydes*). Pinciss assigns another four to the Queen's Men (*A Looking Glass for London and England, The Pedlar's Prophecy, James IV,* and *Alphonsus King of Aragon*) because their authors (George Peele, Robert Wilson) are known to have written for the Queen's Men.[45] McMillin and MacLean, being conservative, do not adopt the assignments by Pinciss unless a title-page advertisement confirms company ownership. Yet the May 1594 acquisitions do coincide with a note by Philip

Henslowe that he had given his nephew Francis £15 on 8 May "for his share to the Quenes players when they brocke & went into the contrey to playe" (*HD* 7).[46] On 14 May, the same day that Creede entered *The Famous Victories of Henry V* and *James IV* in the Stationers' Register, Edward White entered five playbooks, one of which was soon published with a title-page advertisement of the Queen's Men (*Friar Bacon and Friar Bungay*).[47]

The coincidence of the entries by Creede and White with the departure of a group of Queen's players into the country suggests an intentional sale but not necessarily the motive for that sale. Even if one reason was to raise cash for the upcoming tour, the players might not have been selling their only copy of a play. My argument above, that the Queen's Men might have leased the Swan playhouse at its opening in 1595 and revived *The Famous Victories of Henry V* in competition with the "Henry V" offered by the Admiral's Men, depends upon Francis Henslowe and his fellows' retaining a text. Creede, in deciding to print it in 1598, might have known of its stage life since his purchase in 1594, but he might also have been looking at the current market for material on Henry V reflected in the registration of Shakespeare's *1 Henry IV* on 25 February 1598 and printing that same year.

From the viewpoint of company commerce, Blayney's suggestion that publicity was a motive in the sale of playbooks is worth pursuing. Twenty-two of the registrations occurred between December 1593 and July 1594, a time that coincides with the return of companies to London from long periods of touring and the reorganization of players into new companies (or new versions of old ones). Moreover, the fullness of detail on the title pages of a dozen or so of those printed in 1594 and 1595 (including a few printed without registration) suggests a general eagerness to advertise the resumption of business by advertising the popular and sensational narratives being dramatized on public stages. For example, Thomas Millington, when he acquired *1 Contention*, and Thomas Creede, when he acquired *Locrine*, acquired as well a description of the vivid action in these scripts, and they wrote out the descriptions in the Stationers' Register. Creede, who printed both books, repeated that action in title-page advertisements. The title page of *1 Contention*, for example, advertises the death of Duke Humphrey, the banishment and death of the Duke of Suffolk, the tragic end of the Cardinal of Winchester, the rebellion of Jack Cade, and the Duke of York's claim to the throne.

As it happens, the title page of the quarto of *1 Contention* did not name the company owners, but others such as *The Battle of Alcazar* and *The Massacre at Paris* did.[48] In some cases, then, it would appear that companies expected to get publicity specifically for themselves. However, by the time these playbooks reached the bookstalls, much of that company information was out of date or irrelevant. For example, when the *True Tragedy* was published in 1595, it advertised Pembroke's Men, even though the Chamberlain's Men must have acquired it in May 1594 and performed it soon afterward. Likewise, by the time *Titus Andronicus* reached bookstalls in 1594, the aggregation of players indicated by its multiple-company advertisement of Derby's, Pembroke's, and Sussex's Men had dissolved. Richard Jones's advertisement of Edward Alleyn and Will Kempe on the title page of *A Knack to Know a Knave* suggests its company owners in 1592–4 (Strange's Men) but not after May 1594.[49] The Queen's Men, probably on tour in 1594, received the most publicity from title-page advertisements in 1594 but by way of a repertory perhaps retired: *Friar Bacon and Friar Bungay, Old Wives Tale, The True Tragedy of Richard III*, and *Selimus*. Likewise the boys' companies, defunct in 1594, were nonetheless advertised on the title pages of three plays published that year.

Blayney identifies a second period of significantly heavy registration from May 1600 through October 1601. As in the period of 1593–5, twenty-seven playbooks were registered for the first time at Stationers' Hall; seventeen were printed either by the end of December 1601 or within a year of their registration; another three were printed eventually.[50] Three received a second issue in the next year or two, with the initial stationers again profiting. Thus, as in 1593–5, the stationers who invested in these playbooks were at least adequately rewarded; but, as in the earlier period, the playbooks were not the major source of these stationers' revenue. William Leake sold editions of *Venus and Adonis, The Passionate Pilgrim*, and sermons by Henry Smith during 1599–1602, along with *The Downfall of Robert, Earl of Huntingdon* and *The Death of Robert, Earl of Huntingdon* in 1601. Mathew Lownes sold more plays in 1599–1602 than he did sermons or news reports, but his stock was more diverse in later years. James Roberts, for all his interest in plays owned by the Chamberlain's Men, printed only two of them between 1599 and 1602, during which time he was printing thirty-two other works.

In comparison with the plays published in 1593–5, the most

remarkable feature of the publications in 1600–1 is the naming of company owners in title-page advertisements. The accuracy of the information, as well as its formulaic expression, suggests not only that the companies themselves released the texts to stationers but also that they wanted their patrons to be named with the publications. For example, the Admiral's Men were named on the title pages of three of the twenty-seven plays registered in the batch of 1600–1: the first part of *Sir John Oldcastle*; *The Downfall of Robert, Earl of Huntingdon*; and *The Death of Robert, Earl of Huntingdon*. That name reflected the recently acquired title of the company's patron as well as his position: "As it hath been lately acted by the right honorable the Earle of Notingham Lord high Admirall of England his seruants" (title page of Q1600, *1 Sir John Oldcastle*). The Chamberlain's Men were named on the title pages of six plays in the 1600–1 registrations: *A Larum for London, Henry V, Every Man In his Humour, Much Ado About Nothing, 2 Henry IV,* and *A Midsummer Night's Dream*. Their patron, too, was fully advertised: "As it hath bene sundry times playd by the Right honorable the Lord Chamberlaine his seruants" (title page of Q1600, *Henry V*). Seven plays of the twenty-seven registered were published with advertisements of their ownership by boys' companies. Five advertised the Children of Paul's: *The Maid's Metamorphosis, Jack Drum's Entertainment, The Wisdom of Doctor Dodypoll, Antonio and Mellida,* and *Antonio's Revenge*. Two advertised the Children of the Chapel: *Love's Metamorphosis* and *Cynthia's Revels*.

Several additional features suggest that there was more commercial force behind the sales in 1600–1 than in 1593–5. For one, the 1600–1 plays were relatively current repertory items; perhaps the oldest was *Every Man In his Humour*, which had been new in September 1598. For another, their company ownership was current. Also in 1600–1, nine of the plays identified their authors by name or initials; eight of the nine carried the company's name.[51] Curiously, one advertising feature is generally missing from title pages of plays owned by the men's companies: a performance venue. The title page of *The Shoemakers' Holiday* advertised a performance at Court, the title page of *Cynthia's Revels* advertised Blackfriars, and title pages advertising the Children of Paul's necessarily advertised the playhouse at Paul's; but none of the title pages that advertised the Admiral's Men or Chamberlain's Men also advertised the Fortune or Globe.[52]

In order to explore why some companies might have wanted their plays advertised in 1600–1 – and advertised by way of their company name and patronage – it may help to consider the starting point of the sales as well as the rhythm of the registrations (I assume that the plays were registered soon after their purchase). Pollard looked to the Privy Council order of 22 June 1600.[53] However, Blayney starts this second peak period with the entry of "Cloth Breeches and Velvet Hose" on 27 May 1600. For the Chamberlain's Men, therefore, an interest in the sale of playbooks for publication began in late May 1600 (a second play, *A Larum for London*, was registered on 29 May).[54] The company apparently did not sell more playbooks until August, when five were registered. Another was registered in October; then no more appeared for more than a year when *Satiromastix* was registered (11 November 1601). According to Blayney's set of twenty-seven registrations, the Admiral's Men did not join the rush to publication until August 1600, when they sold the two-part *Sir John Oldcastle*. They followed this sale with the offering of the two-part Robin Hood plays in December. The Children of Paul's did not begin to sell plays until July 1600, when *The Maid's Metamorphosis* was registered; they then sold *Jack Drum's Entertainment* (S. R. 8 September) and *The Wisdom of Doctor Dodypoll* (S. R. 7 October). A year later they sold *Antonio and Mellida* and *Antonio's Revenge* (S. R. 24 October 1601). The Children of the Chapel sold only two plays during the eighteen-month span of this peak period: the old play, *Love's Metamorphosis* (S. R. 25 November 1600), and the new play, *Cynthia's Revels* (23 April 1601).

Considering the registrations of 1600–1 from the viewpoint of company commerce, I suggest that – as in 1593–5 – there is no single reason why the companies sold some of their playbooks at particular times. Sales by the Chamberlain's Men in May and August do not by themselves seem significant except in their number, but events in the business of the Admiral's Men provide a suggestive context. By January 1600, the Admiral's players knew that they were soon to have a new playhouse called the Fortune. It is plausible that businessmen in the company decided to generate interest in that new playhouse by getting plays into print that advertised the company and its repertory. Thus they accelerated the rate at which they normally sold texts, selling not only *Old Fortunatus*, which was registered on 20 February, but also *Look About You*, and *The Shoemakers' Holiday*.[55] Having developed language for the advertisement of themselves and their patron with *The Blind Beggar of Alexandria* in 1598 ("by the right honorable the Earle of Nottingham, Lord high

Admirall his seruantes"), they appear to have duplicated the formula on the front of the copies to be sold.

The Chamberlain's Men would have known by May that the opening of the Fortune was imminent. Perhaps therefore their managers decided to sell some of their plays, imitating the Admiral's Men in advertising their business. Since 1597, the Chamberlain's Men had been providing the name of their patron and company with the sale of some of their playbooks (maybe all), and they continued this practice in 1600. The Privy Council order in June 1600 might have given them additional incentive to publicize their business by way of the title pages of plays in print. Richard Dutton, looking back to 19 February 1598 and a similar Privy Council order to allow these two companies only, argues that the Chamberlain's Men and the Admiral's Men began to build into their playtexts reminders of their special privilege as licensed companies. He cites *The Shoemakers' Holiday* and *Old Fortunatus* as examples for the Admiral's Men, and *A Midsummer Night's Dream* for the Chamberlain's Men. In addition, he suggests that *As You Like It*, *Every Man Out of his Humour*, *Twelfth Night*, and *All's Well That Ends Well*, which had roles for Robert Armin, the company's newly acquired player of fools, advertised the company's privilege to audiences.[56] Given that some of these texts were sold in 1600–1, it is reasonable to assume that the Admiral's Men and Chamberlain's Men at this particular moment saw not only the stage but also the bookshop as a venue for advertising their special status.

Despite the commercial importance of the reopening of the boys' playhouses in 1599 and 1600, the men's companies do not appear to have made a significant connection between those reopenings and the sale of playbooks. Nor does it appear that the Children of Paul's looked immediately to book sales to increase revenue or advertise themselves, for their initial sale came in July 1600 (perhaps nine months after their opening). *Love's Metamorphosis* was registered within three months of the opening of Blackfriars, but its printing in 1601 turned out not to be an exclusive advertisement of the Children of the Chapel, for its title page named the Children of Paul's also. In terms of repertories generally, the Children of Paul's could not have advertised their house as the site for satirical comedies, if that was the reputation they sought, by selling the pastoral *The Maid's Metamorphosis* for publication in July 1600; nor could the Children of the Chapel with *Love's Metamorphosis*, also a pastoral. In terms of those plays putatively associated with the War of the Theatres, the Children of Paul's did sell *Jack Drum's Entertainment* to stationers in September 1600, but it could provide little fuel at Richard Oliffe's shop to any quarreling among poets without Marston's name on the title page. *Cynthia's Revels* appeared in May 1601, with a title page that advertised Ben Jonson and Blackfriars; however, Marston's *What You Will*, the play that was supposedly the butt of Jonson's jokes in *Cynthia's Revels*, was not printed until 1607. A similar misfiring occurred with *Every Man Out of his Humour*, which was on sale at William Holme's shop at Sergeant's Inn Gate in Fleet Street in 1600, and *Histrio-Mastix*, its supposed target of satirical pointing, which was not published until 1610. Perhaps within weeks of each other in 1602, *Poetaster* and *Satiromastix* were published, but even they could not have attracted much attention to themselves in bookshops as adversaries on stage. *Poetaster* was sold by Mathew Lownes at his shop in St. Dunstan's Churchyard. It was therefore displayed beside unsold copies of Marston's *Antonio and Mellida* and *Antonio's Revenge* but not beside its playhouse rival, *Satiromastix*, which was on sale two parishes to the east at Edward White's shop in St. Paul's Churchyard.

Obviously, there are many difficulties in assessing the role of stationers in the commerce of the Elizabethan companies. A company might anticipate a commercial advantage to itself, as the Queen's Men might have in the sale of five plays to one stationer in 1594, but those plans would be thwarted when the stationer did not publish the playbooks as the company expected. The rich detail of narrative and spectacle offered to playgoers in the description of "John of Gaunt" – "the famous historye of John of Gaunte, sonne of Kynge Edward the Third, with his conquest of Spaine and marriage of his twoo daughters to the kinges of Castile and Portugale" – apparently never tempted a shopper at White's sign of the Gun to attend a performance. In 1600 the Admiral's Men might reasonably have expected the publication of both parts of *Sir John Oldcastle* to attract playgoers and curry favor with the Cobhams at the expense of the Chamberlain's Men. Their expectations for part one, with its renunciation of Falstaff, were fulfilled; but part two, with the martyrdom of Oldcastle, was apparently never printed.

The periods of playbook registrations identified by Peter Blayney are not the only flash points of commercial activity between stationers and companies. From the perspective of buyers of quartos, 1599 was an interesting year. First editions of the two-part *Edward IV,*

A Warning for Fair Women, Alphonsus King of Aragon, Clyomon and Clamydes, George a Greene, An Humorous Day's Mirth, David and Bethsabe, and *Two Angry Women of Abingdon* appeared in bookshops. In addition, new printings of another eight old plays appeared. Thus, a browser at Cuthbert Burby's shop in Cornhill might have bought not only the newly printed *George a Greene* but also the reprinted *Orlando Furioso, Edward III,* and *Romeo and Juliet.* However, in order to buy all the new plays, such a customer would have had to visit not only Burby's shop but also three shops in St. Paul's Churchyard, one in Thames Street, one on Adling Hill, and one in Coleman Street.

But from the perspective of the companies, Blayney's two peak periods do appear to illustrate that companies on occasion recognized a commercial value to themselves in the availability of their plays in print. McMillin and MacLean, by calling the sale of *The Troublesome Reign of King John* in 1591 an advertisement of the quality of their playing, identify an occasion when a company looked to the bookstall as a site of competition with another company's offerings. The registrations in 1593–5 appear to recognize the need to advertise the return to playing in London after the long plague of 1593. Some of the registrations of 1600–1 appear to respond to the building of the Fortune playhouse, others to the confidence of the Admiral's Men and Chamberlain's Men in their new authority as licensed companies. In the wake of sales in 1600–1, more plays eventually were sold to stationers, and it appears that the companies had recognized and embraced one commercial feature of such sales, for their names as owners now frequently appeared on the title pages of plays printed after 1601.

The middle years of the 1590s were a significant time for the companies in the development of commercial strategies for their own enterprises as well as cooperative relationships with other companies. As the number of London playhouses increased, and as the cessation of plague permitted playing week after week without interruption, the companies came to depend on a large, diverse repertory with frequent infusions of new plays. This created a market for playwrights who could work quickly by themselves or with collaborators to supply a script on a popular subject, perhaps to be followed as rapidly by sequels or spin-offs. The debuts of new plays and the revival of old favorites created a demand for plays with similar motifs to which companies and playwrights alike responded.

In the expanding market of the 1590s, the companies employed many of the same playwrights and playwriting teams without noticeable acrimony. Despite the attempts by the Privy Council to pull down playhouses, or at least limit their number, the business of playing attracted new entrepreneurs and reinvigorated old ones. The boys' companies were a part of this larger market, but there is no evidence to suggest that the reopening of Paul's and Blackfriars caused the men's companies to develop new strategies of addressing competition in terms of playwrights, repertories, and the sale of playbooks to stationers. An oddity of the time, namely the explosion of playbook registrations in 1600–1, may be attributed in part to a jockeying for public attention by the Admiral's Men and Chamberlain's Men, but not, it appears, to their putative rivalry with the boys' companies.

CHAPTER 4

"Histrio-Mastix" and company commerce

True it is, that some bad Poems,
though not all, carry their Owners Marks about 'em.
There is some peculiar aukardness, false Grammar, imperfect Sense,
or at the least Obscurity; some Brand or other on this Buttock,
or that Ear, that 'tis notorious who are the Owners of the Cattel,
though they shou'd not Sign it with their Names.

John Dryden[1]

Histrio-Mastix is an important piece of the narrative of the War of the Theatres and therefore of old notions of commerce among the playing companies. It is most important if its author is John Marston and if it was performed at Paul's playhouse during the late summer or autumn of 1599. It is least important if its author is not Marston, its venue not a commercial playhouse, and its stage run not in the months of August through December of 1599. Whoever its author, *Histrio-Mastix* is no more important to commerce among the Elizabethan playing companies than the hundreds of plays in public and private playhouses, at Court, at the universities, in provincial city halls, at the Inns of Court, and in the banquet halls of noble houses – all sites where the appetite for playgoing was encouraged throughout England in Shakespeare's time. It is no more important to strategies of commerce than the dozens of plays that turn up in dramatic and non-dramatic texts by way of allusions. Stripped of an association with Marston and the boys' playhouses in 1599–1600, *Histrio-Mastix* may be seen for what it is: old-fashioned estate satire enlivened in a few scenes by a troupe of comic players but for the most part burdened with a wooden vocabulary, droning metrics, flat characters, and an inefficient design for the doubling of parts.

Until 1878, the sum of knowledge about the authorship and stage history of *Histrio-Mastix, Or, The Player Whipt* was gleaned from stationers' records: Thomas Thorpe registered the play at Stationers'

75

Hall on 31 October 1610, and it was published in quarto with an advertisement of Thorpe and the date of 1610 on the title page. The early playlists of Rogers and Ley (1656), Archer (1656), and Kirkman (1661) did not suggest an author, nor did Gerard Langbaine in *An Account of the English Dramatick Poets* (1691). But in 1878, in *The School of Shakspere*, Richard Simpson gave *Histrio-Mastix* an author, a reviser, company owners, a playhouse, dates for its debut and revival, and referents for its satirical pointings. Using circumstantial evidence, Simpson named George Peele as the initial author, John Marston as the reviser, a boys' school or university as the initial venue, a boys' playhouse as the venue of the revised production, 1590 as the initial date of performance, early winter of 1599 as the date of the revival, the character of Chrisoganus in the revised scenes as a flattering self-portrait of Marston in imitation of Ben Jonson, and the character of Post-hast as an unflattering portrait of Shakespeare.[2] By identifying Marston as part-author, Simpson expanded the time-frame of Jonson's quarrel with Marston from 1600–1 to 1599–1601 and added *Every Man Out of his Humour* and *Histrio-Mastix* to the plays involved. Simpson's identification also enabled scholars to expand further the tendency in eighteenth-century commentary to perceive theatre history as a cult of personality. Even though many scholars now think of the quarrels as an argument for the moral leadership of drama,[3] few have rejected the model of commerce in the old view, that is, the companies as adversarial rivals in a contest for playgoers.

    In earlier chapters, I have emphasized the cooperative strategies of players, companies, and dramatists, a cooperation similar to that of members in a guild. I have argued that, although there were personal quarrels, those quarrels did not determine business strategies. Here and in subsequent chapters, I pursue the thesis of cooperation indirectly, by dismantling the narrative that has supported a model of theatrical wars. *Histrio-Mastix*, having been assigned to 1598–9, is chronologically the first major piece in that narrative, followed by the "little eyases" passage in *Hamlet* (1599–1600) and the satirical pointing in *Poetaster* and *Satiromastix* (1601). The purpose of this chapter is to remove one foundational block, *Histrio-Mastix*, by arguing that it is a red herring in discussions of company commerce. In the first place, John Marston did not write any of it; it lacks not only the marks of Marstonian prosody and imagery but also the topicality of Marstonian allusions. In the second, none of the men's or boys' companies in London around

1600 could have staged it, even if the most ambitious of doubling schemes were used, because it requires more players than any company would have assembled. In the third, its publication by Thomas Thorpe in 1610 does more to separate it from Marston than to associate it with him. *Histrio-Mastix* did have a role in the economics of the playhouse industry: its stage life at a school, or an Inn of Court, helped to cultivate the habit of playgoing. It also contributed to the debate about the state of the theatre and theatrical poetry by giving Jonson a target for his scorn of pedantic language and traveling players. But it did not initiate Jonson's quarrel with Marston, and it did not accelerate competition among the playing companies *circa* 1599.

STYLE

Since Simpson declared Marston to be part-author of *Histrio-Mastix*, other scholars have also heard the "unmistakeable swagger" of Marston's style in the play.[4] R. A. Small characterized that style as virile, picturesque, and strenuous; Alvin Kernan called it " 'stuttering.' "[5] D. J. Lake argued on the basis of a linguistic analysis of *Histrio-Mastix* that Marston was indeed part-author of the play.[6] To my knowledge, however, the supporters of Marston's authorship have not compared *Histrio-Mastix* with Marston's poetry on stylistic aspects such as prosody and imagery. I make such a comparison here.[7] As texts I use Marston's satires in the collection, *The Scourge of Villanie*, and allegedly Marstonian passages in *Histrio-Mastix*. I choose *The Scourge of Villanie*, which was published in 1598 and republished in 1599 with an additional satire, because scholars who discuss the issue of authorship take for granted that Marston had already written some or all of these poems before he worked on *Histrio-Mastix*.[8] Also, it is the satirist's speeches by the character of Chrisoganus in *Histrio-Mastix* that putatively sound Marstonian. Furthermore, scholars have been persuaded of Marston's authorship because of shared vocabulary in Clove's speech in *Every Man Out of his Humour*, *The Scourge of Villanie*, and *Histrio-Mastix*; however, this coincidence of vocabulary may be no more than generic imitation. Recent scholarly interest in topical subject matter in drama suggests that elements of popular culture may be a fruitful basis of comparison; to illustrate, I develop a criterion I call a "trendiness index" to compare Marston with the author of *Histrio-Mastix*.

Prosody and imagery

Simpson heard Marston's "swagger" primarily in the voice of Chrisoganus, the scholar-pedant who becomes a satirist in *Histrio-Mastix*. Believing Marston to be the reviser, Simpson assigned parts of Acts II and III and all of Acts IV and V to him. Despite F. G. Fleay's giving the entire play to Marston, Simpson's view prevailed until 1958, when Alvin Kernan argued that the play was unified and therefore by Marston alone. Simpson and others pointed to a speech by Chrisoganus in Act II as typical of Marston's voice: "VVrite on, crie on, yawle to the common sort/ Of thickskin'd auditours" [D4]).[9] However, the author of *Histrio-Mastix* differs measurably from Marston in *The Scourge of Villanie* in such aspects of style as prosody and imagery. For example, the author of *Histrio-Mastix* uses mostly medial caesuras, and he rarely enjambs more than one line at a time. Marston, in contrast, frequently uses several caesuras in a line, in part because he is stringing together adjectives and making catalogues, as in "Our aduerse body, beeing earthly, cold, / Heauie, dull, mortall, would not long infold / A stranger inmate" (VIII.185–87).[10] Three- and four-line sets of enjambed lines are common in *The Scourge of Villanie*; Satire VII contains a seven-line enjambment (lines 70–76); Satire IX has an eight-line one (lines 46–53).

Both Marston and the author of *Histrio-Mastix* use iconographic metaphors, but the imagery of the play is almost exclusively emblematic: e. g., "Justice hath whips to scourge impiety" (F4). In contrast, much of Marston's imagery comes from contemporary life: "What Accademick starued Satyrist / . . . with inke black fist / would tosse each muck-heap for som outcast scraps / Of halfe-dung bones to stop his iawning chaps?" (Satire III.111–14). The author of *Histrio-Mastix* associates the poet with drunkenness, imagining ballad-mongers who fill "Their purest organ of inuention" with bottle-ale (D4). In contrast, Marston used a dog metaphor – "sharpe fangd Satyrist" (Satire II. 8; Satire IX. 4) – and it became something of a Marstonian signature. In fact, he believed himself so publicly associated with the dog-whip cluster of images that, in a satire added to *The Scourge of Villanie* in 1599, he took personal offense at an epigram allegedly by Joseph Hall that called for mad dogs to be "cured by cutting & kinsing" and asses to be whipped (Satire X. 50–56). That others associated him with the image is illustrated by a character in *The Second Part of the Returne from Parnassus* who alludes thus to Marston: "What, *Monsier Kinsayder*, lifting vp your legge and pissing against the world?" (1.2.267–8).[11] If that signature is to be found in *Histrio-Mastix*, it is only in the bland wail of Velure, the merchant: "O, I could gnash my teeth, and whip my self" (E2ᵛ).

Vocabulary

A coincidence of vocabulary initially prompted the attribution of *Histrio-Mastix* to Marston. Simpson credited his colleague, Brinsley Nicholson, with having noticed that a character named Clove, in one speech in Jonson's *Every Man Out of his Humour* (3.4.21–30), used words that occur in *The Scourge of Villanie* and in *Histrio-Mastix*. For Simpson, this proved his own hunch that Marston's swaggering style marked the old play. Nicholson noted the shared vocabulary in his edition of Jonson's work in the Mermaid Series in 1894. C. H. Herford, in his own magisterial edition in 1925, repeated Nicholson's note on the vocabulary as proof of Marston's authorship.[12] The relevant words in Clove's speech are "synderesis," "circumference," "intellectual," and "mincing capreall," which are found in *The Scourge of Villanie*; "Zodiack," "Eclipticke line," and "Histriomastix," which are found in *Histrio-Mastix*; and the phrase "port/paunch of Esquiline," which is found in both texts.

However, the problem with an attribution based on shared vocabulary, as S. Schoenbaum makes clear, is that a "testimony of parallels" needs to be more than generic imitation or coincidence; Schoenbaum cites Muriel St. Clare Byrne in the observation that the "mere accumulation of ungraded parallels does not prove anything."[13] The words from *The Scourge of Villanie* and *Histrio-Mastix* on the Nicholson-Herford list have the problem not only of being relatively common in general but of being most common in satirical literature. The phrase "Port Esquiline," which is in fact the only term in Clove's speech shared by *The Scourge of Villanie* and *Histrio-Mastix*, appears to have been popularized by Edmund Spenser, who used the expression to mean "anus" in the allegory of the body in *The Faerie Queene* (II.ix.32). Joseph Hall used it in 1597 in *Virgidemiarum* ("Port-esquiline," IV.I.58). If exactitude of parallels matters, it is worth noting that Chrisoganus's phrase in *Histrio-Mastix*, "paunch of Esquiline," which is also Clove's, is not identical with occurrences in *The Scourge of Villanie*. Marston used "Port Esqueline" (VII.185), "port

Esqueline" (VIII.200), and "muck-pit esculine" (IX.234). William Gifford, Jonson's editor in 1816, called Clove's speech "precious nonsense"; W. David Kay, Jonson's biographer in 1995, called it "learned nonsense."[14] If Simpson and Nicholson had shown a similar restraint, perhaps Marston would never have been mistakenly identified as the author of *Histrio-Mastix* on the basis of vocabulary shared by satirists in general.

Trendiness index

One mark that distinguishes the literature *circa* 1599, especially satirical literature, is its exploitation of literary and theatrical personalities, social fads, vulgar language, bawdry, and the like. Marston's *Scourge of Villanie* is very trendy in this regard; *Histrio-Mastix* is not at all. For example, Marston alludes to a number of contemporary poets including Joseph Hall, Everard Guilpin, Sir John Davies, Thomas Lodge, Thomas Nashe, Barnabe Barnes, Edmund Spenser, Christopher Marlowe, and William Shakespeare (to name a few); the author of *Histrio-Mastix* speaks of playing Tamburlaine on stage but seems otherwise unfamiliar with the literary or theatrical scene.[15] For another example, modern poets *circa* 1599 have learned how to curse. The poems in *The Scourge of Villanie* are outburst on outburst; with a vehemence unmatched in *Histrio-Mastix*, the Marstonian satirist hurls catalogues of insults and vulgar epithets at the objects of his disgust. Chrisoganus, the satirist in *Histrio-Mastix*, has outbursts, but he often turns them back on himself: "Poore foole, leaue prating, enuy not their shine, / Who still will florish, though great Fate repine" (E4^v). The Marstonian satirist is particularly hard on women, who in *The Scourge of Villanie* are scolds, trulls, stales, drabs, occupants, and whores. The one woman abused by language in *Histrio-Mastix* is an abstraction, that "Strumpet warre" (G^v).

There are several missed opportunities for bawdy punning and not much sex in *Histrio-Mastix*. The likeliest scene for such trendy action is in Act III, where the citizens' wives go shopping. Perpetuana, wife of the merchant Velure, asks the jeweler, "Of our three Iewells (sir) which likes you best?" (D3). Bellula orders a loose-bodied-gown for her "iewells maydenhead"; and Perpetuana orders one "tuck't and pinn'd / That powerfull winds may heaue it all a huffe" (D3^v). Fillisella boasts that she will hang "the glorious brightnesse of [her] Globe" on her new dress (D3ᵛ), and Bellula exults that citizens' wives will envy the women's breasts exposed in their new finery. The author of *Histrio-Mastix* may well have expected his audience to associate this chatter with jokes about lovers and genitalia, but the women themselves are merely vain *nouveaux riches*. Marston, in contrast, exploits the bawdy potential of language. His satirists know what the "long slit sleeue" of lechery invites (VII.174). They know that the epic lover who seeks "the inmost nookes of hell" winds up emasculated (VIII.34). An "instrument / Smooth fram'd at *Vitrio*" might save a woman from *"true French pestilence"* (III.94), but she had best be careful using it "in ioulting Coach" (III.32–33, 94, 123). A "busk-poynt" becomes an "itch-allaying pinne" that prompts mock-heroic worship (VIII.100–107).

The author of *Histrio-Mastix* also misses a popular subject in tobacco. Ben Jonson has smokers, anti-smokers, tobacco boys, tobacco boxes, pipes, and tobacco sellers in plays for the Globe and Blackfriars, 1598–1603. Tobacco is brought on stage by George Chapman in *An Humorous Day's Mirth* (at the Rose, 1597); by Thomas Dekker with *Old Fortunatus* and *The Shoemakers' Holiday* (at the Rose and Fortune, 1599–1600) and *Satiromastix* (at the Globe and Paul's, 1601); and by the dramatist of *The Wisdom of Doctor Dodypoll* (at Paul's, 1599–1600). Furthermore, non-dramatic poets refer to tobacco: Edmund Spenser, John Lyly, Joseph Hall, Thomas Nashe, John Donne, Thomas Bastard, Everard Guilpin, and Samuel Rowlands, to name a few. Edward Pudsey has a diatribe against tobacco in his commonplace book. In short, *everyone* is talking about it by 1599. Even the academic plays, parts one and two of *The Returne from Parnassus*, refer to smoking. But not the poet of *Histrio-Mastix*. In the time of Plenty, the gallants go hunting and hawking but they do not take tobacco.[16]

Like his contemporaries (except the poet of *Histrio-Mastix*), Marston characterized flawed personalities by making them smokers. In Satire IX of *The Scourge of Villanie*, for example, "Old Iack of Parris-garden" shops, wears fine clothes, dices, curses, blasphemes, keeps whores, and "Snuffe[s] vp smoak whiffs" (line 77). Feliche, in *Antonio and Mellida*, claims to "take not tobacco much" (3.2.74).[17] In *Jack Drum's Entertainment* (1599–1600), M. Puffe, a foolish wooer, chokes on both compliments and tobacco smoke. In *What You Will*, Quadratus, the railer, calls for "pudding *Tobacco*"; later, in a clownish show by four pages and the pedant, one of the boys announces another who has a grander part: "*Honorificacuminos Bidet Emperor of Crackes, Prince of Pages, Marques of Mumchance, and sole regent ovre a bale of false dice*, to all his under Ministers health, Crownes, Sack, Tobacco, and stockings uncrakt above the shooe."[18] Counting also a reference to tobacco in *Antonio's Revenge* (4.2.41–42), there are smokers in everything Marston wrote, 1598–1601.

There is no external evidence that Marston wrote *Histrio-Mastix*, and the internal evidence of style and vocabulary does not adequately meet S. Schoenbaum's test. There are not "unusual correspondences of language and thought" as measured by prosody, imagery, and topical references between *Histrio-Mastix* and Marston's known work, specifically and most immediately *The Scourge of Villanie*. The few parallels of vocabulary are not sufficient evidence of mutual authorship, for terms such as "Port Esquiline" were familiar to Elizabethans, particularly to satirists. Philip Finkelpearl, though arguing for Marston's authorship, nonetheless astutely observes that *Histrio-Mastix* "is a play written by a satirist with no playwriting experience."[19] Indeed; and I would add that its author – not Marston – had no future in writing for the commercial stage either.

DATE AND VENUE

If Marston did not write part or all of *Histrio-Mastix*, the stage history constructed by scholars disintegrates. The date and venue need not be Paul's playhouse in 1599, which R. A. Small chose because Marston supplied the Children of Paul's with plays after his work for the Admiral's Men in September 1599.[20] The date and venue need not even be the Middle Temple during Christmas 1598/9, which Philip Finkelpearl chooses because Marston was a member of the Middle Temple during his literary career, 1595–1606.[21] The collapse of orthodoxies about the date and venue of *Histrio-Mastix* has implications for the commercial relations of playing companies in 1599. If the play was performed at an Inn of Court or a university, it remains – by virtue of the shared vocabulary in Clove's speech in *Every Man Out of his Humour* and an allusion in *Poetaster* – in narratives of Jonson's campaign to provoke a debate on the language of satire and to involve intellectuals outside the theatre. But if it was not performed at Paul's (or another playhouse in London *circa* 1599), it ceases to be a factor both in company commerce and in narratives about the allegedly fierce rivalry of playing companies.

And *Histrio-Mastix* cannot, I think, have been performed at Paul's or another commercial venue. The evidence is its design. Quite simply, it requires too many players. In the following paragraphs, I discuss charts of doubling options for seven plays known to have been performed at Paul's, 1599–1602, and I compare these to a chart for *Histrio-Mastix* (see tables 2–9). These charts, based on principles of Elizabethan doubling patterns, show how the Children of Paul's might have cast seven of the plays that they certainly performed: *Antonio and Mellida, Jack Drum's Entertainment, Antonio's Revenge, The Wisdom of Doctor Dodypoll, The Maid's Metamorphosis, Satiromastix,* and *Blurt, Master Constable.*[22] Two of these plays, *Antonio and Mellida* and *Antonio's Revenge,* are certainly by Marston; a third, *Jack Drum's Entertainment,* is putatively his. The charts for these three plays suggest that Marston knew the number of players in the Children of Paul's and their level of expertise. The charts for the others in the boys' repertory show that their authors, like Marston, designed plays with the size and expertise of a conventionally sized company in mind. The chart for *Histrio-Mastix* shows the opposite; it reinforces Finkelpearl's observation that the play was written by an amateur dramatist for whom the principles of doubling followed by commercial Elizabethan companies were unknown or irrelevant.

In constructing the charts, I assume that the Children of Paul's used a doubling system similar to that of the men's companies and that they had a comparable number of players available. Practical rules for the Elizabethan doubling system have been developed by scholars such as David Bevington, W. A. Ringler, T. J. King, David Bradley, and Scott McMillin: major parts are not doubled; vague stage directions such as "attendants" or "pages" require two players; players who exit in one role do not return immediately in another (i.e., no "immediate juxtapositions"); a player may alternate between two roles, but no character is split between two players.[23] I modify the rule about immediate juxtapositions by allowing rapid role changes when they occur between acts, because the inter-act music for which the boys' companies were famous would have created extra time for a costume change (or so I assume). No one is quite sure about the number of players in the Children of Paul's. H. N. Hillebrand found the names of ten choristers in a suit in the Court of Exchequer (1554), and the names of nine or ten in various bishops' records (1574, 1594, and 1607).[24] W. Reavley Gair found evidence for eleven choristers in 1598.[25] Trevor Lennam, addressing the number of boys in the company before 1599, observed that seven of the older boys appear to have been retained by the chapel, and he queried whether they were "still useful to [the boys'] theatrical enterprise, perhaps aiding, and some of them even augmenting, the ten choristers in the more spectacular and demanding presentations."[26]

According to my charts, *Antonio and Mellida*, *Jack Drum's Entertainment*, and *The Maid's Metamorphosis*, which may be presented easily with seventeen players, may well represent the number of boys available to the Children of Paul's in the fall of 1599. Reavley Gair suggests that in *Antonio and Mellida* Marston intentionally "presented, in pageant form, the whole of the new Paul's company to the audience" in 1.1, advertising both the players and distinctive features of the playhouse (see table 2).[27] The stage directions of the opening scene (1.1) call for fourteen characters by name, plus one page, plus attendants. This number – seventeen – is sufficient for 5.2, the other scene with heavy demands on the company.[28] As Gair notes, Marston advertises the doubling of two major characters in the Induction, where one of the players says, "The necessity of the play forceth me to act two parts, Andrugio . . . and Alberto" (line 21). In my chart, in addition to the player cast as Alberto/Andrugio, I give six additional players a second part: Matzagente is also Prologue, Galeatzo is also the painter, Attendant 1 is also Lucio, Piero's Page is also Andrugio's Page, Attendant 2 is also the boy with a harp, and Castilio's Page (Catzo) is the extra page in 5.2. *Jack Drum's Entertainment* likewise needs seventeen players (see table 3). Eleven players with speaking roles do no doubling at all; five of the remaining six players take a second part; the sixth takes three parts, which give him collectively forty-eight lines of speech. *The Maid's Metamorphosis* may be played by sixteen players (see table 4).[29]

The charts of *Antonio's Revenge* and *The Wisdom of Doctor Dodypoll* suggest that the Children of Paul's soon had more players at their disposal. *Antonio's Revenge*, which Marston might have written a year or more after *Antonio and Mellida*, requires at least twenty players (see table 5). Ten with speaking roles do not double; four do (Strotzo/ Page 4/Torchbearer; Matzagente/Julio/Page 3; Feliche/Castilio; Mellida/Andrugio's Ghost).[30] In addition, six extras are needed to perform the roles of mute mourners, pages, boys, and waiting women, as well as the minor speaking roles of the senators. As a gauge of the doubling expertise of the Children of Paul's in 1599–1600, I have designed the doubling charts of the plays in the

Table 2. Doubling options: *"Antonio and Mellida"*

	Induction	Prologue	1.1	2.1	3.1	3.2	4.1	4.2	5.1	5.2	Epilogue
Galeatzo	Induction		1.1	2.1		3.2	4.1		Painter	5.2	
Piero	Induction		1.1	2.1		3.2	4.1			5.2	
Alberto	Induction		1.1	2.1	Andrugio		Andrugio	Andrugio	Alberto	Andrugio	Andrugio
Balurdo	Induction		1.1	2.1		3.2	4.1		5.1	5.2	
Forobosco	Induction		1.1	2.1						5.2	
Feliche	Induction		1.1	2.1		3.2	4.1		5.1	5.2	
Antonio	Induction		1.1	2.1		3.2	4.1	4.2		5.2	
Matzagente	Induction	Prologue	1.1	2.1		3.2				5.2	
Castilio			1.1	2.1		3.2				5.2	
Castilio's Page, Catzo			1.1	2.1		3.2	4.1		5.1	(Extra Page)	
Balurdo's Page, Dildo			1.1	2.1		3.2	4.1			5.2	
Mellida			1.1	2.1		3.2	4.1			5.2	
Rossaline			1.1	2.1		3.2				5.2	
Flavia			1.1	2.1		3.2				5.2	
Extra 1		(Attendant 1)			Lucio		Lucio	Lucio		Lucio	
Extra 2		(Attendant 2)			Andrugio's Page		A's Page	A's Page		(Boy w/harp)	
Extra 3		(Piero's Page)								Piero's Page	

Mutes are in parentheses

Table 3. Doubling options: "Jack Drum's Entertainment"

	Introduction	1.1	1.2	1.3	2.1	2.2	2.3	3.1	3.2	3.3	4.1	4.2	4.3	4.4	4.5	5.1
Jack Drum		1.1						3.1			4.1	4.2				5.1
Timothy Twedle		1.1					2.3	3.1			4.1					5.1
Sir Edward Fortune		1.1					2.3	3.1								5.1
M. Mamon		1.1			2.1	2.2							4.3			
Camelia		1.1					2.3		3.2	3.3			4.3		4.5	5.1
Katherine		1.1			2.1		2.3		3.2	3.3			4.3			5.1
Winifride		1.1		1.3			2.3	3.1	3.2		4.1		4.3		4.5	5.1
Flawne		1.1			2.1					3.3				Ms Brabant		
Brabant Jr	as Tyer-man		1.2	1.3			2.3		3.2			4.2			4.5	
Ned Planet	as Child Player		1.2	1.3		2.2			3.2			4.2			4.5	
Brabant Sr				1.3		2.2						4.2		4.4		
M. Puffe				1.3	2.1				3.2							
M. John fo de King				1.3		2.2	2.3				4.1	4.2		4.4		
Pasquill					2.1	2.2	2.3			3.3			4.3			
Extra 1	(Morris 1)		Page 1					Page 1					Country Maid			Page 1
Extra 2	(Morris 2)		Ellis						Ellis				Ellis			Ellis
Extra 3	Fool		Page 2							Page 2			Page 2			

Mutes are in parentheses

Table 4. *Doubling options: "The Maid's Metamorphosis"*

	Prologue	I.I	2.I	3.I	4.I	5.I
Phylander		I.I				5.I
Orestes		I.I	Somnus			
Eurymine		I.I	2.I	3.I	4.I	5.I
Silvio		I.I			4.I	5.I
Gemulo		I.I			4.I	5.I
Ascanio	Prologue		2.I		4.I	5.I
Joculo			2.I	3.I	4.I	5.I
Juno			2.I	Apollo		Apollo
Iris			2.I			Muse I
Morpheus		Shepherd	2.I		Echo	
Mopso		Shepherd	2.I	3.I		
Frisco		Shepherd	2.I	3.I		
Aramanthus				3.I	4.I	5.I
Extra I		Woodman	Fairy	Charity		Muse 2
Extra 2		Woodman	Fairy	Charity		Muse 3
Extra 3		Woodman	Fairy	Charity		Muse 4

first year of the company's reopening, 1599–1600, so that as a rule an extra does not alternate between identities. For example, the extra who plays the attendant in *Antonio and Mellida*, 1.1, becomes Lucio in 3.1 and remains Lucio. Yet there are exceptions: an extra in *Antonio and Mellida* reverts to the role of Piero's Page after having served as Andrugio's Page during the middle scenes of the play; an extra in *Jack Drum's Entertainment*, having been first a morris dancer and then a page, reverts to the identity of the page after an appearance as a country maid. In their second year of playing, however, I believe that the boys could handle a more complicated version of doubling. This development is illustrated by the extra who plays Mellida and Andrugio's Ghost in *Antonio's Revenge*; the boy begins as Mellida, becomes Andrugio's Ghost for two scenes, reverts to the identity of Mellida for one scene, and finishes the play as the ghost.

The Wisdom of Doctor Dodypoll is structured very differently from *Antonio's Revenge*, but it too appears to call for a cast of twenty-one players. In *The Wisdom of Doctor Dodypoll*, thirteen male characters speak twenty-five or more lines, and four women characters speak ten lines or more. There are three character-clusters, which seem to permit doubling, but members of one cluster appear too frequently onstage with those in another cluster for doubling to be easy. Furthermore, twenty-one characters appear in 5.2 (see table 6). Six

Table 5. Doubling options: "Antonio's Revenge"

	1.1	1.2	2.1	2.2	3.1	3.2	4.1	4.2	5.1	5.2	5.3
Piero	1.1		2.1	2.2	3.1		4.1		5.1		5.3
Strotzo	1.1	1.2	2.1	2.2			4.1	Strotzo's Body	(Page 4)		(Torchbearer)
Lucio	1.1	1.2	2.1	2.2			4.1		5.1		5.3
Maria		1.2	2.1	2.2	3.1	3.2	4.1		5.1		5.3
Antonio		1.2	2.1	2.2	3.1	3.2	4.1	4.2	5.1	5.2	5.3
Galeatzo		1.2	2.1	2.2			4.1		5.1		5.3
Matzagente					Julio				(Page 3)		
Balurdo		1.2	2.1	2.2	3.1	3.2	4.1		5.1	5.2	5.3
Pandulpho		1.2	2.1	2.2	3.1			4.2	5.1	5.2	5.3
Alberto		1.2	2.1	2.2	3.1		4.1	4.2	5.1	5.2	5.3
Feliche		1.2	(Castilio)				(Castilio)		(Castilio)		
Mellida				2.2	A's Ghost	A's Ghost	Mellida		A's Ghost		A's Ghost
Nutriche		1.2			3.1		4.1		5.1		5.3
Forobosco		1.2	2.1		3.1				5.1		5.3
Extra 1		Page 1	*M/T/1		Page 1	Page 1		Page 1	Page 1		Page 1
Extra 2			*M/T/2		Page 2	Page 2			Page 2		Page 2
Extra 3			**M/S/1		(Boy 1)		Senator 1		Senator 1		Senator 1
Extra 4			**M/S/2		(Boy 2)		Senator 2		Senator 2		Senator 2
Extra 5			(Herald)				***WW 1		***WW 1		***WW 1
Extra 6							***WW 2		***WW 2		***WW 2

(Mutes are in parentheses)
* Mourner with Torch 1 & 2
** Mourner with Streamers 1 & 2
*** Waiting Woman

Table 6. Doubling options: "The Wisdom of Doctor Dodypoll"

	1.1	1.2	1.3	2.1	2.2	2.3	3.1	3.2	3.3	3.4	3.5	4.1	4.2	4.3	4.4	5.1	5.2
Lassingberg	1.1			2.1			3.1	3.2	3.3					4.3			5.2
Lucilia	1.1			2.1			3.1	3.2	3.3		3.5			4.3			5.2
Haunce	1.1			2.1	2.2		3.1			3.4	3.5			4.3			5.2
Cornelia	1.1			2.1			3.1						4.2				5.2
Dr Dodypoll	1.1				2.2		3.1	3.2					4.2			5.1	5.2
Albertus	1.1		V'Cleeve			V'Cleeve							4.2	V'cleeve			5.2
Flores	1.1			2.1			3.1	3.2		3.4			4.2			5.1	5.2
Alberdure		1.2		2.1				3.2		3.4	3.5	4.1			4.4		5.2
Hyanthe		1.2						3.2							4.4		5.2
Leander		1.2						3.2							4.4		5.2
Motto		1.2		2.1				3.2		3.4		4.1		4.3		5.1	5.2
Cassimere		1.2		2.1				3.2					4.2				5.2
Constantine			1.3											4.3			5.2
Katherine			1.3											4.3			5.2
Ite			1.3						Peasant	Peasant	Peasant	Peasant		Peasant			5.2
Alphonso						2.3		3.2					4.2	4.3			5.2
Hardenbergh						2.3		3.2					4.2				5.2
Hoscherman						2.3			Enchanter		Enchanter						5.2
Extra 1		(Other)		(Other)				(Other)	(Fairy)	(Other)	Spirit	Raphe		Raphe			Raphe
Extra 2		(Other)			(Other)			(Other)	(Fairy)	(Other)	Spirit			(Guard)			Stro
Extra 3		(Other)				(Other)		(Other)	(Fairy)		Spirit						Messenger

Mutes are in parentheses

of the twenty-one are mutes, and I might supply an exit so that one or more of these extras could return as another character, but several of the mutes are referred to during 5.2, or spoken to, by some character on stage. Among speaking roles, I double the part of Albertus with that of Vandercleeve, Ite with the Peasant, and Hoscherman with the Enchanter. The extras ("others," who double as the Enchanter's fairies) are needed in 5.2 to play Raphe, Stro, and the messenger.

By 1602 the Children of Paul's had played *Satiromastix*, perhaps written originally for the Chamberlain's Men at the Globe where Thomas Dekker, the dramatist, could easily have found twenty-three players to fill the roles.[31] Also by 1602 the Children of Paul's had bought *Blurt, Master Constable*. I deduce from the structure of the published texts of these plays that two developments had occurred at Paul's in the year since *Antonio's Revenge* was new: (1) the company had added one more novice player, and (2) continuing members were becoming more adept at handling principal roles and complicated doubling. I draw these conclusions from the gap between the number of players needed for speaking parts and those for mutes, as well as from the proliferation of roles for mutes. The text of *Satiromastix* requires seventeen speaking parts, none of which may comfortably be doubled (see table 7). [32] It requires six extras who cover twenty-one parts. Two of the extras have three identities and four appearances (Extras 1 and 2); one has five identities and five appearances (Extra 6); yet another has six identities and six appearances (Extra 5). The opening scene (1.1) requires thirteen of the players whose parts are not doubled plus all six extras, three of whom exit and return with a new identity; the final scene (5.2) requires sixteen of the undoubled speaking parts and all six extras, two of whom appear in two identities. Twenty-two players may perform all of these tasks, but the pace is less frantic with twenty-three. The text of *Blurt, Master Constable* appears to demand a twenty-fourth player (see table 8). I designate thirteen speaking parts, undoubled, and eleven extras. The stage directions of the final scene (5.3), which call four times for Blurt and his watch, demand twenty-four players if "the Watch" is interpreted as Blurt's entire company (Slubber, Woodcock, and two watchmen); however, because a direction in 4.3 seems to indicate both watchmen ("*Enter* Blurt, Slubber, Woodcock, *and the rest of the Watch*" [4.3.7]),[33] I feel obligated to supply this same group of five in 5.3 also.

Table 7. Doubling options: *"Satiromastix"*

	1.1	1.2	2.1	2.2	3.1	3.2	4.1	4.2	4.3	5.1	5.2
Sr Quintilian Shorthose	1.1		2.1			3.2					5.2
Peter Flash	1.1				3.1		4.1	4.2		5.1	5.2
Sr Adam Prickshaft	1.1		2.1		3.1			4.2	4.3		5.2
Sr Rees Ap Vaughan	1.1		2.1		3.1	3.2	4.1	4.2	4.3		5.2
Mistress Miniver	1.1		2.1		3.1		4.1		4.3		5.2
Blunt	1.1	1.2	2.1		3.1	3.2			4.3	5.1	5.2
Crispinus	1.1	1.2	2.1		3.1	3.2			4.3	5.1	5.2
Demetrius	1.1	1.2	2.1		3.1	3.2			4.3	5.1	5.2
Dicache	1.1		2.1			3.2	4.1		4.3	5.1	5.2
Philocalia	*G1/Philocalia		2.1			3.2	4.1		4.3	5.1	5.2
Petula	*G2/Petula		2.1				4.1			5.1	5.2
Sr Walter Terill	1.1		2.1			3.2				5.1	5.2
Celestine	1.1		2.1			3.2				5.1	5.2
Horace		1.2		2.2	3.1		4.1	4.2	4.3	5.1	5.2
Asinius Bubo		1.2		2.2	3.1		4.1	4.2	4.3		5.2
Tucca		1.2					4.1	4.2	4.3		5.2
King William Rufus			2.1			3.2					5.2
Extra 1	**S1/(O1)		S1								(King's Servant 1)
Extra 2	**S2/(O2)		(S2)								(King's Servant 2)
Extra 3	(Other Lady 1)						Tucca's Boy	Tucca's Boy			Tucca's Boy
Extra 4	(Other Lady 2)										(Sewer)
Extra 5	(S3/Light Bearer 1)		(KT1)			(Attendant 1)					(*BS 1/Officer 1)
Extra 6	(Light Bearer 2)		(KT2)			(Attendant 2)					(*BS 2/Officer 2)

(Mutes are in parentheses)

*Gentlewoman 1 & 2

** Servingman 1 & 2 / Other 1 & 2

KT King's Train

BS Banquet Servers

Table 8. Doubling options: *"Blurt, Master Constable"*

	1.1	1.2	2.1	2.2	3.1	3.2	3.3	4.1	4.2	4.3	5.1	5.2	5.3
Camillo	1.1		2.1	2.2	3.1						5.1		5.3
Hippolito	1.1		2.1	2.2	3.1						5.1		5.3
Violetta	1.1				3.1	3.2						5.2	5.3
Doyt	1.1	1.2	2.1	2.2							5.1		5.3
Dandypratt	1.1	1.2	2.1								5.1		5.3
Fontinelle	1.1				3.1	3.2						5.2	5.3
Lazarillo		1.2	2.1	2.2			3.3		4.2	4.3			5.3
Blurt		1.2								4.3			5.3
Imperia				2.2			3.3		4.2			5.2	
Trivia				2.2								5.2	
Simperina				2.2			3.3	4.1				5.2	
Frisco				2.2	3.1	3.2	3.3		4.2	4.3		5.2	
Curvetto				2.2			3.3	4.1		4.3			5.3
Extra 1	(Baptista)		Truepenny		Truepenny						(Baptista)		(Baptista)
Extra 2	(Bentivoglio)		(Servingman 1)	(Bentivoglio)			*Lady/TB 4				(Bentivoglio)		(Bentivoglio)
Extra 3	Virgilio		(Servingman 2)	Virgilio			*Lady/TB 5				Virgilio		Virgilio
Extra 4	Lady 1			Lady 1			*Lady/TB 1			Woodcock			Woodcock
Extra 5	Lady 2			Lady 2			*Lady/TB 2			Watch 1			Watch 1
Extra 6	Lady 3			Lady 3			*Lady/TB 3			Watch 2			Watch 2
Extra 7		Pilcher		Zany 1		Friar					Asorino		Asorino
Extra 8		Slubber		Zany 2						Slubber			Slubber
Extra 9					Musician 1								Duke
Extra 10					Musician 2								(Gent 1)
Extra 11													(Gent 2)

(Mutes are in parentheses)

*Imperia's Ladies with table books

The two *Antonio* plays by Marston, which illustrate his sense of theatrical design when he had the Children of Paul's in mind, and the plays by Dekker (and Middleton?) in the 1602 repertory, which illustrate the company's additional experience and personnel, provide a perspective from which to view the number of players and the doubling required by *Histrio-Mastix*. According to my chart (see table 9), *Histrio-Mastix*, with about 112 parts, requires fourteen players who do no doubling at all. This number would not have been a problem for the Children of Paul's; the fourteen players with principal roles in *Antonio and Mellida* could have handled these parts easily enough. The problem is the extras. According to my assignments, the 1610 text of *Histrio-Mastix* requires thirty extras to manage about one hundred roles. I might assign some of the cameo roles to the fourteen players who do not double parts, but their characters are onstage so frequently that it seems mean to ask them to take a second part. And little would be gained by Gulch's taking the part of one of the harvest folk, or Peace's taking the role of the ballad singer, or the doubling of Fourcher, Vourcher, Velure, and Lyon-rash with Grammar, Logic, Rhetoric, and Arithmetic. Tinkering with the fourteen major parts will not reduce the number of extras significantly. My chart is conservative, in that I do not assign players different roles in adjacent scenes. Even so, I assign seven roles to one extra (Extra 2), six roles to another (Extra 1), five roles to five more (Extras 9, 10, 14, 15, 16), and four roles to another six (Extras 4, 5, 6, 7, 12, 13). Because of the episodic nature of the plot, in which nearly half of the characters do not reappear once they have had their one-sixtieth of an hour upon the stage, none of the extras has to switch costumes between parts except for Extra 11, who changes between Bougle/Vice and Envy.[34]

Doubts about the playhouse venue run throughout the scholarship of *Histrio-Mastix*. Charts of doubling options confirm those doubts by showing that the play could not have been performed by the company of boys that put on *Antonio and Mellida* and *Antonio's Revenge*, or by another of the professional companies. As confidence in authorship and venue fades, the date of 1599 looks even more questionable. The few apparent clues in the text – the allusion to *Tamburlaine*, Perpetuana's cry about the Spaniards' coming, the reference to Statute rogues – are not topical only in 1599; they are just as plausibly topical in 1588–91.[35] I believe that scholars were on the right track about the stage history of *Histrio-Mastix* when they

Table 9. Doubling options: "*Histrio-Mastix*"

	1.1	1.2	1.3	1.4	2.1	2.2	2.3	2.4	3.1	3.2	3.3	3.4	3.5
Peace	1.1			1.4									
Mauortius	1.1				2.1			2.4		3.2			3.5
Philarchus	1.1				2.1			2.4		3.2			3.5
Chrisoganus	1.1		1.3		2.1							3.4	
Ingle		1.2						2.4					
Belch		1.2				2.2		2.4					
Gutt		1.2				2.2		2.4				3.4	
Posthast		1.2				2.2		2.4				3.4	
Gulch						2.2		2.4				3.4	
Clowt						2.2		2.4				3.4	
Fourcher			1.3				2.3		3.1				
Vourcher			1.3				2.3		3.1				
Velure			1.3				2.3		3.1				
Lyon-rash			1.3				2.3		3.1				
Extra 1	Grammar		HarvestFolk 1		Ballad Singer			Usher of Hall			Jeweler		
Extra 2	Logic		HarvestFolk 2		(Vintner)			Clark of Kitchen			Tirewoman		
Extra 3	Rhetoric		Plenty	Plenty									
Extra 4	Arithmetic		Plutus	Plutus						Vainglory			
Extra 5	Geometry		Ceres	Ceres						Hypocrisy			
Extra 6	Music		Bacchus	Bacchus						Contempt			
Extra 7	Astronomy				Cornbuyer			Helper 3			Bellula	Bellula	
Extra 8	Larius				Clark Market			Landulpho	Landulpho				
Extra 9	Hiletus				Cornseller			Lady	Lady		Tailor		
Extra 10		Scrivener			Merchant Wife			(OtherNoble 1)					(Masquer 1)
Extra 11		Bougle/Vice						Bougle/Vice					Envy
Extra 12					(Merchant Apprentice)			(Other Noble)					(Masquer 2)
Extra 13								(Gent 1)					(Masquer 3)
Extra 14								(Gent 2)					(Masquer 4)
Extra 15								MorrisDancer 1		Servingman 1			
Extra 16								MorrisDancer 2		Servingman 2			
Extra 17								Porter		Servingman 3			
Extra 18								(Sewer)		(Servingman 4)			
Extra 19								(Helper 1)				Champerty	
Extra 20								(Helper 2)				Calamancha	
Extra 21									Page				
Extra 22					Steward						Steward	Steward	Steward
Extra 23									Pride		Perpetuana		
Extra 24											Fillibela	Fillibela	
Extra 25													
Extra 26													
Extra 27													
Extra 28													
Extra 29													
Extra 30													

(Mutes are in parentheses)

R&M = Russetings and Mechanicals

4.1	4.2	4.3	5.1	5.2	5.3	5.4	5.5	6.1	6.2	6.3	6.4	6.5	Epilogue
												6.5	Epilogue
4.1					5.3		5.5		6.2				
					5.3		5.5		6.2				
	4.2				5.3		5.5		6.2				
		4.3					5.5						
		4.3		5.2			5.5					6.5	
		4.3		5.2			5.5					6.5	
				5.2			5.5					6.5	
		4.3		5.2			5.5					6.5	
		4.3		5.2			5.5					6.5	
						5.4	5.5			6.3			
4.1						5.4	5.5			6.3			
4.1						5.4	5.5			6.3			
						5.4	5.5			6.3			
							Soldier						
							(Soldier)						
											Country Servingman 1	Plenty	
		Ambition			Ambition								
		Fury			Fury							Ceres	
		Horror										Bacchus	
Bellula									Bellula				
					Larius								
					Hiletus						Country Servingman 2		
			(Captain)			(Captain)							
						Bougle/Vice							
			Officer									Envy	
				R&M 1		(Peasant 1)							
				R&M 2		(Peasant 2)					Cunstable		
				R&M 3		(Citizen 1)					Sailor 1		
				R&M 4		(Citizen 2)					(Sailor 2)		
		Warre											
Champerty						Champerty						Warre	
C'mancha												(Fame)	
		Ruine										(Fortitude)	
												(Religion)	
												(Virginity)	
Perpetuana						Perpetuana			Perpetuana	Perpetuana		(Artes)	
										Fillibela		Pride	
											Hostess		
						Poverty	Poverty					Poverty	
							Famine					Famine	
							Sicknesse					Sicknesse	
							Bondage					Bondage	
							Sluttishness					Sluttishness	
												Astræa	

guessed at the date and venue of the original play. Simpson, for example, suggested that it "was an academical exercise for young men at the universities or for schoolboys to act" in 1590.[36] Small dated the "old" play in 1596, suggesting that it might have been "privately given at some school."[37] E. K. Chambers, who suggested "a University or possibly an Inns of Court," considered a date between 1585 and 1591.[38] Where they erred, in my opinion, is in theorizing a revision. As Kernan has shown, the play has a unity consistent with a single author. Yet scholars, driven by the desire to promote *Histrio-Mastix* into the narrative of the War of the Theatres, manufactured a revision in 1599 and a revival. Without Marston as author, and without the playhouse at Paul's as venue, that revision and revival have no *raison d'être*. The likeliest scenario for performances of *Histrio-Mastix* is one consistent with internal evidence in the "old" – that is, the only – play: at an institution at some time when Jonson might have become familiar enough with it to remember its quaintly academic language and the players' song about touring.

PUBLICATION

Stripped of an author with commercial and literary appeal (Marston), a recently vital venue (Paul's), and a somewhat recent date (1599), *Histrio-Mastix* is an unlikely piece for Thomas Thorpe to have acquired and published in 1610. Scholars who discuss its role in the War of the Theatres do not comment in detail on its publishing history. Perhaps the assumption is that Thorpe, having done business with Marston in the past, acquired *Histrio-Mastix* from him sometime before 1608; or, that Thorpe, having acquired plays from the children's companies in the past, acquired *Histrio-Mastix* in the diaspora of their plays, 1606–8, when the playhouses at Paul's and Blackfriars closed. However, more than one circumstantial case may be assembled out of the information known about Thomas Thorpe and his business practices. In the context of Thorpe's entire publishing history, in his knowledge of the stage history of the plays he acquired, and in his contacts beyond the playhouse, a case may be made that Thorpe's acquisition of *Histrio-Mastix* had nothing to do with his former contacts among dramatists and playing company agents and therefore nothing to do with literary or commercial aspects of the playhouse world, 1599–1603.

When his entire career was being judged by his allegedly un-authorized publication of *Shake-speares Sonnets* in 1609, Thorpe was disdained as representative of those "shady fellows" in the Eliza-bethan book trade whose "methods of procuring MSS which had passed out of the author's hands were probably none too scrupu-lous."[39] Katherine Duncan-Jones contradicts that opinion, demon-strating by a survey of his business practices that Thorpe "was a publisher of some deserved status and prestige, handling works by close associates of Shakespeare, and producing, in many cases, highly authoritative texts."[40] Duncan-Jones investigates Thorpe's contacts in the world at large and among dramatists, and her conclusions provide no support for those who would argue that Thorpe acquired the manuscript of *Histrio-Mastix* from Marston himself or from a fire sale of playbooks from the defunct Children of Paul's.

In regard to playhouse contacts, Duncan-Jones emphasizes Thorpe's connections with Ben Jonson, John Marston, and George Chapman from 1604 to 1608. She does not make the point, but it is clear also that through these dramatists Thorpe's contact with a playing company was with the Children of the Chapel, not the Children of Paul's. Thorpe and Marston cooperated in 1604 on *The Malcontent*, but by that time Marston was writing for the company at Blackfriars and *The Malcontent* had moved into the repertory of the King's Men at the Globe. Thorpe must have had further contact with Marston in the acquisition of *What You Will*, which he published in 1607 with a title-page advertisement of Marston (but no play-house); and he might have had contact with Marston in 1605 in the acquisition of *Eastward Ho!*, unless he dealt with Jonson or Chapman instead. But more of Thorpe's work, and more of his work just before 1610, was with Jonson and Chapman. Beyond the playhouse, Thorpe had fruitful contacts among academics. In 1603, he pub-lished a speech by Richard Martin of the Middle Temple, the same Martin to whom Jonson dedicated *Poetaster* in the 1616 folio. His work for university men includes the following: 1607, a sermon by Samuel Walsall, "The Life and Death of Jesus Christ" (Cambridge, Corpus Christi); 1608, *Wyttes A. B. C. or A Century of Epigramms*, by Richard West (Oxford, Magdalen College); 1611, *The Preachers Travels* . . . by John Cartwright (Oxford, Magdalen College). Possibly *A Funerall Elegye* . . . (1612) should be added, for William Peter had attended Oxford.[41]

Thorpe's name on the publication of *Histrio-Mastix* in 1610 has seemed to be evidence of Marston's authorship because Thorpe knew Marston. But, if Thorpe did know *Histrio-Mastix* to be Marston's, why did he not advertise that fact on the title page of the quarto? And, if he knew its company owners, why did he not advertise that? Thorpe produced remarkably full title pages, especially of plays. He named the author on the title pages of *The Malcontent, Sejanus, Eastward Ho!, All Fools, The Gentleman Usher, Volpone, What You Will*, and *The Conspiracy and Tragedy of Charles, Duke of Byron*. He named the company or playhouse, or both, on the title pages of four of these eight (*The Malcontent, Eastward Ho!, All Fools*, and *The Conspiracy and Tragedy of Charles, Duke of Byron*). Marston was not shy about having his name advertised, even after he left playwriting in 1608 for the ministry. The title pages of *Antonio and Mellida* and *Antonio's Revenge* carry his initials; the title pages of *The Dutch Courtesan; Parasitaster, Or The Fawn; The Wonder of Women, or Sophonisba; What You Will*, and *The Insatiate Countess* carry his name. He was not shy about his company associations; except for *What You Will*, the plays that appeared in quarto with his name on the title page carried also an advertisement of the company owners. In contrast, the title page of *Histrio-Mastix* is barren. From this absence of information, it is not possible to deduce what Thorpe did or did not know about authorship, company provenance, and playhouse venue; but the barrenness does not support the assignment to Marston, or the Children of Paul's, or the playhouse at Paul's.

If *Histrio-Mastix* was as important to the War of the Theatres as theatre historians have assumed, it was most marketable in 1599–1600, when Jonson ridiculed it through Clove's fustian-speak; and it was most marketable with the name of its dramatist, company owners, and playhouse prominently displayed on the title page of the quarto. What Thorpe did feature on the title page was the name of the play: "*Histrio-mastix, Or, The Player whipt.*" Given that Marston used a "mastix" word to sign himself in an address to the reader of *The Scourge of Villanie* ("Theriomastix"), that Jonson climaxed the litany of Clove's fustian with a gibe at "PLATO's *Histriomastix*," and that Dekker chose "*Satiromastix*" as the title of his riposte to Jonson's *Poetaster*, Thorpe's title has seemed yet another sign that more than linguistic coincidence connects *The Scourge of Villanie, Histrio-Mastix, Every Man Out of his Humour*, and *Satiromastix*. That may be (even without Marston's authorship of *Histrio-Mastix*), but neologisms formed with "mastix" as suffix were not rare. Andrew Willet, parish priest and theologian, knew a number of such words, or claimed to. In 1604 Willet published a pamphlet entitled *Limbo-mastix*. Richard Parkes of Brasenose College, responding in *An Apologie: of Three Testimonies of Holy Scripture* (1607), toyed with Willet's pseudonym, suggesting that "Symbolo-mastix" and "Clero-mastix" were more appropriate than "Limbo-mastix."[42] Highly incensed, Willet answered Parkes in *Loidoromastix: that is, A Scovrge for a Rayler* (1607), in which he defended his choice of "limbo-mastix" and argued for the currency of "mastix" words: "though *Limbomastix* may seeme a new name for the *application*, yet in respect of the manner of *deriuation* and composition, it is not new: as the vsuall words, *Homeromastix*, *Rhetoromastix*, doe shew."[43] In 1623, Ben Jonson coined the term "Chronomastix" to ridicule George Wither for being an ineffective satirist, and Wither guaranteed that the insult would survive by objecting to it in *Britain's Remembrancer*, 1628.[44] Perhaps most telling of all, in the text of *Fucus Histriomastix*, a Cambridge play in 1623 that mocks an anti-theatrical prejudice, characters ridicule the title character (Fucus Histriomastix) by making up "mastix" words:[45]

Villanus: Rogitas? vnicus est quem novi Vtriculariomastix.
Ingenium: Vtriculariomastix: Ha ha he.
Mimus: et maypolemastix quoque. . . .
Comes 1:   vale mastix.
Comes 2:   vale histriomastix.
Comes 3: Vale vtriculariomastix.
Hirsutus: vale festomastix.
Mimus: vale maypolemastix sane.   (5.6.8–10, 31–35)

Commentators have argued that the title of *Histrio-Mastix* is appropriate because the play is "really about" Sir Oliver Owlet's Men: to Simpson, *Histrio-Mastix* "was to show the utter unworthiness of actors to any place in the commonwealth, in peace or war, plenty or poverty."[46] To Kernan, it "is a satiric treatment of the Elizabethan provincial touring companies."[47] But for theatre historians to argue that the play privileges the players is a self-serving argument. A scholar with another agenda – for example, Philip Finkelpearl, who believes that the play was constructed for "an audience of lawyers" – has no trouble finding evidence that the play privileges the role of the law in a moral commonwealth.[48] Objective readers might agree that the liveliest parts of *Histrio-Mastix* are its scenes with Owlet's Men, but that too reflects modern taste. An academic audience might well have preferred Chrisoganus's lesson with the four would-be scholars; a Court audience might have preferred the masque-like inter-acts with the iconographic figures. In fact, play titles do not always advertise content, theme, or best parts. For plays with multiple agendas, such as *Satiromastix*, the title advertised its role in the flash of hot anger called the Poetomachia, not its more general appeal as a folk romance or its social commentary on the marriageability of widows. Likewise *The Second Part of Henrie the Fourth* advertised itself first as a historical sequel and second as a showcase for the great clown, Falstaff. The author of *The Second Part of the Returne from Parnassus* (or, *The Scourge of Simony*) apparently chose to associate his play with its earlier parts and to advertise a minor story line (not, however, by using "Raderick-mastix"). How *Histrio-Mastix* acquired its title, when *The Triumph of Peace and Plenty* is a far more logical one, is a mystery. If the play was conceived in 1590 (or thereabouts) with its subsequently published title, its name is unintentionally appropriate to the burst of satirical literature beginning in 1595 and Marston's use of "Theriomastix" to identify himself. Its author may have meant nothing more than to associate himself with an academic fashion in neologisms.

Ben Jonson recalled the title of *Histrio-Mastix* and four words from its 1610 text ("Zodiack . . . Eclipticke line . . . Tropicks . . . Esquiline") in a single ten-line speech by Clove in *Every Man Out of his Humour*. In *Poetaster*, in a scene with the player Histrio (3.4), Jonson quoted a line from the players' song in *Histrio-Mastix*, but in the vomiting scene (5.3), he did not purge Crispinus of a single word from the play. Jonson thus apparently knew the play by 1599 and certainly recalled it in 1601. But what evidence does this fact provide of the extent of the debate among writers about the decorum of satirical literature and the implications of that debate for the commercial relations among the Elizabethan playing companies? First, Jonson's allusions may suggest Marston's name in the hunt for the author of *Histrio-Mastix* because words from *The Scourge of Villanie* are mixed in Clove's speech with the words from *Histrio-Mastix*, but it does not turn that suggestion into proof. In *Poetaster* Jonson mixed allusions to *The Spanish Tragedy* and *The Battle of Alcazar* (if not also *A Warning for Fair Women*) within a twenty-line passage without suggesting that the texts had the same author. Perhaps similarly, Jonson was casting a wide net with a collage of verbal pointings in *Every Man Out of his Humour*.

Second, only Jonson of those writers associated with the debate seems to have been intrigued by *Histrio-Mastix*. Marston himself did not use distinctive phrases from the play, and no vocabulary or references are so construed in *Satiromastix* or *The Second Part of the Returne from Parnassus*. Writers such as John Weever, Nicholas Breton, and Everard Guilpin who chimed in with "The Whipping of the Satyre," "No Whipping," and "The Whipper of the Satyre his Pennance" respectively seem not to have had *Histrio-Mastix* in mind. Thus the role of the play in the networks of satirical pointings in dramatic and non-dramatic literature, 1598–1603, was limited to the allusions by Jonson.

Histrio-Mastix had an even more limited role in the commercial relations of the Elizabethan playing companies, in that its role was shared by many other plays. If it was an academic play, it helped to cultivate an appetite for theatricals in English schoolboys and youths, an appetite to which the professional playing companies (both men's and boys') would cater. Wherever it was played, it helped to maintain the popularity of medieval literary forms such as estate satire. Scott McMillin and Sally-Beth MacLean, assessing the puzzling decline of the Queen's Men after 1588 despite their privileged status in the royal household, conjecture that their repertory and acting style could not compete with the stage-rattling new breed of drama in the repertory of the Admiral's Men characterized by the plays of Christopher Marlowe.[49] But even an all-Marlowe repertory was not the ideal; diversification was. Companies thrived by mixing super-heroic drama with domestic comedies, revenge tragedies, comedies of humour, English chronicle plays, and the like. To have the moral play and estate satire available increased narrative and didactic options. The Admiral's Men made good money in 1595–6 with "Seven Days of the Week," apparently a moral play.[50] In repertory in 1599–1600, the Chamberlain's Men had "Cloth Breeches and Velvet Hose," which featured a parade of estates with satirical commentary (if it followed its source of *A Quip for an Upstart Courtier* by Robert Greene). The company thought well enough of it commercially to sell it for publication with a batch of other successes in the summer of 1600, though the actual printing apparently never took place. One of the boys' companies performed the moral play, *The Contention Between Liberality and Prodigality*, before Queen Elizabeth, possibly as late as 1601. Its commercial appeal to the stationers who produced a quarto in 1602 suggests that texts with virtually no stage history or acclaim were nonetheless attractive properties, perhaps merely for their celebration of royalty. Perhaps similarly, the celebration of Queen Elizabeth in the epilogue of *Histrio-Mastix* was enough to make Thomas Thorpe think it worth publishing.

Histrio-Mastix does represent one aspect of dramatic and literary criticism in the years of 1599–1601. In the way that Pistol parodied Tamburlanean language, generating both nostalgia and mockery, Jonson's allusions to Chrisoganus's pedantic diction invited critical listeners to choose between the debased rhetoric of the academy and the witty newspeak of an Asper, Crites, or Horace. In *Satiromastix* Dekker focused the argument specifically on the variety of everyday fare in the playhouse world at large by turning Jonson's ridicule of *The Spanish Tragedy* and *The Battle of Alcazar* into a commemorative reprise of former hits on the London public stages such as "Long Meg of Westminster," "Hercules," and "George Scanderbeg." Therefore, even though it was not itself an offering on a London stage and did not have the role awarded to it in old narratives of company commerce, *Histrio-Mastix* is not utterly insignificant in its contribution to commercial theatre, for it helped Jonson to construct a debate that in time enhanced the self-conscious artistry of English drama.

CHAPTER 5

"Hamlet" and company commerce

This passage, notwithstanding the pains bestowed on it by the commentators, I do not understand.

John Lord Chedworth

While it seems to be agreed upon all hands that *Hamlet* is the most topical play in the whole corpus, unhappily when it comes to interpreting the supposed allusions, agreement almost entirely vanishes.

John Dover Wilson[1]

Two issues – text and theatre history – govern the interpretation of lines in *Hamlet* known as the "little eyases" passage, in which Rosencrantz banters about "an eyrie of children" who "cry out on the top of question, and are most tyrannically clapped for't" (2.2.337–39).[2] The textual issue addresses the specifics of composition: when was the "little eyases" passage written and entered into Shakespeare's *Hamlet*? The issue of theatre history concerns the events to which the passage alludes: what was happening in the playhouse world that prompted the lines to be composed? In traditional as well as recent scholarly opinion, the issues have come together to enforce an interpretation that locates the event in 1601 when the War of the Theatres reached its height in an exchange of barbs between Ben Jonson's *Poetaster* at Blackfriars and Thomas Dekker's *Satiromastix* at the Globe.

This interpretation seems at first beyond challenge. It is based on textual decisions and an aggregate of commentary beginning with Nicholas Rowe in 1709. Yet consensus in the critical history of the "little eyases" passage is more apparent than real. Eighteenth-century editors agreed that the best *Hamlet* text was published in folio from 1623 to 1685 (F-F4). They raided the *Hamlet* text published in quarto from 1604/5 to 1676 (Q2-Q6) for lines variant or missing from F, but for the "little eyases" passage, they did not have to compare readings since the passage appears only in the Folio. However, eighteenth-century editors disagreed on the commercial theatrical events to which the lines alluded. The variorum-style commentary in Edmond Malone's *Plays and Poems of William Shakespeare* (1790, 1821) reflected these differences as well as Malone's own opinion, but that commentary was undermined almost immediately by the discovery in 1823 of another document, the 1603 quarto of *Hamlet* (Q1). Initially Q1 was presented as Shakespeare's first draft;[3] but in 1843 John Payne Collier dismissed Q1 as a corruption of Q2 or F.[4] Although opinion remained divided on the legitimacy of Q1,[5] it seemed obvious that certain Q1 lines – lines about the novelty of children players – were a variant of the "little eyases" passage. Consequently, many nineteenth-century scholars made the plausible assumption that Shakespeare, in the Folio, was alluding to the boys' companies collectively. Persuaded by such reasoning, theatre historians by 1900 had assigned the "little eyases" passage to the event of alleged commercial rivalry between the men's and children's playhouses *circa* 1600 known as the War of the Theatres.

In previous chapters, I have argued that the cut-throat rivalry implicit in the War of the Theatres has been overvalued as a model of commerce among the Elizabethan playing companies. On the one hand, an argument can be made that the players, companies, dramatists, and stationers worked cooperatively and legitimately with one another to expand their respective markets. On the other hand, narrative elements of the War of the Theatres such as the attribution of *Histrio-Mastix* to John Marston are erroneous. I argue below that the "little eyases" passage, long considered proof of a war between the men's and boys' companies, is a response not to the reopening of Paul's playhouse in 1599 and Blackfriars in 1600 but to actions by the Children of the Chapel at Blackfriars in 1606 or shortly thereafter. Those alarming actions were to perform several plays that contained political satire aimed at powerful nobles. The boys' misbehavior drew severe criticism from the Court, and it cost the company its identification with the queen and her chapel. It threatened to cost all of the companies their license to play. The King's Men, attempting to take control of the situation, acted as falconer to the little eyases, calling on them publicly to curtail their flights over politically dangerous territory. The proposed new date of 1606–8, eliminating the value of the "little eyases" passage to the War of the Theatres, enables the extant texts and stage runs of

Hamlet to be aligned with shifting commercial agendas in the life of Shakespeare's company.

Nicholas Rowe, in his 1709 *Works of Mr. William Shakespear*, based his text of *Hamlet* on the folio of 1685 (F4); the "little eyases" passage reproduces the Folio passage except for minor spelling and punctuation changes, and appears in his edition as follows:

Ham. How comes it? do they grow rusty?

Ros. Nay, their endeavour keeps in the wonted pace; But there is, Sir, an airy of Children, little Yases, that cry out on the top of Question; and are most tyrannically clapt for't; these are now the Fashion, and so be-rattle the common Stages (so they call them) that many wearing Rapiers, are afraid of Goose Quills, and dare scarce come thither.

Ham. What are they Children? Who maintains 'em? How are they escoted? Will they pursue the Quality no longer than they can sing? Will they not say afterwards if they should grow themselves to common Players, as it is like most, if their Means are no better, their Writers do them wrong to make them exclaim against their own Succession.

Ros. Faith, there has been much to do on both sides; and the Nation holds it no Sin, to tarre them to controversie. There was for a while, no Mony bid for Argument, unless the Poet and the Player went to Cuffs in the Question.

Ham. Is't possible?

Guild. Oh there has been much throwing about of Brains.

Ham. Do the Boys carry it away?

Ros. Aye, that they do, my Lord, *Hercules* and his load too.[6] (TLN 1384–1408)

Rowe drew on Q6 (1676) for seven passages not in F4,[7] but for the lines immediately preceding the "little eyases" passage – lines that are found in both folio and quarto – he appears to have followed F4:

Ham. How chances it they travel? their residence both in Reputation and Profit was better, both ways.

Ros. I think their Inhibition comes by the means of the late Innovation?

Ham. Do they hold the same Estimation they did when I was in the City? Are they so follow'd?

Ros. No indeed, they are not. (TLN 1376–83; Q2, F2^v)

In the years after 1709, editors of *Hamlet* drew increasingly on the quarto versions that began with Q2, but they retained most Folio-only material, including the "little eyases" passage. Malone followed Rowe and the rest by choosing the Folio as the best *Hamlet* text, and the codification of the "little eyases" passage in Shakespeare's *Hamlet* was thus completed. In 1934, John Dover Wilson argued that Q2 was set from Shakespeare's manuscript, whereas F was set from "a transcript of a transcript," which had been heavily marked by a "bookholder of the theatre" and "a slovenly playhouse scribe."[8] Dover Wilson therefore adopted Q2 as control text, but he included the "little eyases" passage, which he perceived as a deletion from Shakespeare's foul papers that must be restored to achieve the authorial manuscript behind Q2.[9] Recent editors such as Harold Jenkins (Arden edition) and Barbara Mowat and Paul Werstine (New Folger edition) have followed Dover Wilson's choice of Q2 plus F-only passages.[10] However, George Hibbard (Oxford edition) reverts to the folio as control text. Defending that choice, Gary Taylor commends Hibbard for disposing "of the argument that extended passages present in F but not Q2 were present in the foul papers."[11] The Taylor-Hibbard position is liberating, but it does not address the issue of when these passages entered the Folio. Taylor implies that all were in place by 1603; for evidence of dating the "little eyases" passage in that time frame, however, he offers only the alleged link to the War of the Theatres.

None of the eighteenth-century editors, including Malone, knew of a third text of *Hamlet*, the quarto published in 1603 (Q1). Sir Henry Bunbury discovered the quarto in 1823, and a reprint was issued in 1825.[12] In the preface to the reprint, the text was identified as "originally written by Shakespeare, which he afterwards altered and enlarged."[13] Many Shakespeareans were horrified. James O. Halliwell, for one, called Q1 "a surreptitious and imperfect transcript of portions of the tragedy, taken probably from short-hand notes made at the theatre and partly completed from memory."[14] In 1941, George I. Duthie added a motive to what had become the orthodox position, declaring that Q1 was "made for provincial performance."[15] Its inferiority thus established, Q1 nevertheless continued to be raided by editors for words, phrases, and action, such as the appealing stage direction, "*Enter Ofelia playing on a Lute, and her haire downe singing*" (G4ᵛ).

In making the case for Q1 as a touring script, Duthie had nothing to say about the following passage, which has not acquired the authority given other bits of Q1:

Ham. How comes it that they trauell? Do they grow restie?
Gil. No my Lord, their reputation holds as it was wont.
Ham. How then?
Gil. Yfaith my Lord, noueltie carries it away,
  For the principall publike audience that
  Came to them, are turned to priuate playes,
  And to the humour of children. (E3)

If acknowledged at all, this passage is considered a derivative of its counterparts in Q2 and F, shortened and misremembered. Hibbard calls the "humour of children" passage "a much abbreviated and typically garbled version of [the 'little eyases' passage]."[16] E. A. J. Honigmann applies beliefs about the workings of the memorial process when he says that "the pirates of the First Quarto of *Hamlet* understood 'innovation' [in Q2] to mean 'novelty.'"[17] In order to explain the derivation of the "humour of children" passage from F, scholars have expended a great deal of energy constructing scenarios to explain the appearance of the "little eyases" passage in Shakespeare's manuscript, and its subsequent disappearance. For example, Philip Edwards conjectures that the "little eyases" passage existed in the foul papers from which Q2 was set, but on a "separate slip" or "interleaved sheet" that had "become separated or lost by 1604" when the text behind Q2 reached the printer.[18] Honigmann says that the "little eyases" passage was added in 1601 to the company's prompt-copy, from which F was set.[19] Among the new revisionists, however, there is a willingness to give the "humour of children" passage an independent textual life in 1600. Grace Ioppolo, for example, suggests that it "may imperfectly represent Shakespeare's first attempt, after the play had originally been composed, to mock his private-theatre competition."[20] Ioppolo's suggestion revitalizes the 1825 theory of provenance for Q1, that the text is – or approximates – Shakespeare's first *Hamlet*. A corollary of this theory is that the "humour of children" passage reflects events in the playhouse world around 1600.

On issues other than provenance, more of Q1 has been rehabilitated. The most recent and diversified treatment appears in Thomas Clayton's *The Hamlet First Published (Q1, 1603)*. In that collection Alan Dessen explores "some key assumptions behind the arguments about Q1's relationship to Q2/F and the kinds of evidence that can be used to buttress or challenge such assumptions."[21] George Hibbard does a braver thing, questioning his own argument in the

Oxford *Hamlet* that Q1 stems from F. Dessen and Hibbard point out anomalies that demonstrate an independence of Q1 from F: for example, the designations of Osric, who is *"a Bragart Gentleman"* in Q1; a *"Courtier,"* then *"young Ostricke"* in Q2; and *"Osricke"* in F.[22] The anomalies are present in several aspects of the text such as stage directions, exposition, scene sequence, onstage characters, imagery, jokes, and psychology of character. Looking at the textual implications, Hibbard points out that "There is . . . no inherent logical reason why the version represented by F should have preceded that for which our only witness is Q1";[23] still, he does not place Q1 before Q2. Dessen does, inclining to consider Q1 "a reasonably faithful rendition" of the text for the performances in London and in the college towns that are advertised on its title page.[24]

Hibbard's admission that there is "no inherent logical reason" for one assumption about the chronology of the *Hamlet* texts may be applied as well to assumptions about the relation between the "humour of children" and the "little eyases" passages. If the Q1 passage is a duplicate or paraphrase of a passage marked for deletion in the copy from which Q2 was set, instead of a botched recollection of the "little eyases" passage in F (for example), each *Hamlet* text may be seen to indicate a different commercial event: Q1 may reflect the attitude of the Chamberlain's Men toward boy players in 1599–1600; Q2 may reflect playhouse disruptions in 1603–4; and F may reflect the company's attitude toward the boy players at a date after 1604/5. The textual transmission for this scenario is as follows:

Script behind Q2	Q1	Q2	F
"humour of children"	"humour of children"	CUT "humour of children"	"inhibition . . . innovation"
(or a passage very like it)		ADD "inhibition . . . innovation"	ADD "little eyases"

A comparison of the three *Hamlet*s shows another feature of the above sequence: the similarity of the several lines that frame the "humour of children" and "little eyases" passages. These framing passages are printed below, with asterisks marking the places where the passages I am here tracing appear: in Q1, the seven-line "humour of children" passage; in Q2, the seven-line "inhibition . . . innovation" passage; and in F, the thirty-three-line combined "inhibition . . . innovation" and "little eyases" passages. I have moved the part of Hamlet's Q1 speech that begins "For his picture" so that it can be seen in comparison with the other texts; brackets mark the transposed text.

Q1	Q2	F
[Ham. For his picture: but they shall be welcome, He that playes the King shall haue tribute of me, The ventrous Knight shall vse his foyle and target, The louer shall sigh gratis, The clowne shall make them laugh That are tickled in the lungs, or the blanke verse shall halt for't, And the Lady shall haue leaue to speake her minde freely.]	Ham. He that playes the King shal be welcome, his Maiestie shal haue tribute on me, the aduenterous Knight shall vse his foyle and target, the Louer shall not sigh gratis, the humorus Man shall end his part in peace, and the Lady shall say her minde freely: or the black verse shall hault for't.	Ham. He that playes the King shall be welcome; his Maiesty shall haue Tribute of mee: the aduenturous Knight shal vse his Foyle and Target: the Louer shall not sigh *gratis*, the humorous man shall end his part in peace: the Clowne shall make those laugh whose lungs are tickled a'th'sere: and the Lady shall say her minde freely; or the blanke Verse shall halt for't:

Q1	Q2	F
Ham. Players, what Players be they? Ros. My Lord, the Tragedians of the Citty, Those that you tooke delight to see so often.	What players are they? Ros. Euen those you were wont to take such delight in, the Tragedians of the Citty.	what Players are they? Rosin. Euen those you were wont to take delight in the Tragedians of the City.
* * * * *	* * * * *	* * * * *
Ham. I doe not greatly wonder of it, For those that would make mops and moes At my vncle, when my father liued, Now giue a hundred, two hundred pounds (E3)	It is not very strange, for my Vncle is King of Denmarke, and those that would make mouths at him while my father liued, giue twenty, fortie, fifty, a hundred duckets a peece, for his Picture in little, s'bloud there is somthing in this more then naturall, if Philosophie could find it out. (F2–F2^v)	It is not strange: for mine Vnckle is King of Denmarke, and those that would make mowes at him while my Father liued; giue twenty, forty, an hundred Ducates a peece, for his picture in Little. There is something in this more then Naturall, if Philosophy could finde it out. (TLN 1366–1375, 1409–1414)

The lines of the framing passages suggest to me a moment of stability in a set of texts known for their instability. If Q1 is a memorial reconstruction, the alleged reporters are remembering with some accuracy. They are abbreviating, but they are not substituting synonyms liberally or distilling meaning into summary and paraphrase. They transpose one passage but maintain a high incidence of its words and phrases. In short, Q1 sounds here very like Q2 and F. The unstable sections are the "humour of children" passage, the "inhibition . . . innovation" lines, and the "little eyases" passage. Therefore, I do not look ahead to the copy acquired by F's printer to find the original of the "humour of children" passage;

rather, I look back to Shakespeare's manuscript before it was altered into the copy from which Q2 was set. In a "conjectural history of Q1," Albert B. Weiner also argues for a text-based descent of Q1 from Shakespeare's foul papers; in his mind's eye, he sees the "adapter-abridger" of the Chamberlain's Men paraphrasing and making deep cuts in Shakespeare's foul papers to construct a script for use on tour by a handful of sharers and a fair number of inexperienced youths.[25] Harold Jenkins, too, argues for cuts in the foul papers, but he holds the traditional view that it is the "little eyases" passage that was cut.[26] However, the "humour of children" passage slips as comfortably into Jenkins's gap as does the "little eyases" passage.

Nearly everyone now agrees that Shakespeare was composing his first *Hamlet* in 1599–1600.[27] It might have been ready for staging by the spring of 1600, and it was almost certainly in repertory by the fall. This period (1599–1600) was a busy time in the theatrical world. Derby's Men were playing at the Boar's Head playhouse, which had recently been expanded to accommodate larger crowds. Although the Theatre had been dismantled, a company had taken up the lease on the Curtain playhouse, which the Chamberlain's Men had left vacant when they moved to their newly built Globe in late spring or summer of 1599, across the street from the Admiral's Men at the Rose. In the midst of this activity, one "noueltie" of the winter season was the reopening of the private playhouse at Paul's, where a company of boys gave performances once a week (at least). No doubt the Children of Paul's were initially fashionable, taking some playgoers away from the public playhouses. Perhaps it was their success that encouraged Richard Burbage and Henry Evans in the spring or summer of 1600 to make plans for Blackfriars to be used again for a boys' company (Evans had managed that company there previously). In the context of an expanding public theatre and a renewed private one, it is plausible that Shakespeare, in his new version of the old "Hamlet" story, conceived a scenario in which a men's company – despite the excellence of their playing – would be driven out of London by a company of boys, merely because of playgoers' taste for novelty. The jest in the "humour of children" passage is that kings and players alike were at the mercy of a shallow public. The unambiguous reference to public audiences and private plays, plus a pun on "humour" as a kind of play and as the whimsical appeal of boy players, catches precisely the spirit of the allusion: bemused, tolerant, confident that the fashion will pass, but disappointed by the fickleness of playgoers. The tone of the jest is consistent with the degree to which one or both boys' companies might have been seen as a commercial threat in 1600.

A textual issue remains: the red herring of the "bad" quartos. Q1 has, of course, been given that label. Since A. W. Pollard developed the concept of "good" and "bad" quartos in *Shakespeare Folios and Quartos* (1909), members of the orthodox school of textual criticism have supported and refined his distinction. Increasingly, however, respected voices are attacking Pollard's concept from several directions. There is now a body of commentary that undermines many of the bases – including the revision of older plays, piracy, reconstitution from shorthand notes, and memorial reconstruction – on which "bad" quartos are deemed bad.[28] In addition, scholars of the book trade are looking again at the idea that inconsistencies in the registration and production of playtexts are signs of actor-pirates and dishonest stationers, the results of which were the publication of "bad" quartos. They are finding that inconsistencies are signs not of disreputable practices but rather of unregularized ones.[29] Furthermore, inconsistencies that were once thought to be peculiar to the handling of plays are found to be typical of the handling of publications in general. Gerald Johnson, for one, has studied the business habits of a number of stationers who produced quartos of plays. In regard to the registration and publication of Q1 and Q2 of *Hamlet*, Johnson exonerates Nicholas Ling and John Trundle from the charge of dishonesty in the publication of Q1 after James Roberts had registered "the Revenge of Hamlett" on 26 July 1602. Johnson demonstrates that Ling "often in his career financed the publication of copy that had been procured by other stationers," and he posits as "usual" an arrangement between Trundle and Ling in which Trundle would provide the copy and Ling would "claim the copyright."[30] Although the details are unclear on Ling's agreement with Roberts, Johnson points out that Ling and Roberts had worked together many times. Johnson conjectures, as does Albert Weiner, that Roberts and Ling expected to collaborate on Q2, which could be advertised as "enlarged . . . [and] perfect Coppie."[31]

One use to which scholars have consistently assigned "bad" quartos is touring. In *Two Elizabethan Stage Abridgements* (1922) W. W. Greg published two scenarios in which the texts of plays taken on tour were abridged to permit a smaller cast and rewritten to entertain a rural audience.[32] In his opinion, alterations of these kinds produced a corrupt text. However, one problem with the assignment of short texts with extra clown scenes to a provincial venue is that there is no supporting material evidence. Not a single record book from Ipswich or York or Coventry or any other town along the players' circuits identifies a performance by naming a play for which a text survives.[33] In volumes of Records of Early English Drama (REED), scholars are making available new data on touring, and the history of provincial performance is being revised. It is now clear that dozens of companies were playing outside of London and that towns were more likely to welcome players than turn them away. However, none of the REED data has turned up a small-cast abbreviation of a London text dumbed down for a provincial audience. Scott McMillin considers the relationship of play length to casting, and of both to scripts for touring. In an examination of several plays owned by Pembroke's Men and allegedly representative of the poor quality of tour texts, he suggests that the altered texts of *2 Henry VI* (*1 Contention*), *3 Henry VI* (*True Tragedy*), and *The Taming of A Shrew* did not produce scripts peculiarly suited for touring; the shortened history plays, for example, still require a substantial cast (11 players), a number of costumes, and "more than 100 speaking roles."[34] Addressing these issues in terms of *Hamlet*, McMillin shows that Q2, despite its length (indeed, perhaps because of it), requires as few players as Q1 and thus is as suitable for touring on the basis of company size.[35]

For my argument, I reiterate that there are two passages in texts of *Hamlet* that allude to the boy players: the "humour of children" in Q1 and the "little eyases" passage in F. Nothing may be said for certain about the date of composition of the latter except that it existed by 1623. The former, however, must have been written prior to the late spring of 1603. Many scholars have thought it likely that the alleged reporters of Q1 took the convoluted and obtuse "little eyases" passage and turned it into something as plain and clear as the "humour of children" passage. But an alternative is that the manuscript Shakespeare wrote in 1599–1600 was altered in a process of deletions and additions that produced Q1, Q2, and F (more or less directly, at different times, for different reasons). Even editors generally resistant to the concept of authorial revisions concede that Shakespeare's *Hamlet* underwent changes. Harold Jenkins, who thinks Shakespeare "had no call to rework his previous plays,"[36] considers the Q2/F line about an innovation as well as the "little eyases" passage to be additions. Therefore, as it has been from the beginning of the editorial tradition of *Hamlet*, the question is not *whether* Shakespeare's manuscript was revised but *when* and *in what ways*. I suggest the following textual history: a passage very like the "humour of children" passage existed in the *Hamlet* that was staged at the Globe in 1600; that passage was cut by 1604 and its place filled with the line about an inhibition, caused by an innovation; at a still later date (*circa* 1606), the "little eyases" passage was added in the place formerly occupied by the "humour of children" passage in the *Hamlet* of 1600.

THEATRE HISTORY ISSUES

George Hibbard takes for granted that the "little eyases" were the Children of the Chapel at Blackfriars, but this identification has been reached over several hundred years of commentary. The process began in 1725 with Alexander Pope, who placed a dagger (†) just before the word "Airy" ["aerie"] and noted the following: "Relating to the playhouses then contending, the Bankside, the Fortune, &^{tc} – play'd by the Children of his majesty's chappel."[37] As succeeding editors added notes to the "little eyases" passage, the commentary became a site for the discussion of Elizabethan theatre history. Below, reconsidering issues that have bound it to a story of hostile competition between the men's and boys' companies between 1599 and 1601, I suggest a new date and commercial agenda for the "little eyases" passage and its textual variants. I argue that the Q1 passage about the "humour of children" (or one very like it) represents the response of Shakespeare and the Chamberlain's Men to the reopening of Paul's and Blackfriars playhouses with companies of boys; that the Q2/F line, ". . . their inhibition comes by the means of the late innovation," represents their response to the closure of the playhouses in the summer of 1603 due to the accession of James I and the onset of plague; and that the F-only "little eyases" passage represents their response to the wayward behavior of the Blackfriars company after 1604.

I. To which company or companies does the allusion refer?
Pope's identification of the "little eyases" with the Children of the Chapel prevailed until George Steevens suggested in 1778 that the

passage also referred to the Children of Paul's.[38] In 1790 and 1821, Edmond Malone, having considered Steevens's conflation of the allusion to both children's companies, settled on the Children of Paul's as the true identity of the "little eyases."[39] By 1877, when H. H. Furness published the Variorum edition of *Hamlet,* Shakespeareans had returned to Steevens's position. They might have been influenced in this by the publication in 1825 of Q1 and its "humour of children" passage. The vagueness of the plurals – "children," "little eyases" – enabled scholars to avoid choosing between the boys' companies by conflating them into a single adversary. E. K. Chambers perpetuated this reading by linking the "little eyases" passage to "the theatrical competition set up by the establishment of boy companies at St. Paul's in 1599 and at the Chapel Royal in 1600."[40] Alfred Harbage further sealed the association by joining the enterprises at Paul's and Blackfriars in "a theatre of a coterie."[41] Thus by 1952 theatre historians had transformed the eighteenth-century editors' identification of the "little eyases" as either the Children of Paul's or the Children of the Chapel into an identification of them as both.

In *Shakespeare's Blackfriars Playhouse* (1964) Irwin Smith changed that opinion. Smith argued that the Children of the Chapel were the dominant of the two boys' companies because they had the larger playhouse and more prestige at Court.[42] As part of his evidence, he discussed the decision of Richard Burbage to lease Blackfriars to Henry Evans in September 1600. Burbage knew that Evans planned to bring in a company of boys; and, to guarantee his investment, Burbage obtained a bond of £400 to secure the terms of the twenty-one-year lease by which he was to be paid £40 per year rent.[43] For Smith, this contract meant that the "little eyases" passage had to refer to the Children of the Chapel. For commerce among playing companies in 1600, it means that Burbage had a stake in the success of a company other than his own.

It is possible that other sharers in the Chamberlain's Men also saw an advantage to themselves if the venture at Blackfriars prospered. This possibility rests on evidence that in 1600 some of those sharers were taking a wider financial interest in the business of playing. On 21 February 1600, five of the Chamberlain's Men – William Shakespeare, Augustine Phillips, Thomas Pope, John Heminges, and William Kempe – signed the lease on the Globe and its property and thus joined Burbage and his brother Cuthbert as householders. They did not become householders in the Blackfriars enterprise until 1608, at which time they were joined by fellow player-sharers Henry Condell and Will Sly.[44] Even though the Globe sharers did not have the same investments in 1600 as Burbage, they might have admired him as an entrepreneur and anticipated that opportunities for him now might be opportunities for themselves at some later date.[45] And, if playing companies looked on one another as partners in the enterprise of expanding the customer base (as I have argued in previous chapters), sharers in the Chamberlain's Men might have seen the opening of Blackfriars as well as the remodeled Boar's Head and new Fortune playhouses as stimulants to the growth of the industry. In this commercial climate, a jest about the "humour of children" conveys the dynamic of a theatrical world with an increasing number of venues from which to choose.

II. What circumstances caused the Crown to issue an "inhibition" of playing?
In the Q2/F line, ". . . their inhibition comes by the means of the late innovation," the theatre history issues have been the meaning of "inhibition" and "innovation." In the nineteenth century, scholars sought a governmental inhibition that was close chronologically to the maiden run of *Hamlet*. They found it in an order on 22 June 1600 by the Privy Council to restrict the number of men's playhouses to two (the Fortune and Globe), the number of companies to two (the Admiral's Men and Chamberlain's Men), and the number of playing days to twice a week. J. P. Collier published a full text of the order in *The History of English Dramatic Poetry* (1831), and he made the connection with the "inhibition" in Shakespeare's line in his *The Works of William Shakespeare* (1843). Collier's thesis, which was included in the 1877 Variorum *Hamlet*, was widely endorsed, but support has weakened recently. In a classroom edition of Shakespeare's works, David Bevington backs away from a direct link between the 1600 order and the Elsinore troupe's touring, glossing "inhibition" as a "formal prohibition (from acting plays in the city)."[46] Bevington does not explain his lack of enthusiasm for the old interpretation, but a good reason would be that the Privy Council order in fact did not inhibit playing. In a letter dated 31 December 1601, the Privy Council complained to the justices of Middlesex and Surrey that its June order had been "so farr from takinge dew effect, as in steede of restrainte and redresse of the former disorders the multitude of play howses is much encreased, and . . . no daie passeth over without

many stage plaies in one place or other . . . publiquelie made."[47] Another reason is that the June 1600 order did not threaten Shakespeare and his company, whose business was specifically exempted and whose playhouse was specifically sanctioned.

Over time, editorial opinion on the meaning of "innovation" has also shifted. Formerly, most scholars agreed that the "innovation" had some relation to the children's companies and their repertory of satirical comedies in 1599–1601. Many commentators focused on the children themselves as the novelty. According to Joseph Rann, the innovation arose from "the modern taste for *infant performers*, the children of *the chapel and St. Paul's*."[48] In 1826 Samuel W. Singer cited "the humour of children" passage in a gloss on "travel" and added that the hindrance of the Elsinore troupe "comes from the late innovation of *companies of juvenile performers*, as the children of the revels, the children of St. Paul's, &c."[49] However, it is a drawback that neither satires nor child performers were innovations in 1599 or 1600. Nevertheless, an identification of "innovation" with the children's companies and their repertory of satires has persisted. E. A. J. Honigmann identifies the innovation as "the renewal of acting by the boys," and, as one of three possible meanings, Bevington cites "the new fashion in satirical plays performed by boy actors in the 'private' theaters."[50]

The second of Bevington's three glosses on "innovation" is "political uprising," which refers to an interpretation popularized by John Dover Wilson in the 1930s. Citing Frederick Boas's claim that the word in Shakespeare "always means a political upheaval of some kind," Dover Wilson asserted that the innovation could "hardly be other than that of the Earl of Essex," in February 1601.[51] But there is a drawback to this interpretation too: there is no evidence of an inhibition of playing in the wake of the Essex rebellion. Moreover, for those who argue as Jenkins does that the "little eyases" passage was deleted from the manuscript behind Q2 because "by 1604 the war of the theatres was no longer a burning topic,"[52] the identification of "innovation" with the Essex rebellion raises the question of why the political allusion was not also deleted. The Chamberlain's Men had been implicated in the treason by the performance of *Richard II* at the Globe. They escaped punishment at the time, and their fortunes were recovered by 1604/5 when Q2 of *Hamlet* was published. However, earlier in that very year Samuel Daniel had gotten into serious trouble over perceived parallels between his

Tragedy of Philotas and the career of Essex, and he had had to defend himself before the Privy Council.[53] If Shakespeare and his company cut the "little eyases" passage because it was outdated, but retained an Essex allusion even though the subject was still highly sensitive, they showed an uncharacteristically foolhardy sense of priorities.

In 1785 John Monck Mason had offered another possible explanation of "innovation." Noting that Francis Beaumont and John Fletcher used the word to refer to the coronation of a new monarch, Mason had suggested that Shakespeare used "innovation" to mean "the late *change* of government," that is, the accession of James I.[54] Although added by Malone to the commentary on *Hamlet* in the 1821 edition of Shakespeare's plays, Mason's suggestion was thereafter ignored. However, this explanation deserves consideration, for it offers a solution to the clash of textual issues and theatre history. In the first place, "innovation" as "the accession of a new monarch" enables Q2 to be seen as a feature of the political world of 1604/5, as it is by its date of publication. In the second, it links chronologically an "innovation" to an actual inhibition: a closure of the playhouses due to an outbreak of plague in the summer of 1603. For some years now, theatre historians have recognized that Privy Council orders rarely caused disruptions in London playing. Indeed, the evidence suggests that few orders of closure were issued and fewer were honored. Where scholars once saw paradigms of official inhibition, they now see coincidence.[55] The one occasion on which the government successfully suspended playing was during a time of plague. Even then companies seem to have calculated the possible resumption of playing from day to day. In May of 1603, for example, the scattered dates of Henslowe's payments for texts and apparel, plus the heading "Begininge to playe Agayne" (*HD* 225), make it appear that Worcester's Men kept themselves in readiness to open as soon as the plague ban was lifted.

The inhibition of May 1603 lasted until Easter Monday, 1604. Thus the autumn season of 1604 was effectively the first chance in a year for Shakespeare's company to offer a normal battery of plays at the Globe. They could not have known then that their reprieve was to be brief. Outbreaks of plague occurred in 1605–6, 1606–7, and 1607–8; and, as Leeds Barroll argues, even a mild epidemic was sufficient to cause the Privy Council to suspend public recreations.[56] The long stretch from May 1603 to April 1604 no doubt reminded the players that their professional life in plague time was uncertain.

The charge of their royal patent as the King's Men licensed the company to play not only at the Globe but also in the provinces. Indeed, Alan Somerset suggests that "touring under the King's name was probably part of their expected duties, as was entertaining the monarch at court or the London populace at the company's permanent theatres."[57] In the minds of the players, then, the "late innovation" that established James I as their king and themselves as his servants, coupled with an "inhibition" against playing in London during plague time, might logically have come together to produce a reason for touring that finds expression in the travel of the Elsinore troupe. If, as I argue, the "little eyases" passage did not yet exist in a script played by the Chamberlain's Men and one about the "humour of children" (or its counterpart) did; and if the Q2 text of *Hamlet* could have been used for touring (as Scott McMillin suggests); and if the company script was revised at that time (summer, 1603), then it is plausible that the following alterations were among those revisions: (1) a passage was dropped that alluded to a novelty no longer novel (the opening of boys' playhouses); and (2) a passage was added that alluded to the accession and the plague, conditions both immediate and relevant to provincial audiences in 1603.

III. When did the aerie of children cry out on the top of question?
From Pope to Malone, eighteenth-century commentators offered different chronologies for the events behind the "little eyases" passage. By specifying the Fortune as one of the playhouses "then contending," Pope implied a date after August 1600. Malone added new evidence to clarify the meaning of the "little eyases" passage, but in so doing he further confused the issue of chronology. In his notes on "inhibition," "innovation," and "aerie," he cited events dating from 1596 to 1620.[58] After Malone, scholars continued to grope for the historical and theatrical referents of, and therefore the right date for, the "little eyases" passage. F. G. Fleay assigned parts of the allusion to different dates: the reference to "aerie," 1601; "the innovation," 1603–4 (connecting it to both the Essex rebellion and petitions by Puritans); and the growth of the youths into adulthood, 1610.[59] Yet even as contrary opinions proliferated, a consensus of sorts developed for the date of 1601, largely because there was power in the coincidence of the narrative of theatrical wars and the June 1600 Privy Council order. Speaking with a confidence bred of that consensus, Alfred Harbage explained the allusion in *Hamlet* unequi-

vocally in terms of a rivalry between the men's and boys' companies, 1599–1602. Apparently because of that alleged company rivalry, Jenkins, Hibbard, Taylor, and Ioppolo assign the "little eyases" passage to 1601, even though their opinions differ on numerous other issues concerning the *Hamlet* texts.

A common denominator in old as well as new scholarly commentary is that the boys' companies produced satirical comedies. Richard Dutton, in his study of the role of the Revels Office in the licensing of plays, argues that the offense most likely to draw the ire of the master was the "guying of famous people," or "the particularizing of private mens humours (yet alive) Noble-men, & others" (as Thomas Heywood put it in *An Apology for Actors*); the worst invective, according to Heywood, came from "the mouthes of Children, supposing their iuniority to be a priuiledge for any rayling."[60] Proponents of the assignment of the "little eyases" passage to 1600–1 argue in effect that by that time either the boys' company at Blackfriars or the boys' companies together had achieved a record of offensive plays sufficient to prompt Shakespeare's company to lash out at them in a sustained diatribe. However, this record was achieved from 1604 through 1608 solely by the Blackfriars company and their performances of plays such as *Philotas* (1604), *Eastward Ho!* (1605), *The Isle of Gulls* (1606), the two-part *Byron* (1608), and a lost play about mines in Scotland (1608). Unlike the children's offerings of 1600–1, these plays angered influential noblemen who pressured the court of James I for reprisals (that is, for the boys to be forcibly reprimanded).[61] One contemporary witness in April 1608, M. de la Boderie, thought that the king had closed "all the London theatres" and would not open them again until the companies paid "100,000 francs to lift the ban."[62] Such behavior was sufficient to set off alarms of industry-wide restraints and provoke a warning voice from elders within the profession.

The King's Men had another reason to be disturbed by events at Blackfriars: by 1606 the boys were passing puberty. Hamlet seems inordinately interested in the long-term career expectations of the baby birds: "Will they pursue the quality no longer than they can sing? Will they not say afterwards, if they should grow themselves to common players – as it is most like, if their means are no better – their writers do them wrong to make them exclaim against their own succession?" (2.2.343–49). Nathan Field was thirteen in 1600; by 1606 he was nineteen. By 1610 if not earlier, boys such as John

Underwood and William Ostler had grown to be men, as the Burbage faction claimed in 1635. This maturity was obvious to all. In a record of performance before the king in 1606, the Children of Paul's were called "the Youths of Paul's." In 1600–1 Shakespeare and the Chamberlain's Men might have anticipated that the troublesome children would become adult players, but in 1606 that eventuality was imminent. After the demise of the Children of Paul's in 1606–7, there might be only adult companies, and one of them might be making trouble at Burbage's own Blackfriars.

IV. How did popularity become rivalry?

Pope introduced the concept of a heated competition when he used the verb "contending" in a note on "Airy." In 1726 Lewis Theobald emended Shakespeare's phrase, "These are now the fashion, and so berattle the common stages," to this: "These are now the FACTION, and so berattle the common STAGERS."[63] In Theobald's mind, "faction" expressed not only that the children appealed to audiences (they had "Fashion and Esteem") but also that they had a position of rivalry "against the other Playhouses, or had a Faction made by the Town in their Favour."[64] In his 1733 edition of Shakespeare's plays, Theobald attached that meaning to a note on "aerie," and he made the rivalry aggressive, giving Shakespeare a satirist's weaponry and attitude: "The Poet here steps out of his Subject to give a Lash at home, and sneer at the prevailing Fashion of following Plays perform'd by the Children of the Chapel."[65] In the same note Theobald greatly exaggerated the children's success by describing playgoers as "abandoning the establish'd Theatres" in order to follow the children's plays. Malone, enlarging the annotation of "Hercules and his load," raised the issue of numbers of playgoers; he supposed that the quip meant that the boys' playhouses attracted "greater audiences" than did the men's.[66]

In the nineteenth century, various factors conspired to transform the children's popularity into a narrative of rivalry with the adult companies. I have pointed out two such factors above: (1) the interpretation of "aerie" as a reference to both of the boys' companies, and (2) the discovery of government documents that encouraged scholars to see 1600–1 as a time when the Privy Council was keenly interested in the number of playhouses in London and the kind of satire being brought to the stage. I have pointed out another factor in preceding chapters: the inclination to read theatre history as personality. Steevens betrayed a contemporary hostility toward Ben Jonson by noting that he "should have been very much surprized" if Jonson were not one of the dramatists alluded to in the phrase, "their writers do them wrong."[67] Although William Gifford and others attempted to exonerate Jonson, the momentum favored the development of a theory of adversarial relations among the poets and, by association, among companies. The "little eyases" passage appeared then to confirm the rivalry, and it appears to do so for many scholars now. Harold Jenkins, although separating the "innovation" from the reappearance and quick success of the boys' company at Blackfriars, maintains an explicit association of the "little eyases" passage with a rivalry; his comment on the phrase "Hercules and his load" reads: "Shakespeare's word-play not only represents the boys carrying the whole world with them but wittily allows them a complete triumph over his own fellow-actors at the Globe."[68] Joseph Loewenstein argues that even more of *Hamlet* than the "little eyases" passage belongs on "the front lines of the War of the Theaters."[69]

In the next chapter, I address a fourth factor in the transformation of the children's popularity into company rivalries: the commercial effect of the boys' companies on the men's. At the heart of that argument is Histrio's complaint in *Poetaster*: "this winter ha's made vs all poorer, then so many staru'd snakes: No bodie comes at vs" (3.4.328–29). The orthodox reading of this quip is that Jonson was publicizing (and bragging about) the fact that the men's companies were losing money during the winter of 1600–1 because of the popularity of the Children of the Chapel at Blackfriars (and the Children of Paul's). The orthodox reading of the "little eyases" quip is that Shakespeare was lamenting that same loss of custom in 1600–1. On the issue of competition for playgoers, however, Histrio's complaint is as appropriate to the "humour of children" passage in Q1 as to the "little eyases" passage in F. Moreover, there is a rhetorical appeal in the assignment of Jonson's sniping to the "humour of children" passage rather than the "little eyases" one. Jonson took pride in having sharper teeth than his adversaries. As a retort to the mild complaint of playgoers being "turned to priuate playes, / And the humour of children," Jonson's image of the men players as "staru'd snakes" escalates the wit and hostility of the exchange, but it is tepid as a retort to the length and detailed anatomy of boy players in the "little eyases" passage.

Whatever the commercial effect of the poets' sparring in 1601, a commercial *and* political crisis for the companies began in 1604. There is evidence of it in the following documents: an Apology printed in the quarto of *Philotas* (1605) and a pair of letters by Samuel Daniel; ten letters collectively from Ben Jonson and George Chapman on their imprisonment in connection with performances of *Eastward Ho!* in 1605; and a letter between courtiers about imprisonments due to the performance of *The Isle of Gulls* in February 1606.[70] On the surface, the issue was similar to the one raised by Steevens and others to explain the "innovation" – namely, drama of personal abuse. But there is a significant difference in the public stature of the persons being abused. The Blackfriars plays in 1604–6 offended important noblemen who attributed political meanings to characterizations, jokes, costumes, and stage gestures that the dramatists claimed not to have intended.[71] The offended noblemen who were members of the Privy Council or who had friends on the Council could cause trouble for the playwrights. By November 1606 the company at Blackfriars had been punished in the form of patronage withdrawn: no longer identified by name with the queen or her chapel, the players had become merely the Children of Blackfriars. However, the company managers either did not recognize or did not heed these signs of danger. As Dutton puts it, the "Blackfriars Company . . . seem to have been totally unabashed . . . by what happened to the authors of these plays and continued to stage the most controversial works."[72] In 1608 two more plays at Blackfriars caused offense (the two-part *Byron* and the lost play about mines in Scotland).

I suggest that it was in this context that the King's Men stepped in, admonishing the Blackfriars company in public. Several years earlier, in 1603, they had done so on another issue. When the Children of the Chapel played "Jeronimo" at their playhouse, thereby violating a protocol among companies not to pirate one another's scripts, the King's Men took the Blackfriars play, *The Malcontent*, and, in a new Induction, told playgoers as well as customers of the bookshops that they were justified in taking revenge.[73] Now the threat from the children was both political and commercial. The King's Men had themselves offended some powerful nobles in the winter of 1604 when they presented the tragedy of "Gowrie"; "some great Councellors" were "much displeased with it," and there were rumors that the play would be "forbidden."[74] Thus the King's Men knew from immediate experience that a company provoked a clique of royal favorites at its peril. They knew that, since 1603, business had already been disrupted for months at a time by outbreaks of plague, that there was always opposition from churchmen and civic officials, and that the Children of Blackfriars and the poets who wrote for them were persisting in willful behavior. The King's Men therefore spoke out publicly in an attempt to limit the damage to themselves and the industry as a whole. In the "little eyases" passage, the King's Men could make fun of the loud, shrill voices of the children and trivialize their misbehavior by making them appear to be nestlings not yet properly trained. At the same time, should the councilors not be mollified, the King's Men could advertise their own displeasure at the children's mischief and distance themselves from it.

By assigning the "little eyases" passage to 1606–8, I bring issues of theatre history and textual revision together at a juncture of commerce and politics. For decades textual scholars and theatre historians have given reasons why a company might commission alterations or a dramatist on his own might mend part of his manuscript: they have suggested, for example, expansion of popular stage business, revision of topical allusions, updating of generic elements, second thoughts, and second drafts. The new revisionists suggest that a dramatist might have rewritten his old plays for artistic improvements in characterization, motivation, and the like. I call attention to an occasion for which revisions were political and commercial. In addition, my version of events enables a reinterpretation of the passages in Q1 and Q2 that are counterparts of the "little eyases" allusion. I suggest that – like the protest against the Blackfriars children in F – the variant passages in Q1 and Q2 mark a place in the sequential *Hamlet*s where the Chamberlain's/King's Men felt economic pressure. In the following scenarios I coordinate stage runs of Shakespeare's *Hamlet* with events current in the commercial and political environment of the company:

1600–1: The maiden run of Shakespeare's "Hamlet" at the Globe

In the fall of 1599 the Chamberlain's Men moved to their new playhouse, the Globe, across the lane from a company of old friends and competitors, the Admiral's Men. This physical relocation increased the opportunity for habitual playgoers to see a new or favorite play on a given day. At the same time, playhouses such as the Boar's Head and Curtain were operating with adult companies. A playhouse with a boys' company opened in the fall of 1599 at Paul's, and another opened in the fall of 1600 at Blackfriars (on lease from Richard Burbage). Making its debut in the spring or summer of 1600, *Hamlet* enjoyed a successful run and was retired by the fall of 1601.[75] For that stage run, the script of *Hamlet* contained a passage that alluded to a climate for commerce in which public audiences, who had been exclusively the customers of the men's companies for nearly a decade, were drawn to the private houses by the novelty of children's companies and their repertory of "humor" plays. The allusion – the "humour of children" passage in Q1, or one very like it – expressed the company's mock despair that playgoers could be so fickle.

1603–4: A revival of Shakespeare's "Hamlet"

Newly patented as the King's Men after May 1603, the company left the Globe, which was closed due to plague, and went on tour, visiting Bath, Shrewsbury, and Coventry among other towns. The alterations advertised on the title page of Q2 indicate that *Hamlet* had been revived recently, and it was kept in repertory after April 1604 when the plague ban was lifted in London. Presumably it was also revised with the tour of 1603–4 in mind. The extent of that revision might have been the addition of any or all of the Q2-only passages, but it included the deletion of the "humour of children" passage and the insertion of a new explanation for touring. The new explanation was topical and commercial, as the reference to children had once been. It alluded to a fact of professional life well known to provincial audiences: the impossibility of conducting business in the usual way due to the plague of 1603 ("inhibition"). In this case, that inhibition was conflated with another new feature of life throughout England in 1603, the change in monarchs ("innovation").[76]

1606–8: Another revival of Shakespeare's "Hamlet"

Sometime later still, perhaps between 1606 and 1608, the King's Men revived *Hamlet* again. One circumstance that made a revival attractive was that revenge plays were enjoying another wave of playgoer interest. In 1605–6, the King's Men had played *The Devil's Charter*, and in 1606–7, they offered *The Revenger's Tragedy*.[77] For this revival, the text of *Hamlet* was again revised. Some Q2–only passages were dropped, and the F-only "little eyases" passage was added. The "little eyases" addition imitated the "humour of children" passage in commenting on the phenomenon of boy players; at this time, however, the King's Men had a more urgent agenda: to disavow the behavior of a particular boys' company, the Children of Blackfriars. The addition implied that the children had irritated a powerful royal constituency and that, as a result, they had been punished by the heavy hand of the Crown ("and are most tyrannically clapped for't"). The addition implied that other prominent playgoers were also afraid of being lampooned by the children's dramatists ("many wearing rapiers are afraid of goose-quills"). It implied that the boy players argued with their poets over controversial material in the new scripts ("no money bid for argument, unless the poet and the player went to cuffs in the question"). And it implied that – while audiences were enjoying the mischief, perhaps thinking that the boys were tweaking upstart courtiers with impunity ("Do the boys carry it away?") – in fact the company was headed for a fall that might bring down their elders in the playhouse world with them ("Hercules and his load").[78]

The belief that the "little eyases" passage belonged to the *Hamlet* of 1600–1 has linked it to a narrative of commercial rivalry; and, once in place, the passage became the proof on which the narrative itself was authorized. However, the ubiquitous model of commercial competition in Shakespeare's London was the guild. In that system, when a young man was made free of the apprentice system, he joined a fraternal business that was designed to protect him from foreign competition and encourage his prosperity. Records for the Court of Assistants of individual guilds show that fines were imposed on wayward freemen, established as well as new, but the intent of the disciplinary action was not to drive away legitimate members of the trade but to regulate the industry and punish destructive behavior. In terms of this model, the meaning of "rival" in the sixteenth century is pertinent. The word occurs in the *Oxford English Dictionary* in the context of lovers and combatants, not in a context of commerce. But a sense in which "rival" might apply to sixteenth-century businesses occurs in *Hamlet*. In the opening scene on the battlements in Q2/F, Barnardo says to Francisco: "Well, goodnight.

If you do meet *Horatio* and *Marcellus*, the Riuals of my Watch, bid them make hast" (TLN 16–17). In the playtext of Q1, the line captures the same meaning; it is rendered: "And if you meete Marcellus and Horatio, / The partners of my watch, bid them make haste" (B). Like other businessmen who thrived in a widening market for their wares, the players in Shakespeare's London bristled at lapses in protocol; as seniors in the profession, the members of the King's Men made their views public when they were sufficiently alarmed. The "little eyases" passage, which was an overreaction to normal working conditions such as the opening of a new playhouse in 1600, is an appropriate response to the Children of Blackfriars in 1606–8, whose flight over certain political terrain put the entire theatrical industry at risk.

CHAPTER 6

"Poetaster," "Satiromastix," and company commerce

Hee wold have slong iests at him as hard as stones till he had
pelted him out of this place
Poetaster, as quoted by Edward Pudsey, in his Commonplace Book[1]

In an entry dated 3 November 1600, Henry Travice, steward to Sir
William Cavendish, recorded in an account book an expenditure of
18d. for his master's "going to a play at paules."[2] Over the next two
years, Travice made additional entries of payments for his master's
playgoing. As in the entry for 3 November 1600, Travice sometimes
named the playhouse that Cavendish attended: Paul's in October
1601, June 1602, and November 1602; Blackfriars in October and
November 1601. The Cavendish records are new evidence of a long-
assumed phenomenon, namely, attendance by persons of noble birth
at the boys' playhouses after their opening in 1599 (Paul's) and 1600
(Blackfriars). During the nineteenth century, scholars became con-
vinced that the nature of company commerce in Shakespeare's time
could be deduced from this moment of competition for the better
class of playgoer. The "little eyases" passage in Shakespeare's *Hamlet*
seemed to reveal the fear of the Chamberlain's Men that men such
as Cavendish now would not only prefer the private theatres but also
choose them exclusively. The complaint by the player Histrio in
Jonson's *Poetaster* that his company's players were like starving snakes
seemed to reveal that such fear was justified. Drawn to the satirical
pointing in plays such as *Poetaster* and *Satiromastix* because of Jonson's
quarreling with other playwrights, R. A. Small in 1899 linked
playwrights to companies and quarreling to company commerce. In
1952 Alfred Harbage further construed the satirical pointing as
evidence of a commercial rivalry between the men's and boys'
companies.

In recent years many scholars have come to view as quaint the over-identification of characters with real people,[3] but they have left largely unchallenged the perception of the theatrical marketplace that underlies Harbage's declaration of commercial rivalry. In the previous chapter, I presented arguments to remove the "little eyases" passage from events in 1600–1, substituting the far milder quip about the "humour of children" in Q1 (1603) as a measure of the commercial anxiety of the Chamberlain's Men at the reopening of Paul's and Blackfriars playhouses. Here I raise again the issue of competing repertories, looking now specifically at the commercial context and theatrical content of *Poetaster* and *Satiromastix*. I accept the opinion of W. David Kay that Jonson's quarrel with John Marston and Thomas Dekker as carried on through the satirical pointings in plays "reveals much about the tensions in the Elizabethan literary system,"[4] but I note that Kay's emphasis is personal and literary (i.e., the dramatist's self-image, the dramatist as poet), mine commercial and theatrical (i.e., the business of playing). I argue that, in the competition for playgoers waged by *Poetaster* and *Satiromastix*, Jonson and Dekker used similar weaponry. Both exploited the affection of their audience for the golden oldies of the Elizabethan repertory and their continuing taste for the theatrics that had made many a pot-boiler successful.

Cavendish might have attended a performance of *Poetaster* when it was new. In an entry dated October 1601, his steward, Travice, recorded an expenditure of 12d. for his master's "going into a plea at blacke frayers."[5] The title page of the quarto of *Poetaster* advertises performances at Blackfriars by the Children of the Chapel and carries the date of 1602 (S. R. 21 December 1601); the title page of the text in the 1616 folio edition claims that the play was acted in 1601. As a rule, scholars of Jonson's professional life have agreed that *Poetaster* was on stage by late spring or early summer of 1601. Their opinion is based on the belief that Jonson heard about Dekker's plans to satirize him in a play (*Satiromastix*) and hurriedly composed *Poetaster* "as a pre-emptive strike."[6] However, in the 1995 Revels edition Tom Cain challenges received opinion by suggesting that *Poetaster* made its debut in "performances over the Michaelmas/ winter season of 1601–2."[7]

Unfortunately, little is known of the repertory that Cavendish might have seen at Blackfriars if he did not see *Poetaster*. Advertisements on the title pages of quartos identify only two plays staged at Blackfriars near the time of *Poetaster*: *Cynthia's Revels*, which was probably new in the winter of 1600–1 (S. R. 23 May 1601, Q1601); and an old play by John Lyly, *Love's Metamorphosis*, which, according to the title page of its quarto, had been played by the Children of Paul's but was played "now by the Children of the Chappell" (S. R. 25 November 1600, Q1601). *The Case is Altered*, the 1609 quarto of which advertises the boys' company at Blackfriars, probably existed in 1597, but it is not clear when it traveled to Blackfriars. Scholars of the boys' companies have generally agreed that the Children of the Chapel had one or more plays by George Chapman in repertory, possibly as early as 1600–1. Plausible choices are *All Fools*, originally written for the Admiral's Men (Q1605), *Sir Giles Goosecap* (S. R. 10 January 1606, Q1606), *May Day* (Q1611), and *The Gentleman Usher* (S. R. 26 November 1605, Q1606).[8] Taking literally the King's Men (formerly Chamberlain's Men) in the Induction to *The Malcontent*, these scholars also agree that the boys' company at Blackfriars had a play featuring Hieronimo; Hillebrand called it "the old and famed *Jeronimo*."[9]

Even into the 1980s, the scholarship on *Poetaster* focused almost exclusively on its role in the War of the Theatres. Cain, summarizing that commentary, tells the familiar narrative about Marston's and Jonson's taking offense at satirical portraits of themselves in each other's plays and retaliating with more caricatures. Cain's mantra-like recitation of plays (*Histrio-Mastix*, *Every Man Out of his Humour*, *Jack Drum's Entertainment*, *Cynthia's Revels*, *What You Will*, *Poetaster*, and *Satiromastix*) and characters (Chrisoganus, Clove, Brabant Sr., Hedon, Anaides, Lampatho Doria, Crispinus, Demetrius, and Horace) signals that the narrative is moribund.[10] Recently Jonson scholars have reinvigorated discussion of *Poetaster* by turning to issues such as politics, patronage, censorship, venues, and audience.[11] Inseparable from the issue of audience is Jonson's use of *Poetaster* as a vehicle for his opinions on the playwright-poet as moralist, himself as superior in that category, and the relationship of the poet to the state.[12]

Theatrical commerce is one subject that links discussions of Jonson's image of himself and the playwright-poet, the competition for audiences, and performances of *Poetaster*. Having inherited the narrative of the War of the Theatres, scholars discussing the theatrical-commercial environment of Jonson and *Poetaster* and that of Dekker and *Satiromastix* typically emphasize the differences: at Blackfriars, a company of boys entertained a coterie audience indoors once a week with satirical comedies at prices designed to exclude the riff-raff; at the Globe, a company of men entertained outdoors daily with pulp drama by hack writers (except Shakespeare) at prices designed to include anyone.[13] Reflecting that legacy, Alan Sinfield observes that Jonson appears in *Poetaster* to reject the theatrical marketplace by rejecting "the trivializing pressures of the public playhouses."[14] This attitude toward commercial drama may be deduced from the bluster of Pantilius Tucca, Jonson's skeldering captain and tear-mouth, in a street scene in which he prevents the arrest of Crispinus, the newly-minted poet and thus poetaster. Tucca notices Histrio, a player, passing by and calls him over: "you, player, rogue, stalker, come backe here: no respect to men of worship, you slaue? What, are you proud, you rascall, are you proud? ha? you grow rich, doe you?" (3.4.122–25). Seeing opportunity in bringing together the player and the new poet, Tucca recommends the service Crispinus can provide: "he pens high, loftie, in a new stalking straine" (3.4.161–62). Tucca boasts that with such a playwright Histrio and his fellows will grow so rich that they can abandon touring in the provinces: "If hee pen for thee once, thou shalt not need to trauell, with thy pumps full of grauell, any more, after a blinde iade and a hamper" (3.4.167–66).[15] Tucca, a playgoer himself, would come to Histrio's playhouse if a good new bawdy play were in production; however, he has heard that there is "nothing but *humours, reuells,* and *satyres,* that girde and fart at the time" (3.4.190–91). Histrio assures him that there is "as much ribaldrie in our plaies, as can bee, as you would wish," and consequently "All the sinners, i' the suburbs, come, and applaud our action, daily" (3.4.194–96). A shabby fellow comes along, and Histrio introduces him as "Demetrivs, a dresser of plaies about the towne" who has been hired by Histrio's company to satirize Horace by misrepresenting him and his gallants in a play (3.4.321–24). Histrio relishes the "huge deale of money" such a play will bring, profits desperately needed because "this winter ha's made vs all poorer, then so many staru'd snakes: No bodie comes at vs; not a gentleman, nor a – " (3.4.327–30).

Editors of *Poetaster* routinely cite these passages as evidence of Jonson's contempt for common players and their playhouses, and from an Olympian viewpoint they do depict a grubby, artless existence. But from the everyday perspective of the marketplace, this theatrical matter suggests Jonson's grudging admiration for the commercial stage. As Sinfield observes, *"Poetaster* is itself a market product; like many of Jonson's plays, it communicates the excitement of writing for the popular London theatre."[16] This theatricality is evident at the beginning of the play when Envy rises from the middle of the stage, caressing her snakes: "Cling to my necke, and wrists, my louing wormes, / And cast you round, in soft, amorous foulds" (Induction 6–7). Perversely, she invites playgoers to "hiss, sting, and teare" the author's work, and she offers them her playmates: "Here, take my snakes among you" (Induction 44). When rebuffed, she begins to sink, and Prologue, armed, steps forward to set his foot upon her head, thus acting out an emblem of her defeat. Having used the trap to effect, Jonson confiscates a playgoer's stool so that Crispinus may both watch and participate in the comedy of manners at the house of Chloe and Albius (2.1.1–2). Jonson uses the aside to dramatize Horace's increasing desperation to escape the parasitic Crispinus (i.e., 3.1.44). Sinfield cites the trial scene in which Crispinus vomits offensive vocabulary as evidence of Jonson's theatricality, declaring that the "device shows as much inventive exuberance as the marvelous verbal excesses of Crispinus."[17] But the violent emetic is not Jonson's only trick here. As the pills begin to work, members of the on-stage audience comment on the action: "O terrible windy words!" (5.3.497). Horace, holding the barber's basin, repeats the words as they are spit up, also giving a progress report: "No: there's the often *conscious dampe* behind, still" (5.3.504–505). Horace suggests an action that will void Crispinus completely: "Force your selfe then, a little with your finger" (5.3.511–12), and at Caesar's request someone steps forward to hold Crispinus's head: "Again, hold him: hold his head there" (5.3.524).

Equally exuberant in stage business, and even more theatrical because of the subject matter, are the performances by Tucca's pages (the *pyrgi*), whose impromptu recitations from old plays give their master an opportunity to gossip in the street with Histrio about theatrical matters. Jonson's choice of play-scraps is often interpreted as satire of the repertories of men's companies,[18] but this opinion underestimates the commercial value of the advertising in that satire. Collectively, the play-scraps allude to old offerings newly current. The piece from Chapman's *The Blind Beggar of Alexandria –* *"Who calls out murder? lady, was it you?"* (3.4.246) – looks back to the most popular new play in the repertory of the Admiral's Men at the Rose in 1595–6, but it also looks out to the Fortune and a revival for which the Admiral's Men paid £9 3s. 4d. for apparel and "divers thing*es*" in May and June 1601 (*HD* 169–70).[19] Likewise, Peele's *Battle of Alcazar* was in revival in 1601, if it was the play Henslowe called "Mahomet."[20] Not new when it was staged by the Admiral's Men at the Rose in 1594–5, "Mahomet" was apparently revived at the Fortune in the fall of 1601, for Henslowe recorded the purchase of apparel and the text in August and September (*HD* 178, 180). Even if not an allusion to the revived "Mahomet," the scrap from *The Battle of Alcazar* serves as a metonymy, evoking Mediterranean plays in performance.[21] The cry of "*Vindicta!*" functions similarly, collecting theatrical moments from ghosts and revenge plays such as *Antonio's Revenge*, which was perhaps currently on stage at the adjacent playhouse at Paul's. A tragedy at the Globe in 1600–1 did not itself have a ghost crying "Revenge!" according to its published texts; but its precursor apparently did, if Thomas Lodge's recollection of Hamlet's ghost in *Wits Miserie and the Worlds Madnesse* (1596) is trustworthy. Another old play was Thomas Kyd's *Spanish Tragedy*, from which the pages perform two scraps (4.3.215–22, 247–54); it had been on stage in London since 1587 or thereabouts, with revivals at the Rose in 1592 and 1597. However it was soon to be new again, with additions by Ben Jonson.[22] The pages' comic performances might well have suggested to some of Jonson's playgoers at Black-friars, as they did to Alfred Harbage, that "[o]nly the brainless admire *The Spanish Tragedy.*"[23] But for other playgoers, the play-scraps in *Poetaster* might have revived their former interest in the old play and prompted their attendance at the Fortune a year later.

Behind these allusions are echoes of several playwrights but none more theatrically present to Jonson than Christopher Marlowe and William Shakespeare. In *Rival Playwrights* (1991) James Shapiro explores Jonson's anxiety over Marlovian and Shakespearean influences. He points out Jonson's appropriation of Marlowe's translation of Ovid in *Poetaster*, but there might also be echoes of *Tamburlaine* and *Doctor Faustus*.[24] Reminders of Tamburlaine's mighty line permeate the page's selections from *The Battle of Alcazar*, and the plaintive "Where is Calipolis?" recalls Tamburlaine's beloved Zenocrate.[25] Memories of *Doctor Faustus* might have been triggered in the first scene of *Poetaster*. William Gifford inserted a stage direction for the entire first act that locates Ovid, Jr., "*in his study.*" The discovery of a character in such a place was common, but *Doctor Faustus* had had more stage exposure by 1601 than any of the plays in the entry on "study" in Alan Dessen and Leslie Thomson's *Dictionary of Stage Directions* (1999). Jonson's audience might have been reminded further of Faustus when Ovid-the-character recites the Marlovian translation of Ovid-the-poet's elegy (*Amores*, I.xv), for the poem rejects various literary models as a means to fame in a rhetorical sequence similar to Faustus's rejection of various academic means. Dekker found this opening moment significant in establishing theatrical parallels, and he replicated it in *Satiromastix*: Horace is discovered, composing a poem, "*sitting in a study behinde a Curtaine, a candle by him burning, bookes lying confusedly*" (1.2.0.s.d.). According to Cain, scholars have not traced the cries of "*Veni*" in the pages' performances (3.4.234–35), but playgoers who had seen *Doctor Faustus* might have remembered Faustus's summons – "*Veni, veni, Mephostophile!*" – at the beginning of the contract scene.

There are no specific allusions to Shakespeare's plays in *Poetaster*, but playgoers who had attended performances at the Globe might have remembered Cinna the poet's fate in *Julius Caesar* in the call by Envy to tear the poet and his verses (Induction 52–53), repeated by Luscus's threat against Ovid's verses (1.1.11). As commentators on the play generally note, the farewell scene of Ovid and Julia recalls the balcony scene in *Romeo and Juliet*, which Shakespeare himself recalls in the elopement of Jessica and Lorenzo in *The Merchant of Venice* (and behind both is the balcony scene from *The Jew of Malta*). Herford and Simpson heard Falstaff vaunting in "King Cambyses' vein" (*1 Henry IV*, 2.4.387) behind Tucca's boast that his page will "speake, in king Darivs dolefull straine" (3.4.208–9). In the oration that follows, however, Jonson's playgoers might have remembered another comic stage moment. The page begins, "*O doleful days! O direfull deadly dump!*" (3.4.210). He thus evokes the alliteration and apostrophe in "A tedious brief scene of young Pyramus and his love Thisby" in *A Midsummer Night's Dream*: for example, Prologue's "Whereat, with blade, with bloody blameful blade, / He bravely broach'd his boiling bloody breast" (5.1.146–47), and Pyramus's "O grim-look'd night! O night with hue so black!" (5.1.170) and "Quail, crush, conclude, and quell!" (5.1.287).[26]

The performances of the pages also gave Jonson opportunities in meta-theatre, similar to Shakespeare's meta-theatrical matter in *1 Henry IV, Hamlet*, and *A Midsummer Night's Dream*. Tucca becomes the pages' director, calling for stock oratorical declamations: the "dolefull straine" of the mourner, the "amorous vaine" of the lover, and vaunts of "the horrible fierce Souldier" (3.4.209, 214, 223). He calls for specific characters (the ghost, the Moor) and properties (a drum). The pages appropriate Tucca's scarf in their second round of playing, and they press Minos, the apothecary, into service. Tucca becomes a critic of audience reaction, asking Histrio and Demetrius "art not rapt? are not tickled now? do'st not applaud, rascall?" (3.4.270–72). Histrio, turned playgoer, calls for a favorite bit: " 'Pray, sweet Captaine, let one of them doe a little of a ladie" (3.4.259–60). After a brief off-stage rehearsal, one of the pages enters on the shoulders of Minos, who stalks about the stage as the page declaims. His stalking for Jonson's audiences is an example of David Mann's point that a now-lost category of theatrical allusion is the mimicking of well-known stage players by trademark gestures.[27]

In the comic performances of the pages and the stage business in various scenes, Jonson relied on theatrical strategies that were attracting playgoers to the Fortune, Globe, Boar's Head, Curtain, and even Blackfriars when his plays were not on offer. As Sinfield puts it, "Blackfriars was not *so* different from the public theatres."[28] Neither, in fact, was Paul's. The repertory offerings there in 1599–1602 matched offerings at the men's playhouses in such pairings as Marston's *Antonio and Mellida* and *Antonio's Revenge* with Shakespeare's *Hamlet* at the Globe, and *The Maid's Metamorphosis* with "The Golden Ass & Cupid and Psyche" at the Rose. Richard Dutton points out that the reputation for "biting" satires at the boys' playhouses was unjustified for Paul's at any time and unjustified for Blackfriars until 1604, when Samuel Daniel was appointed licenser of the Children of the Chapel; only then did the repertory at Blackfriars become "distinctly different from that of Paul's Boys and the adult companies."[29] Yet there were differences between the boys' and men's playhouses in the business of playing that would have affected the relative profitability of each enterprise. The scale of business at Paul's and Blackfriars was smaller than that at the men's playhouses: a shorter season (Michaelmas into Trinity Term), fewer performances weekly, fewer plays in repertory, a smaller playhouse. It appears, therefore, that the boys' playhouses were less profitable for their investors than the men's, even though they had higher prices and fewer expenses for personnel.[30]

In the same month of October 1601 that he recorded the expenses of Sir William Cavendish's attendance at Blackfriars, Henry Travice entered the expense of 18d. for his master's "going into a plea at

Poles."[31] There Cavendish might have seen *Satiromastix*, Dekker's counterpart to *Poetaster*, for it was played both at Paul's and the Globe, according to the title page of its quarto published in 1602. But *when* it was staged at either playhouse is one of the unknowns of playhouse commerce. Opinions on the debut of *Satiromastix* are entangled with other issues of provenance including the circumstances of its composition and authorship. All explanations start with the passage in *Poetaster* in which Histrio confides to Tucca that Demetrius has been hired "to abuse HORACE, and bring him in, in a play, with all his gallants" (3.4.323–25). The line is considered evidence that Jonson rushed *Poetaster* to the stage before a production of *Satiromastix* could be mounted. According to the Induction to *Poetaster*, Jonson took "fifteene weekes" to compose the play (Induction 14), finishing sometime in late spring or summer. Dekker did not need another fifteen weeks after that to complete *Satiromastix*, but he did need access to Jonson's play in manuscript or performance in order to appropriate its stage business and characters (Tucca, Horace-Jonson, Crispinus-Marston, Demetrius-Dekker). By the time he began work on *Blurt, Master Constable* for the Children of Paul's late in 1601 (perhaps with Thomas Middleton), *Satiromastix* was in production, for it was registered at Stationers' Hall on 11 November 1601.

The quarto of *Satiromastix* advertises on its title page the solo authorship of Thomas Dekker. Nonetheless, Marston is usually given a role in the composition because he supposedly had the greater sense of injury, having been lampooned in Jonson's plays since the staging of *Every Man Out of his Humour* in 1599. Alfred Harbage and O. J. Campbell referred to *Satiromastix* as "Marston and Dekker's"; Hoy gives "the actual writing" to Dekker.[32] However, Dekker's motive for satirizing Jonson is obscure, unless he took offense personally at the portrait of Anaides in *Cynthia's Revels*. But the prior question is why Jonson might have targeted Dekker at all. A possible explanation is that something happened in the fall of 1599 to irritate Jonson when he, Marston, and Dekker were writing for the Admiral's Men.[33] Whatever that "something" was, it allegedly had to do with Jonson's desire to distinguish himself from ordinary dramatists and his dramatic poetry from their pulp fare. Cyrus Hoy projects a role in the composition for the companies involved. He suggests that Dekker acquired "a joint commission" from the Chamberlain's Men and Children of Paul's for the attack.[34] Hoy finds a motive for the

Chamberlain's Men in their disappointment over the "failure of their production of Jonson's *Every Man Out of his Humour.*"[35] He attributes the interest of the Children of Paul's in a commission to their support of Marston because of recent performances of *Jack Drum's Entertainment* and *What You Will.* Harbage, focused on the rivalry between the men's and boys' playhouses, avers that the Children of Paul's were willing to perform *Satiromastix* "in the cause of Marston" despite their contempt for popular drama.[36]

Few scholars have had much good to say about Dekker and *Satiromastix* except to praise the satire of Jonson. Gerard Langbaine observed in 1691 that *Satiromastix* was "far inferior" to *Poetaster*, a judgment he based on Dekker's "abilities in Poetry," which he believed were far poorer than Jonson's.[37] R. H. Shepherd could have become Dekker's apologist in his 1873 edition of the plays, but in the accompanying memoir, he struck a decidedly melancholy note. He called Dekker "one of those unfortunate poets to whom the Muse is a cruel stepmother."[38] Shepherd appreciated the "considerable pungency" of Dekker's satire, but he deferred to Disraeli in the opinion that Dekker was a "subordinate author" who had luckily "caught some portion of Jonson's own genius" in the one instance of this play.[39] The satire thus generally praised was both biographical and literary. Dekker targeted Jonson's working-class background, penchant for fighting, undistinguished former career as a player, backbiting in the guise of moral correction, exaggerated sense of his appeal to patrons, addiction to generic form, self-promotion, and self-pity.[40]

Many critics have not been able to overcome a distaste for the form of *Satiromastix.* They object to its mix of tragedy, comedy, and satire, yet they excuse Dekker by assuming that he was working on the story of King William Rufus when the idea of responding to Jonson arose. Then, as Hoy puts it, Dekker "appears to have met the request for a satiric action directed against a contemporary literary personality by the simple expedient of inserting it, at whatever cost to dramatic congruity, into his pseudo-historical romance."[41] Larry Champion calls *Satiromastix* "notoriously ill-constructed," and concludes that it "has probably done more to damage Dekker's reputation as a playwright than any other single work."[42] However, Robert C. Evans finds thematic parallels that connect the plots of Horace-Jonson and King William Rufus. He argues that both poet and king, though similarly corrupt and selfish, differ in their acknowledgement of wrong-doing: Horace's confession is forced and insincere; the king's is spontaneous and redemptive.[43] Evans also finds theatrical parallels, as in the rhyming stage action of bringing Horace to Court to be punished and bringing Cælestine to Court to punish King William Rufus.

I suggest that there is another unifying theme in *Satiromastix*, one more significant to commercial relations among the companies than Dekker's whipping of Jonson. This theme is the defense of pulp drama. Dekker, recognizing Jonson's gambit of jesting with popular repertory materials, seized the advantage: he used the text of *Satiromastix* to remind playgoers of the repertorial diversity in subject and kind that had been drawing them to playhouses since the 1570s. It may be, as Hoy supposes, that the Chamberlain's Men and the Children of Paul's "commissioned" Dekker to knock Jonson down a few pegs, but Dekker's artistic invention gave them more than they could have imagined by complementing the satire with a bombardment of allusions to the very drama that Jonson had seemingly lampooned. Further, Dekker's call in the epilogue for serial retaliatory plays advertised the collaborative strategy of competition by which the London playhouse enterprise had flourished.

As in *Poetaster*, Tucca is a unifying figure in the action, moving freely between the poet's and courtiers' worlds.[44] But unlike in *Poetaster*, where Jonson concentrates the theatrical allusions in a few scenes, Dekker weaves play titles, characters' names, and snatches of lines throughout Tucca's speeches.[45] This strategy enables him to remind his audience continuously of the successful history of drama and its diverse venues. One cluster of allusions looks back to the 1550s and 1560s: "mother Mumble crust" (3.1.139–40), "King Gorboduck" and "ô royall Porrex" (1.2. 339, 392), "Gammer Gurton, I meane to bee thy needle" (3.1.200), and "King *Cambises*" (5.2.249). Mage (or Madge) Mumble-crust is a character in *Ralph Roister Doister* (Q1566?), which was probably first played by Nicholas Udall's schoolboys at Eton (1545–53?); *Gammer Gurton's Needle* (Q1575) was performed at Christ's College, Cambridge, in the 1550s; *Gorboduc*, or *Ferrex and Porrex* by Thomas Sackville and Thomas Norton (Q1565), was performed at the Inner Temple for revels at Christmas, 1561–2; *Cambyses* by Thomas Preston (Q1569) was a public play written for a commercial company. These allusions might have been lost on a number of Dekker's playgoers, even though the characters of Roister Doister and Cambyses had become synonymous with the very type to which Tucca himself belonged. Some in the audience might have remembered a more recent version of Gorboduc's story in the "Ferrex and Porrex" written by William Haughton for the Admiral's Men in the late spring of 1600.

Another set of Dekker's allusions represents the golden age of commercial theatre in the 1580s and early 1590s. Several answer *Poetaster* directly, for they recall the same plays by Kyd, Marlowe, and Peele to which Jonson alluded: "thou ranst mad for the death of Horatio," "Goe by Ieronimo, goe by," and "my smug Belimperia" (1.2.355–56, 372; 3.1.131); "my name's Hamlet reuenge" (4.1.121); "*Sultane Soliman*" (5.2.165); "thou must run of an errand for mee Mephostophiles" (1.2.297–98); "thou seest my red flag is hung out" and "dost stampe mad Tamberlaine, dost stampe?" (4.2.29, 4.3.169–70);[46] "Feede and be fat my faire Calipolis" (4.1.150); and "while we haue Hiren heere" (4.3.243–44). A few scraps performed by the pages in *Poetaster* appear to reflect plays now unknown, but the allusions in *Satiromastix* are identifiable due to Dekker's strategy of calling names. Thus, plays documented by Henslowe's entries of performances at the Rose from 1592 through 1597 – though now lost – are recognizable in Tucca's speeches: "Huon of Bordeaux" ("noble Huon," 4.2.42), "Machiavel" ("*Monsieur Machiauell*," 4.2.80), "Long Meg of Westminster" ("Long Meg a Westminster," 3.1.174), the two-part "Hercules" ("Death of Hercules," "thou shalt be *Perithous* and *Tucca Theseus*," and "th'art a little Hercules," 4.1.126; 4.2.93–94, 107), "Crack Me this Nut," ("with his Squirrell by his side cracking nuttes," 4.2.53–54), the two-part "Tamar Cham" (ô royall *Tamor Cham*," 5.2.182), and "Alexander and Lodowick" ("thou and I hence forth will be *Alexander* and *Lodwicke*, the Gemini, sworne brothers," 4.2.92–93). For long-time playgoers in Dekker's audience in 1601, a few of these names might have recalled an earlier generation of companies: "Machiavel" and the two-part "Tamar Cham" belonged to Strange's Men in 1592; "Huon of Bordeaux" belonged to Sussex's Men in 1593–4.

Yet another cluster of Dekker's allusions identify plays on stage at the Rose dating from the fall of 1597. These include "Mother Redcap," purchased in December 1597; *The Downfall of Robert, Earl of Huntingdon* and *The Death of Robert, Earl of Huntingdon*, purchased in February 1598; "King Arthur," purchased in April 1598; "The Civil Wars of France," purchased from September 1598 through January 1599; "Tristram of Lyons," purchased in October 1599; "Ferrex and

Porrex," purchased in April 1600; and "Damon and Pythias," purchased in May 1600. Allusions to plays of 1597–1600 answered Jonson not only by reminding audiences of the bread-and-butter offerings that made up a commercial repertory but also by defending the poets who had produced them: Anthony Munday, Michael Drayton, Henry Chettle, Richard Hathaway, and William Haughton. Further, Jonson had been associated with the Admiral's Men at the Rose, 1597–9. He had collaborated with Henry Porter and Henry Chettle on "Hot Anger Soon Cold" in August 1598; with Dekker on "Page of Plymouth" in August–September 1599; and with Dekker, Chettle, and a dramatist not named on "Robert II, King of Scots" also in September 1599. Through the allusions, therefore, Dekker reminded audiences that Jonson himself had been partially responsible for the variety and quality of theatrical offerings in London.

Along with a sweeping view of play offerings at the Rose, Dekker's allusions embraced commerce at the Swan, Boar's Head, Globe, Paul's, and Blackfriars (at least). There is one specific reference to the event that first brought Jonson to the attention of the theatrical world – the infamous "Isle of Dogs" affair ("the Stagerites banisht thee into the Ile of Dogs," 4.1.132–33) – and two references to Paris Garden, the site of the Swan (4.1.122, 134–35). There is a reference to "The True History of George Scanderbeg," which was staged somewhere in the summer of 1601 by the Earl of Oxford's Men, perhaps at the Boar's Head playhouse. There may even be a line from that now-lost play in the allusion: "whir, away, I goe vpon life and death, away, flie Scanderbag flie" (4.2.23–24). Dekker included his own recent work at Paul's in Horace's complaint that Demetrius had "cut an Innocent Moore i'th middle, to serue him in twice; and when he had done, made Poules-worke of it" (2.2.39–42). An allusion to *The Wisdom of Doctor Dodypoll* further advertises the offerings by the Children of Paul's ("Doctor Doddipol," 5.2.323). Dekker referred specifically to *Poetaster* and its venue at Blackfriars in Tucca's accusation that Horace had "arraigned two Poets against all lawe and conscience; and . . . turn'd them amongst a company of horrible blacke Fryers" (4.3.197–99). By direct quotes from *Cynthia's Revels* (1.2.149–51, 154–56) as well as by naming Criticus (1.2.312–13), Dekker included Jonson's earlier work for the Children of the Chapel. Dekker recalled the repertory at the Globe through this same allusion to Criticus, which includes other Jonsonian pseudonyms, specifically in the allusion, Asper, from *Every Man Out of his Humour*, staged by the Chamberlain's Men at the Globe. Tucca links *Every Man Out of his Humour* with *Every Man In his Humour* (which Jonson wrote for the Chamberlain's Men in pre-Globe days) in a passage complaining against Jonson's practice of satirical pointing: "A Gentleman, or an honest Cittizen, shall not Sit in your pennie-bench Theaters . . . but he shall be Satyr'd, and Epigram'd vpon, and his humour must run vpo'th Stage: you'll ha *Euery Gentleman in's humour*, and *Euery Gentleman out on's humour*" (4.2.52–57). Other allusions to the repertory of the Chamberlain's Men include the naming of Justice Shallow (2.2.35), Hal's exit line to Falstaff in *1 Henry IV* ("I owe God a death," 4.1.211), Tucca's kinship with the Falstaff of *The Merry Wives of Windsor* as a go-between who woos for himself, and the echo of *Romeo and Juliet* in Cælestine's sleeping potion.[47]

In the same month of October 1601 that he recorded his master's going to plays at Blackfriars and Paul's, Henry Travice recorded the expense of 3d. for "Hallams going into the plea." Hallam, being Cavendish's personal servant, might well have accompanied Sir William, but given that the entry is separate in the ledger and the expense of 3d. is less than the putative custom at a private house, it is tempting to imagine that Hallam attended a public playhouse when his master was otherwise occupied.[48] If that playhouse was the Fortune, Hallam might have seen the lavish new production, "Cardinal Wolsey," for which the Admiral's Men spent more than £37 for apparel; or his taste might have run more to the folk material of "Friar Rush and the Proud Woman of Antwerp" and "The Wise Man of West Chester" (newly revived). He might also have gone to the Boar's Head to see Worcester's Men, whose repertory included work by Heywood, but evidence of specific offerings is lost. The Curtain, despite having faced sanctions in May for pointing satirically at distinguished public figures, might have been open in the fall of 1601; however, its resident company and repertory are unknown.

Or, Hallam might have attended the Globe. There he could have seen Shakespeare's new play, *Twelfth Night*, or a continuation from the spring, perhaps *Hamlet*. But he could also have seen *Satiromastix*. He might therefore have been among the playgoers whom Tucca addressed in the epilogue of *Satiromastix*, promising to dance for joy if they will spend their "two pence a piece agen" to return to the playhouse (line 15). Tucca assumes that the audience knows him from having seen *Poetaster* at Blackfriars, and in mock-confession to these friarites, he blames "the Deuill and his Angels" and that "Hereticall Libertine *Horace*" for causing raillery that he now recants (lines 6–11). He knows that some have come from Blackfriars to hiss him, but he offers a better way to vent their anger: "Are you aduiz'd what you doe when you hisse? you blowe away *Horaces* reuenge: but if you set your hands and Seales to this, *Horace* will write against it, and you may haue more sport: . . . No, my Poetasters will not laugh at him, but will vntrusse him agen, and agen, and agen" (lines 19–24). Tucca is suggesting that *Poetaster* and *Satiromastix* are parts one and two of a serial drama in which arraignments and untrussings become the centerpiece of a theatrical game that guarantees revenue at the participating playhouses. Thus Dekker caps his defense of pulp drama and common playwrights with an advertisement of the commercial strategy by means of which the companies might all profit, namely, the exploitation of one another's repertorial successes.

The company to pick up the challenge of a sequel, or "Poetaster II," was not the Children of the Chapel but the Children of Paul's. Perhaps during the very season that *Satiromastix* was playing at the Globe, or perhaps in the spring of 1602, the Children of Paul's acquired and staged Dekker's play. This production would have been their most ambitious to date by far. According to my doubling charts, *Antonio's Revenge* and *The Wisdom of Doctor Dodypoll*, which were in production in 1600–1, required twenty and twenty-one players respectively (see tables 5 and 6) In *Antonio's Revenge*, three players had parts of 250 lines or more, and two had one hundred lines or more; in *The Wisdom of Doctor Dodypoll*, four players had parts of 250 lines or more, and two had one hundred lines or more. *Satiromastix*, in comparison, required twenty-three players (see table 7), eight of whom had parts of 150 lines or more. Perhaps in production with *Satiromastix*, Dekker's new play – *Blurt, Master Constable* – might have used twenty-four players (see table 8), six of whom had over 150 lines and two of whom had over one hundred lines. Given that the Children of Paul's had fewer plays in production per season and fewer performances per week than the Chamberlain's Men, *Satiromastix* probably had a higher visibility among their offerings than at the Globe.[49]

Word of Tucca's challenge reached Cambridge (or Cambridge students, in London on holiday, learned of *Poetaster* and *Satiromastix* through performance or publication), and allusions to both plays appear in the published text of *The Second Part of the Returne from Parnassus*. The title page of the quarto in 1606 (S. R. 16 October 1605) advertises public performance by the students of St. John's College, Cambridge; J. B. Leishman and Alan Nelson date these performances *circa* 1601–3.[50] The relevant passage occurs in a scene between Dick Burbage and Will Kempe, in which Kempe quips that university students write bad plays. He then brags, "our fellow *Shakespeare* puts them all downe, I and *Ben Ionson* too. O that *Ben Ionson* is a pentilent fellow, he brought vp *Horace* giving the Poets a pill, but our fellow *Shakespeare* hath giuen him a purge that made him beray his credit."[51] Two students, Studioso and Philomusus, join Burbage and Kempe, who audition them by way of passages from *The Spanish Tragedy* and *Richard III*. Directly through the names of Jonson, Shakespeare, and players with the Chamberlain's Men, and indirectly through imitation of the impromptu performances in *Poetaster* and *Satiromastix*, the playwrights of the second *Returne from Parnassus* thus continue the game of serial satire, even if their connection of Shakespeare to the purge of *Satiromastix* is off the mark.[52]

Dekker and Jonson each added a postscript to the satirical exchange. Dekker's is an address, "To the World," which accompanied *Satiromastix* into print in 1602. In it Dekker appears to renew Tucca's challenge by goading Jonson into a sequel. Dekker exaggerates the competition by calling it a "*terrible* Poetomachia" (line 7). He claims victory in having "*answer'd* [Jonson] *at his owne weapon*" (lines 17–18) and imagines that in a trial he and the poetasters would be declared as having acted in self-defense. He pretends that he will laugh off insults (lines 41–42), yet he taunts Jonson as being characteristically base: "*Enuy feede thy Snakes so fat with poyson till they burst*" (lines 51–52). Jonson had a retort prepared, an Apological Dialogue, which was read once on the stage as an epilogue to *Poetaster* but not published until the 1616 folio. In the Apological Dialogue, the character of the author scornfully dismisses his accusers, "these vncleane birds, / That make their mouthes their clysters" (lines 219–20). He will rise above them through his superior talent in pursuit of the muse of tragedy; he will not pander for audiences but be vindicated if this next play "proue the pleasure but of one" (line 226). For all his hauteur, however, what Jonson actually did next was routine commercial work: he earned 40s. on 25

September 1601 from the Admiral's Men for revisions to *The Spanish Tragedy* and another 20os. on 22 June 1602 for more revisions and for the book of "Richard Crookback" (the story of which undoubtedly appropriated Shakespeare's *Richard III*, published for the third time in 1602). *Sejanus*, the tragedy that presumably was the play-in-expectation in the Apologetical Dialogue, was acquired in 1603 by the Chamberlain's/King's Men at the Globe, not by the Children of the Chapel at Blackfriars.

There was another possible witness besides Sir William Cavendish and his servant Hallam to the rivalry of *Poetaster* and *Satiromastix*. Edward Pudsey, a Derbyshire gentleman, kept a commonplace book in which he entered scraps of plays (along with extracts from other kinds of literature). Side by side in the commonplace book are quotations from *Poetaster* and *Satiromastix*. J. O. Halliwell-Phillipps and Richard Savage, who first studied the commonplace book, were primarily interested in Pudsey's jottings from plays by Shakespeare. In *Shakespearean Extracts from "Edward Pudsey's Booke"* (1888), influenced by the accuracy of Pudsey's quotations, Savage posited a friendship that enabled Pudsey to copy from Shakespeare's manuscripts.[53] Halliwell-Phillipps, on the other hand, found the jottings relatively inaccurate and posited that they were probably "copies of brief short-hand or other notes taken by Pudseye at the theatres."[54] Differences of opinion remain on Pudsey's sources,[55] but whether Pudsey came to know these plays by way of the playhouse or the bookshop, two observations about the play-scraps in his commonplace book appear unarguable: (1) he had no interest in those parts of *Poetaster* and *Satiromastix* that are typically associated with the War of the Theatres or Stage Quarrel, and (2) many of the plays of interest to him represent repertory offerings at four or five playhouses in London around 1600–1.

Pudsey quoted nothing from *Poetaster*, 4.3, the scene in which Tucca discusses theatrical matters with Histrio and Demetrius and in which the two pages perform scraps from plays by Kyd, Peele, and others. Pudsey took five citations from 5.3, in which Crispinus and Demetrius are arraigned and punished for their offenses; however, none indicates an interest in the issue central to Horace and to proponents of theatrical wars, namely, the scorn of Crispinus's vocabulary and the injunction not to harass Horace or pretend to be poets. Pudsey must have heard or read the trial scene, for he quoted "let yo[r] matte[t] run before yo[r] words" (f 42[v]), which is a piece of Virgil's advice to Crispinus ("But let your *matter* runne before your *words*," 5.3.551). Without its context, though, the advice is neutered to a maxim on wise speech. A few of the scraps in the commonplace book from *Poetaster* suggest that Pudsey intentionally avoided all the fleers about poets and poetry. For example, in the first entry, "The envyous have Basiliske eys & forked tonges steept in venom as their harts in gall" (f 41ᵛ), he could have provided Jonson's subject for basilisk eyes and forked tongues ("Are there no players here? No poet-apes," Induction 35), but he substituted "the envious" instead. Similarly, in his entry on ignorance, "The spawne of ignorance may beslime his name" (f 41ᵛ), he omitted the phrase "Our frie of writers" ("How ere that common spawne of ignorance, / Our frie of writers, may beslime his fame," Pro. 18–19). Pudsey read (or heard) the Apologetical Dialogue all the way to the end to lift the phrase, "Commest thy thought" (f 42); but he skipped both the complaint by the author that he had been provoked by poetasters for three years and his pledge to turn his back on his detractors by inventing a new form of tragedy.

Pudsey was equally uninterested in topical theatrical references in *Satiromastix*. He quoted nothing from 1.2.1–157, in which Horace and Asinius Bubo exult in the perfection of Horace's epithalamium for Sir Walter Terrill and Cælestine; he quoted nothing from 1.2.158–404, in which Crispinus and Demetrius complain to Horace that he has maligned them. Pudsey quoted Tucca a few times but skipped every theatrical allusion. Pudsey also skipped the jibes at Jonson's undistinguished background and career. He quoted nothing from the untrussing of the poet (5.2.159–342), although he used the phrase, which is the sub-title of the play, to head his own set of entries on *Satiromastix*. So it is not surprising that he quoted nothing from the epilogue and its call for another round of satirical pointing. He quoted nothing from "To the World," printed with the quarto in 1602, in which Dekker justified at length his quarrel with Jonson. However, Pudsey did quote extensively from the pair of poems on baldness by Horace and Crispinus.[56]

In the section of his commonplace book with scraps from *Poetaster* and *Satiromastix* (f 39ᵛ-SBT1ᵛ), Pudsey wrote down lines and phrases from eighteen additional plays.[57] All but one (*Othello*) had been published by 1602, and were thus available to him in print.[58] But they had also been recently on stage (again, with the exception of *Othello*). If Pudsey saw the plays in performance, he went to many playhouses, perhaps over several years. He could have seen *The Blind Beggar of Alexandria* during its maiden run at the Rose (12 February 1596–1 April 1597), or he could have seen it at the Fortune in the spring of 1601, for which revival Henslowe paid £9 3s. 4d. for apparel and divers things. If he saw *Every Man In his Humour* and *Much Ado About Nothing* in their maiden runs at the Globe, he probably saw them sometime in 1598–9. If he saw *Every Man Out of his Humour* in its maiden run at the Globe, he saw it sometime in 1599–1600.[59] At Paul's that same year he could have seen *Antonio and Mellida* and *Antonio's Revenge* as well as *Jack Drum's Entertainment*. In 1600, when Blackfriars opened, Pudsey could have seen *Cynthia's Revels* and *Love's Metamorphosis*. In 1600–1 he could have seen Worcester's Men perform *How a Man may Choose a Good Wife from a Bad* at the Boar's Head. In 1601 he could have seen *Poetaster* at Blackfriars, *Satiromastix* at the Globe or Paul's, and *Blurt, Master Constable* at Paul's. From this evidence Pudsey – if he did see these plays in performance – seems to have been exactly the kind of customer Dekker called for in the epilogue of *Satiromastix*: the kind who would go regularly to different playhouses and enjoy the wide range of fare.

In August 1608, just as the plague returned to London, the King's Men acquired the lease on Blackfriars playhouse. Andrew Gurr is the most recent historian of playing companies to repeat the venerable opinion that the acquisition enabled the company to play at the Globe in the summer and at Blackfriars in the winter.[60] Gurr is interested in the financial repercussions of the company's choice to play alternately at both playhouses. G. E. Bentley was interested in the repertorial choices; he argued that the King's Men staged their new plays from fashionable dramatists such as Francis Beaumont and John Fletcher at Blackfriars and relegated their hackwork and revivals to the Globe.[61] However, the playgoing habits of the three men identified here raise questions about class-based and taste-based repertory offerings. *Poetaster* and *Satiromastix*, supposedly representative of an upper-class taste for satirical comedy, are in fact as similar in their exploitation of popular theatrical materials as they are in the slinging of stone-hard jests.

The Cavendish records do not reveal the titles of plays seen by Sir William and his servant at Paul's, or Blackfriars, or elsewhere; but the commonplace book of Edward Pudsey does reveal the plays he knew. When Pudsey went to the playhouse or bought a play in quarto, he appears to have been looking for sententiae, witty similes, and cultural opinion on clothing, jewelry, baldness, music, women, and boorish behavior, not for the latest fashion in genre or the greatest dramatic poetry. Pudsey's omnivorous appetite for dramatic literature suggests that the strategy of company commerce in Tucca's epilogue was sound: the successful theatrical marketplace invited audiences diverse in class and taste to enjoy what they would of the variety available to them. If the King's Men had heeded Dekker's commercial advice when they took over the lease of Blackfriars, they would have acquired a few more players, divided the company into two playing units, and staged a mix of offerings in genre and subject matter at both Blackfriars and the Globe for as much of the year as officialdom permitted.

Conclusion: Hot Anger and company commerce

> deare Captaine thinke
> I writ out of hot bloud, which (now) being colde,
> I could be pleas'd (to please you) to quaffe downe,
> The poyson'd Inke, in which I dipt your name.
> Horace, in *Satiromastix*, 4.2.65–68

Among the lost documents that might illuminate the personality of Ben Jonson is "Hot Anger Soon Cold," a playscript for which the Admiral's Men paid £6 to Jonson, Henry Porter, and Henry Chettle on 18 August 1598. Nothing more is known of the play, but it is hardly surprising that Jonson was drawn to a story about quarreling. Ian Donaldson argues "that anger meant a great deal to Jonson, both morally and creatively."[1] In discussions of theatre history, however, Jonson's anger has not been viewed so positively, nor has it been assumed to have grown cold. Apologists such as William Gifford, reacting at the turn of the nineteenth century to a deification of Shakespeare at Jonson's expense, believed that they had to justify Jonson's temper, and they did so by accusing others, specifically John Marston and Thomas Dekker, of being the provocateurs. Over time, these poets' quarrels acquired commercial significance. *Poetaster* and *Satiromastix* were taken to be proof of verbal attacks in other plays, and rivalries were assigned to the plays' company owners to match the intensity of the satirical pointing. The discovery of an episode of hot anger between John Alleyn and James Burbage prompted C. W. Wallace and others to presume that subsequent business decisions by the Alleyns and Burbages were predicated on outbursts of verbal heat. As one scholar's presumption became another's fact, the quarrels among players and quarrels among dramatists were accepted as the personal equivalent of a cut-throat rivalry among the companies, or a War of the Theatres.

But a translation of hot anger into adversarial commerce is not the only way to interpret the evidence on business relations among the companies. Donaldson sees a sociability in Jonson's anger. Speaking of characters in *Bartholomew Fair*, he notes that "many of the play's characters come to the fair precisely in order to enjoy the exhilaration of a public quarrel."[2] Thomas Dekker captured the moral force of anger in the untrussing of the humorous poet in *Satiromastix*; he captured as well the Jonsonian exhilaration of quarreling in Tucca's call for the game of hurling insults to be continued. Of more significance here, Dekker recognized the commercial implications of the game: playgoers could be drawn to the playhouse again and again to enjoy serial quarrels. This sociable commerce, in which companies might participate merely by joining the current game or starting another, suggests that a paradigm of cooperative business such as the guild is a fruitful way of perceiving the relationship of the companies to one another.

The analogy of the guild calls attention to certain inclusive and cohesive features of the playhouse world that are neglected in narratives of commerce based on quarreling dramatists and warring theatres. The guild recognized a fraternity among its members. Similarly, members of playing companies were friends, neighbors, fellow parishioners, and former or future colleagues; they married players' widows, sisters, and daughters, and they chose players to be godparents to their children. There were of course personal as well as professional disputes among individuals. In the guild, personal quarrels were separated from business decisions: the Court of Assistants monitored personal and commercial behavior; and by means of fines and privileges withdrawn, it pressured its uncivil and fraudulent members to accommodate themselves to the larger enterprise of the guild. Similarly, the behavior of companies, not their individual members, affected business decisions. The need for men skilled in crafts and trades wherever people carried on the activities of daily life suggests that there was room in the theatrical marketplace across England for lords' companies who rarely traveled a day's distance beyond their patron's provincial manor house as well as for companies in royal livery who were most often at their playhouse in London.

After having spent the previous decades seeking patrons who could provide protection from charges of vagrancy as well as status through association with the Crown, playing companies at the start of the reign of King James found themselves being absorbed into the

Crown's own patronage system. This authorization afforded the companies security, but it also discouraged the formation of new companies and thus the expansion of the theatrical enterprise in quite the explosive manner of the 1570s and following. Nevertheless the commercial common cause made by the companies during the 1590s in particular continued to serve them well. Their recognition of marketable features of their own repertory and the repertory of their competitors – as well as their readiness to best each other's offerings in subject, genre, and style – provided a creative environment for playwrights who might duplicate or improve the latest hit on a rival stage.

The company under the patronage of Queen Anne in 1604 illustrates the commercial energy that the economic protocols developed in previous decades could provide. Queen Anne's Men had a tireless producer of popular scripts in Thomas Heywood; they had experienced players in Robert Lee, Robert Pallant, and John Duke, plus talented newcomers in Thomas Swinnerton and Richard Perkins; they had a succession of famous clowns in Will Kempe and Thomas Greene. They acquired a new playhouse, the Red Bull, in 1605 or thereabouts. In Christopher Beeston they had an ambitious entrepreneur in the mold of a James Burbage, and in 1617 Beeston added the Cockpit as a second playhouse to the company's use of the Red Bull.[3] The King's Men were similarly positioned in 1603 with royal patronage, successful commercial dramatists, experienced players, a large, open-air, relatively new playhouse, and a stock of golden oldies. In 1608 they acquired the lease on Blackfriars, a playing site the company had not previously used, although it had been bought in 1596 by James Burbage and was owned subsequently by Richard Burbage. It may be, as scholars have assumed, that the King's Men squandered the advantage of two playhouses by opening only the smaller one, Blackfriars, during the long seasons from Michaelmas through Trinity Term.[4] But if they followed the commercial logic of the previous decades of a growth industry based on cooperative competition, they would have kept both playhouses open for as much of the year as possible. By making such a choice, they would have shown theatrical entrepreneurs such as Beeston how a company might flourish if it were willing to become its own partner and rival in the business of playing.

Notes

1 Jacobean Commonplace Book, Folger Shakespeare Library, v.a.381, p. 20.
2 Wallace, *The First London Theatre*, pp. 101–2. I retain the spellings and contractions in Wallace's transcript (I have modernized the "s").
3 *Ibid.*, p. 100.
4 *Ibid.*, p. 101.
5 *Ibid.*, p. 123.
6 *Ibid.*, p. 127. There is disagreement among scholars about the date of the quarrel. Wallace chose November 1590 (*ibid.*, p. 19), and Herbert Berry agrees in *Shakespeare's Playhouses* (p. 9). Chambers chose May 1591 (*The Elizabethan Stage*, vol. II, p. 392), and Andrew Gurr agrees in *The Shakespearian Playing Companies* (p. 7).
7 Wallace, *The First London Theatre*, p. 19.
8 *Ibid.*, p. 21.
9 Sharpe, *The Real War of the Theaters*, p. 5.
10 Gurr, "Intertextuality at Windsor," pp. 189, 190.
11 Herford and Simpson, *Ben Jonson*, vol. I, pp. 131, 140. Jonson also related an event concerning *Sejanus* in terms of a dispute: he called the Earl of Northampton "his mortall enimie" for having him summoned before the Privy Council and "accused both of popperie and treason" (p. 141). All quotations from Jonson's works are taken from this edition unless otherwise noted.
12 Rowe, ed., vol. I, pp. xii–xiii.
13 *Ibid.*, p. xiii.
14 Gilchrist, *An Examination of the Charges . . . of Ben Jonson's Enmity*, p. 7. Gilchrist's attack was not the only scholarly quarrel at the time, as Peter Martin observes in *Edmond Malone, Shakespearean Scholar*. George Chalmers attacked Malone in *An Apology for the Believers in the Shakspeare-Papers* (1797) and *A Supplemental Apology* (1799), as much for Malone's superior tone as for the right of reasonable men to disagree on questionable points (see Chalmers's "Advertisement" to the *Apology*). Similar feuds

marked the proceedings of the New Shakspere Society, founded by F. J. Furnivall in 1874. It is tempting to conclude that eighteenth- and nineteenth-century scholars were influenced by the bickering among their ranks to exaggerate the bickering in the subject of their research, the Elizabethan playhouse world. Herbert Berry's account in *Shakespeare's Playhouses* of the contest in the Round Room of the Public Record Office between Charles W. Wallace and Mrs. C. C. Stopes for discoveries of documents carries the adversarial relationship among scholars into the twentieth century (pp. 20–22.)

15 Gifford, ed., *The Works of Ben Jonson*, vol. I, p. ccli.
16 *Ibid.*, p. liii, n. 9.
17 *Ibid.*, p. xlvii.
18 Langbaine, *An Account of the English Dramatick Poets*, p. 123.
19 Gifford, ed., *The Works of Ben Jonson*, vol. II, p. 453, note to *Poetaster*, 3.1, "Dost thou know that Pantalabus there?" Peter Whalley, editor of *The Works of Ben Jonson* in 1756, had repeated Langbaine's opinion that Jonson meant for Dekker to be satirized in the character of Crispinus.
20 Cartwright, *Shakspere and Jonson*, pp. 2–5.
21 Simpson, *The School of Shakspere*, vol. II, p. 3; I spell *Histrio-Mastix* as it appears on the title page of the quarto in 1610, but I follow recent scholarly preference by spelling *Satiromastix* without the hyphen of its 1602 title page.
22 Fleay, *A Chronicle History of the London Stage*, p. 119.
23 Small, *The Stage Quarrel*, p. 11.
24 Chambers, *The Elizabethan Stage*, vol. I, p. 381, note 1.
25 Harbage, *Shakespeare and the Rival Traditions*, p. 90.
26 Sharpe, *The Real War of the Theaters*, p. 1.
27 Ingram, *The Business of Playing*, pp. 84–5, especially p. 84. Rather than inhibit playing, however, "regulation by the lord mayor and the Court of Aldermen seems not to have had any adverse affect on the continuing expansion and prosperity of the enterprise" (p. 75).
28 Ingram, *The Business of Playing*, p. 90.
29 McMillin and MacLean, *The Queen's Men and their Plays*, pp. 24–36, especially p. 28. McMillin and MacLean also argue that the Queen's Men were formed to "help to consolidate the theatre industry by reducing the personnel and influence of the other companies" (p. 17). If this is true, there was a miscalculation on the part of the politicians, for the Queen's Men were to be overtaken in five short years by companies that were quicker and smarter in making entrepreneurial choices such as a permanent London playhouse and a diversified, electrifying repertory.
30 *Ibid.*, p. 44.
31 *Ibid.*, p. 33.
32 Gurr, *The Shakespearian Playing Companies*, p. 65. Gurr's perception of a shared agenda between Howard and Hunsdon in twin playing com-

panies is at odds with R. B. Sharpe's view that the Howard-Cecil-Admiral's Men alliance fought with that of the Hunsdon-Essex-Chamberlain's Men for ascendancy in the London market, 1594–1603.

33 Gurr, *The Shakespearian Playing Companies*, p. 67. "Duopoly" is Gurr's word; the image of the companies as embracing the whole of London from their locations at the Rose and Theatre is Gurr's in "Intertextuality at Windsor," p. 190.

34 Malone Society *Collections*, vol. i.i., item XXVI, p. 82.

35 *Ibid.*, item XXVI, p. 83.

36 Dutton, *Licensing, Censorship and Authorship in Early Modern England*, p. 26. "Cartel" is Dutton's word.

37 Ingram, *A London Life in the Brazen Age*, pp. 207, 208.

38 Malone Society *Collections*, i.i., item XXVII, p. 84. The quoted phrase is from the Privy Council's answer to the lord mayor and aldermen; it repeats the civic officials' complaint. A letter from the lord mayor in 1602 prompted the Privy Council on 31 March to authorize Oxford's Men and Worcester's Men, now combined under the latter's patron (*ibid.*, item XXVIII, pp. 85–6). Noting the disorderly behavior whereby the players "do chainge there place at there owne disposition," the Privy Council specified that the company was to play henceforth at the Boar's Head (p. 86).

39 Ingram, *The Business of Playing*, p. 75.

40 Mullaney, *The Place of the Stage*, pp. 8, 30.

41 Yachnin, *Stage-Wrights*, p. 3.

42 Bruster, *Drama and the Market in the Age of Shakespeare*, p. 8.

43 Malone Society *Collections*, vol. i.ii., item X, p. 174.

44 Cerasano, "Edward Alleyn: 1566–1626," p. 21.

45 Ingram thinks it possible that the Swan continued to offer plays in the wake of the "Isle of Dogs" affair (*A London Life in the Brazen Age*, p. 208). Richard Vennar advertised a performance of "England's Joy" to take place at the Swan in 1602; the condition of the playhouse apparently was not a factor in the aborted show. See Herbert Berry's article on Vennar in the new edition of the *Dictionary of National Biography*, forthcoming.

46 Somerset, " 'How chances it they travel?' " p. 50.

47 Beckerman, "Philip Henslowe," pp. 19–62. In an 1845 edition of Henslowe's business diary kept at the Rose playhouse, Collier criticized Henslowe as "an ignorant man, even for the time in which he lived, and for the station he occupied"; Collier didn't like Henslowe's handwriting, or his spelling, or his bookkeeping: "[Henslowe] wrote a bad hand, adopted any orthography that suited his notions of the sound of words . . ., and he kept his book . . . in the most disorderly, negligent, and confused, manner" (*The Diary of Philip Henslowe*, p. xv).

48 Ingram, *A London Life in the Brazen Age*, p. 238.

49 Blayney, "The Publication of Playbooks," pp. 384–7.

50 Quoted here from Chambers, *The Elizabethan Stage*, vol. IV, p. 332.
51 Dutton, *Mastering the Revels*, p. 128.
52 Quoted from E. K. Chambers, *The Elizabethan Stage*, vol. I, p. 322, n. 2. In the siege of Turnhout in January 1598, the Dutch and English overthrew the Spanish; see also James Shapiro, "*The Scot's Tragedy* and the Politics of Popular Drama."
53 Bate and Strauss, ed., *The Yale Edition of the Works of Samuel Johnson*, vol. IV, p. 288.
54 *Ibid.*, p. 287.
55 White, "The Value of Narrativity in the Representation of Reality," p. 4.
56 *Ibid.*, pp. 4, 5.
57 Simpson, ed., *The School of Shakspere*, vol. II, p. 5.
58 Fleay, *A Biographical Chronicle of the English Drama*, vol. II, p. 70; Small, *The Stage Quarrel*, p. 83.
59 Bednarz, "Marston's Subversion of Shakespeare and Jonson," p. 104.
60 Supposedly Anthony Munday was considered a laughing stock and was mocked by Jonson in the character of Antonio Balladino in *The Case is Altered* and by Marston in the character of Post-hast in *Histrio-Mastix*. Recently, however, David Bergeron has challenged the targeting of Munday in "Thomas Middleton and Anthony Munday: Artistic Rivalry?"; he argues that the targeting began with scholars' interpretations of another supposed rivalry, that between Thomas Middleton and Munday, and gravitated to an assumption that Jonson and Marston similarly ridiculed Munday.
61 Cook, *The Privileged Playgoers of Shakespeare's London*, p. 129.
62 Cain, ed., *Poetaster*, p. 40.
63 White, "The Value of Narrativity in the Representation of Reality," p. 11.
64 The Admiral's Men's *Sir John Oldcastle* (in two parts) was paid for on 16 October 1599 (Foakes and Rickert, eds., *Henslowe's Diary*, vol. II, p. 125). The Chamberlain's Men's "Oldcastle" was performed for the Lord Chamberlain on 6 March 1600 (Collins, ed., *Letters and Memorials of State*, vol. II, p. 175; letter of 8 March 1599 [1600] from Rowland Whyte to Sir Robert Sidney).
65 Bate and Strauss, eds., *The Yale Edition of the Works of Samuel Johnson*, vol. IV, p. 288, *The Rambler* No. 122.

2 PLAYERS AND COMPANY COMMERCE

1 Morley, ed., *Plays and Poems by Ben Jonson*, p. 7.
2 Wallace, *The First London Theatre*, pp. 19–21.
3 In *Dramatic Documents from the Elizabethan Playhouses*, Greg looked at the name of Richard Burbage in the Plot of "2 Seven Deadly Sins," and he decided that the play could be dated from a time when Burbage

and Alleyn might have played together (the titles of lost plays named in this chapter are indicated by quotation marks; titles of surviving plays are indicated by italics). Because Greg believed in the family feud, that time had to have been before "the quarrel of 1590–1" (vol. I, pp. 17–18 and 111–13, especially p. 111). He also dated the Plot of "The Dead Man's Fortune" according to his assumptions about the feud (vol. I, pp. 44–50). For a different interpretation, see McMillin, "The Plots of *The Dead Man's Fortune* and *2 Seven Deadly Sins*" and "Building Stories."

4 Gurr, *The Shakespearian Playing Companies*, p. 244. Gurr inadvertently illustrates the confusion in identities that has contributed to the linkage of personal quarrels and company commerce. Gurr says: "Richard . . . separated from Strange's when Alleyn quarrelled with his father and helped to set up the new Pembroke's as a company . . . when Alleyn and Strange's moved to the Rose" (p. 74). It is clear that Gurr is thinking of Edward Alleyn, not John, because he says next that Burbage was "a year or so younger than Alleyn," and he provides a footnote with Edward Alleyn's date of birth in 1566 and Richard's in 1567 (p. 74, n. 40). But of course it was John who "quarrelled" with Richard's father.

5 Nungezer's *Dictionary of Actors* is my source for players' biographies unless otherwise noted. For more recent information, see Berry, *The Boar's Head Playhouse*; Ingram, *The Business of Playing* and "Abstract and Brief Chronicles" (a web site in development); Eccles, the series entitled "Elizabethan Actors"; Cerasano, "Anthony Jeffes, Player and Brewer," "Edward Alleyn's Early Years," and "New Renaissance Players' Wills"; Honigmann and Brock, *Playhouse Wills*; and David Kathman, "A Biographical Index to the Elizabethan Theatre" (web site).

6 Ingram, *A London Life in the Brazen Age*, pp. 11–28.

7 Berry, "The First Public Playhouses"; see also Ingram, *The Business of Playing*, pp. 182–218.

8 Berry, *The Boar's Head Playhouse*, p. 26.

9 Ingram, "Inside *and* Outside in Tudor London." Ingram points out that guild membership conveyed status, even if – as in the case of most of these men – one left the trade to do something else such as playing. One player, Anthony Jeffes, left playing to join the Brewers' guild (Cerasano, "Anthony Jeffes").

10 Gurr, *The Shakespearian Playing Companies*, pp. 65–71, especially pp. 70, 71.

11 McLuskie and Dunsworth, "Patronage and the Economics of Theater," p. 432.

12 Here, however, I use the list provided by Greg in *Dramatic Documents from the Elizabethan Playhouses*, vol. I, pp. 43–50.

13 For a transcript of the license, see Chambers, *The Elizabethan Stage*, vol. II, p. 123.

14 I use the list compiled by McMillin in "Casting for Pembroke's Men," p. 157.

15 McMillin, "Building Stories," p. 54.

16 McMillin, "Casting for Pembroke's Men," p. 158.

17 *Playhouse Wills*, edited by Honigmann and Brock, is the source here of all information and citations from wills.

18 Berry, "The Player's Apprentice," p. 77. According to Berry, "the normal practices of the commercial world" probably governed the apprenticeships of players (p. 74).

19 Honigmann and Brock explain why Cooke's apprenticeship was probably in playing rather than grocering (*Playhouse Wills*, p. 3).

20 Smith, *Shakespeare's Blackfriars Playhouse*, Item 46, pp. 553–59, especially p. 557.

21 Greg, ed., *Henslowe Papers*, pp. 153–4. Some or all of these boys might have been servants, not apprentices.

22 All citations from Henslowe's diary are taken from the edition by Foakes and Rickert unless otherwise noted; I designate these in the text by the abbreviation, *HD*.

23 Berry, *The Boar's Head Playhouse*, p. 195.

24 Until S. P. Cerasano published the will of William Bird (alias Borne) in "New Renaissance Players' Wills," theatre historians could imagine that Augustine's sister Margery was the player's wife. However, Bird's will, dated 17 January 1623, names Marie Bird as wife and executrix; further, the bequests to sons William (christened in St. Saviour's, Southwark, 18 May 1600), Theophilus (christened in St. Leonard Shoreditch, 7 Dec. 1608), and Thomas (christening date unknown) indicate that the man named Borne who married Phillips's sister Margery and the player, William Borne (Bird) were different people. Theophilus Bird married Christopher Beeston's daughter, Anne.

25 Guildhall Library, MS 17,607; 22 September 1604.

26 These articles, " 'Neere the Playe Howse' " and " 'The Globe Playhouse and its Neighbors in 1600," address issues such as demography, urban growth, civic order, and the attractiveness of various residential properties. To the latter essay, Ingram appends a diagram showing the families resident in Brend's Rents, 1598–1603.

27 Ingram, *A London Life in the Brazen Age*, pp. 118–19, p. 110.

28 Denkinger, p. 91. Citations from the registers of St. Botolph Aldgate are from Denkinger (duplicated in Nungezer) unless otherwise documented. In " 'Borrowed Robes,' Costume Prices, and the Drawing of *Titus Andronicus*," S. P. Cerasano calls attention to a second business of Philip Henslowe – pawn-broking – and its trade in second-hand clothing; she makes clear that new clothing was beyond the budget of common people. Cerasano's argument implies that the sale of previously owned clothing, far from being the activity of indigents only, is comparable in Elizabethan society to the sale of previously owned cars in our own.

29 For details of Tunstall's presence in the parish books of St. Botolph Aldgate, see Ingram, *The Business of Playing*, pp. 26-7.

30 Guildhall Library, MS 9234/5.

31 Ingram, *The Business of Playing*, p. 29.

32 Guildhall Library, MS 9234/5; 16 November 1595.

33 Guildhall Library, MS 9234/5; 30 April 1595.

34 Guildhall Library, MS 9234/5; 25 Jan 1598/99. Christenings of "Allstide Darbie" (1 May 1602) and "Margaret Darleye" (1 Dec. 1604) may also be for Darloe children (Guildhall Library, MS 9220).

35 Greg, *Dramatic Documents from the Elizabethan Playhouses*, vol. 1, pp. 44-50.

36 Mary Edmond, who discovered and published the will, identifies the patronage of Jewell's company with the Pembroke family ("Pembroke's Men"). Scott McMillin identifies several players in the will with the Queen's Men ("Simon Jewell and the Queen's Men").

37 Guildhall Library, MS 7499/1.

38 Downton's presence with Strange's Men in 1594 is established in a letter by John Pyk, a boy player (*HD* 283).

39 Cerasano, "Anthony Jeffes," p. 222.

40 Players with no known theatrical business in St. Giles Cripplegate turn up in the parish register in the following entries: 10 February 1586/7, christening of "Comedia baseborne Daughter of Alice Bowker and as she saithe the fathers name is William Iohnson one of the Queens plaiers"; 3 March 1593, Comedia's burial (Guildhall Library, MS 6418); 24 September 1606, christening of "John, son of Wyllm Sly (player) baseborn of the body of Margaret Chambers"; 4 October 1606, John's burial. Information from the St. Giles register is taken from G. E. Bentley, "Records of Players in the Parish of St. Giles, Cripplegate" unless otherwise documented.

41 Wallace, *The First London Theatre*, p. 149.

42 *Ibid.*, p. 149. Ingram explores possible meanings of "Esore" in *The Business of Playing*, pp. 230-32.

43 Rutter, ed., *Documents of the Rose Playhouse*, p. 25.

44 The letter is transcribed in Greg, ed., *Henslowe Papers*, p. 49 (Article 27).

45 Cerasano, "Edward Alleyn:1566-1626," p. 19.

46 Ingram, *A London Life in the Brazen Age*, p. 106.

47 *Ibid.*, p. 285.

48 *Ibid.*, p. 238.

49 The two companies on 1 January were Derby's Men and the Children of Paul's; the four on 6 January were the Chamberlain's Men, the Admiral's Men, the Children of the Chapel, and Derby's Men.

50 Malone Society *Collections*, vol. II.3, "The Players at Ipswich," p. 277; Johnston and Rogerson, ed., *York*, vol. I, p. 455; Anderson, ed., *Newcastle*, p. 90 (the entry says that the players were "all in one companye");

Somerset, ed., *Shropshire*, vol. I, p. 277; and Stokes, *Somerset including Bath*, vol. I, p. 17.

51 See McMillin, "Sussex's Men in 1594," p. 222.

52 Bennett, "The Word 'Goths' in 'A Knack to Know a Knave,'" p. 462. McMillin, "Sussex's Men in 1594," subscribes to the theory of serial, not joint, company ownership for *Titus Andronicus* (p. 216).

53 See Berry, *The Boar's Head Playhouse*, on the "use and . . . control" of the Boar's Head, pp. 29–36, 124, and 51.

54 Equally peculiar is that Browne, after he leased the Boar's Head to Worcester's Men, took his own Derby's Men on tour. New narratives of touring made possible in large part by data published in cooperation with REED give reasons other than financial exigency for a company's choosing to tour.

55 Fleay, *A Chronicle History of the London Stage*, p. 140.

56 Greg, ed., *Henslowe's Diary*, vol. II, p. 85.

57 Rutter, ed., *Documents of the Rose Playhouse*, p. 82.

58 Gurr, *The Shakespearian Playing Companies*, p. 66. Gurr does not choose between the companies' giving "joint or alternate performances" at the Newington playhouse (p. 75).

59 Hotson, "The Adventure of the Single Rapier," p. 28.

60 Archer, *The Pursuit of Stability*, p. 141.

61 Marsh, *Records of the Worshipful Company of Carpenters*, vol. III, pp. 181, 90, 53, 68, 67, 100, and 162.

62 Guildhall Library, MS. 11,588/1; 23 October, and 22 December, 1581.

63 Guildhall Library, MS. 11,588/1; 1 March 1580/1.

64 Guildhall Library, MS 7090/3.

65 *Ibid.*

66 Archer, *The Pursuit of Stability*, p. 143.

67 Chambers, *The Elizabethan Stage*, vol. IV, p. 323. See also Ingram, *A London Life in the Brazen Age*, pp. 178–86.

68 Wallace provided a transcription of the suit in "The Swan Theatre and the Earl of Pembroke's Servants." For a discussion of the suit, see Ingram, *A London Life in the Brazen Age*, pp. 187–91.

69 Wallace, "The Swan Theatre and the Earl of Pembroke's Servants," pp. 353, 352.

70 On 10 December Shaa purchased apparel – possibly from Langley – for "Alice Pierce," a playbook apparently brought over from the repertory at the Swan. To the list of plays brought in by Pembroke's Men, Greg included "Hardicanute," "Friar Spendleton," "Bourbon," "Branholt," "Stark Flattery," and "Black Joan" (*Henslowe's Diary*, vol. II, p. 90).

71 The company apparently meant to revive "Hercules" right away, for Downton was authorized to buy a robe for the production on the very day Slater was paid for the text.

72 Ingram, "What kind of future for the theatrical past," p. 221.

73 Archer, *The Pursuit of Stability*, pp. 146–7.

3 PLAYWRIGHTS, REPERTORIES, AND THE BOOK TRADE

1 The epigraphs are from Henslowe's diary, Foakes and Rickert edition, p. 288 (cited in the text as *HD*), and Collier, ed., *King Edward the Third*, p. i.

2 Peter Thomson uses the 1635 contract of Richard Brome to suggest the "smaller jobs" of an in-house dramatist (*Shakespeare's Professional Career*, p. 117).

3 Fleay, *A Chronicle History of the London Stage*, p. 118; Sharpe, *The Real War of the Theaters*, p. 10.

4 In *Shakespeare at the Globe, 1599–1609*, Beckerman called the idea that the company might have competed with a small, primarily Shakespearean repertory the product of "an idolatrous love of Shakespeare" (p. 14).

5 The titles of lost plays are indicated by quotation marks; the titles of surviving plays are indicated by italics.

6 Bentley, *The Profession of Dramatist in Shakespeare's Time*, p. 62. Scholars no longer associate that employment with a debasing servitude. For a history of opinion on Henslowe's treatment of dramatists, see Beckerman, "Philip Henslowe," and Neil Carson, "Literary Management in the Lord Admiral's Company, 1597–1603."

7 Carson, *A Companion to Henslowe's Diary*, p. 59.

8 In a few cases, the multi-part plays appear to have been package deals. The two plays on Robin Hood, for example, were paid for within three weeks of each other. The payment in full for *1 Sir John Oldcastle* included a payment in earnest on the second part, which was completed in two months. In contrast, there is a gap of eight months between payments for part one of *The Blind Beggar of Bednal Green* and its second part.

9 Chettle might have had these partners all along, even though only his name occurs in the entries of payments.

10 Bentley, *The Profession of Dramatist in Shakespeare's Time*, p. 64.

11 Cyrus Hoy thought it possible that the Chamberlain's Men (or the Children of Paul's) commissioned Dekker to write *Satiromastix* (*Introductions, Notes, and Commentaries . . . Thomas Dekker . . .* , vol. 1, p. 180); yet nothing but a fondness among scholars for a war of the theatres suggests a scenario in which a company wanted to punish a playwright (here, Jonson) and hired another (here, Dekker) to do it by representing the offender satirically in a play.

12 Quoted from Bentley, *The Profession of Dramatist in Shakespeare's Time*, p. 74.

13 See Dutton, "*Hamlet, An Apology for Actors*, and the Sign of the Globe," p. 39, and Dutton, *Licensing, Censorship and Authorship in Early Modern England*, pp. 28–40.

14 Robbins, ed., *Thomas Dekker's A Knights Conjuring*, p. 157.

15 Harbage, *Shakespeare and the Rival Traditions*, p. 71.

16 McMillin and MacLean, *The Queen's Men and their Plays*, p. xii.

17 Greg has an invaluable chapter (Chapter III) on the plays in vol. II of his *Henslowe's Diary*. I rely heavily on his analyses except when he identifies plays on similar subjects as versions of the same text (see the note on "Godfrey of Boulogne," below).

18 I consider the revivals to be *The Jew of Malta*, "Fortunatus," and the two parts of "Tamar Cham" (even though they are marked "ne").

19 The principle of a spin-off explains the promotion of Falstaff into the central character of *The Merry Wives of Windsor* and Tom Strowd into the title character of "3 Tom Strowd" (from *The Blind Beggar of Bednal Green*) as well as the existence of plays featuring minor characters from larger story complexes such as "Buckingham" (Sussex's Men, 1593–4), *Thomas of Woodstock* (company and date unknown), "Mortimer" (Admiral's Men, 1602–3), and "Shore's Wife" (Worcester's Men, 1602–3).

20 Greg, ed., *Henslowe's Diary*, vol. II, p. 166. In *A Bibliography of the English Printed Drama*, Greg included the 19 June 1594 entry in the Stationers' Register with the entry of *Four Prentices of London* (no. 333); I use Greg's *Bibliography* throughout this book for title-page information.

21 Greg, ed., *Henslowe's Diary*, vol. II, p. 166 (headnote to the entry on "Godfrey of Boulogne"). Greg's discomfort with the entry of a "Godfrey" play in the Stationers' Register before the play appears in Henslowe's playlists (and thus, presumably, before its maiden performance) appears to be a result of his decision to collapse both parts of "Godfrey of Boulogne" into a single play, new on 19 July 1594. Yet the entry in the Stationers' Register may be the entry of part one of the play, which is not marked "ne" when it first appears in Henslowe's playlists on 26 July 1594. The absence of the "ne" suggests that the first part was already old, when it was acquired by the Admiral's Men, by which time its previous owners had already sold a copy to stationers (in June).

22 The Admiral's Men followed a similar strategy at the resumption of playing after Easter, 1596, relying for more than two weeks on popular old plays.

23 On 17 and 19 December, as well as on 30 December 1594 and 1 January 1595, the two *Tamburlaines* were scheduled without an intervening play; on 27 and 29 January 1595, "A Seat at Maw" was scheduled between them.

24 The "Hercules" plays appeared as singletons on 25 October 1595 (part one) and 2 November (part two).

25 In the diary, performances of each part of "Tamar Cham" are dated 8 July 1596, as if the parts formed a double bill. At least one of the entries is surely a mistake, but a serendipitous one, in that it reinforces the idea that serials played together had excellent commercial appeal.

26 See Knutson, "Marlowe Reruns," forthcoming in *Marlowe's Empery*, for

further discussion of the marketing strategies by which the Admiral's Men exploited the popularity of their holdings by Marlowe.

27 Ingram, *A London Life in the Brazen Age*, pp. 108–20.

28 McMillin and MacLean, *The Queen's Men and their Plays*, p. 51.

29 If the Admiral's Men used here a standard Elizabethan economy of action (which would give Abigail two bags of gold and jewels to throw down to her father), Shakespeare might be adding a visual joke to the linguistic one when the young Venetians mock Shylock for bewailing the loss of his stones.

30 For a discussion of "The Tartarian Cripple" as a Chamberlain's play, see Knutson, "Evidence for the Assignment of Plays to the Repertory of Shakespeare's Company," pp. 78–89.

31 Dutton, "The Revels Office and the Boy Companies 1600–1613," forthcoming in *English Literary Renaissance*.

32 Collier expressed these opinions in *King Edward the Third*, pp. i–ii.

33 *Ibid.*, p. i.

34 See Blayney, "The Publication of Playbooks," pp. 383–4, for a summary of myths that persist about the relations between companies and stationers.

35 Blayney discounts "all masques, pageants and entertainments, closet and academic plays, Latin plays and translations published as literary texts" ("The Publication of Playbooks," p. 384). "Peak periods" is Blayney's phrase (p. 385).

36 For clarity, I list here Blayney's twenty-seven, with dates of initial publication as applicable: (1) *Orlando Furioso*, Q1594; (2) *A Knack to Know a Knave*, Q1594; (3) *Cornelia*, Q1594; (4) *Titus Andronicus*, Q1594; (5) *A Looking Glass for London and England*, Q1594; (6) *The First Part of the Contention Between the Houses of York and Lancaster*, Q1594; (7) *The Taming of A Shrew*, Q1594; (8) *The Pedlar's Prophecy*, Q1595; (9) *The Famous Victories of Henry V*, Q1598; (10) *James IV*, Q1598; (11) *Friar Bacon and Friar Bungay*, Q1594; (12) *King Leir*, Q1605; (13) "John of Gaunt"; (14) *David and Bethsabe*, Q1599; (15) "Robin Hood and Little John"; (16) *The Jew of Malta*, Q1633; (17) *The Wounds of Civil War*, Q1594; (18) *The Cobler's Prophecy*, Q1594; (19) *Mother Bombie*, Q1594; (20) "Godfrey of Boulogne"; (21) "Heliogabalus"; (22) *The True Tragedy of Richard III*, Q1594; (23) *Locrine*, Q1595; (24) *George a Greene, or the Pinner of Wakefield*, Q1599; (25) *Old Wives Tale*, Q1595; (26) "Ninus & Semiramis"; (27) "Valentine and Orson."

37 For clarity, I provide those titles here, with publication dates and company owners: (1) *The Battle of Alcazar*, Admiral's Men, Q1594; (2) *Dido, Queen of Carthage*, Children of the Chapel, Q1594; (3) *Edward II*, Pembroke's Men, Q1594; (4) *Selimus*, Queen's Men, Q1594; (5) *The Wars of Cyrus*, Children of the Chapel, Q1594; (6) *The Massacre at Paris*, Admiral's Men, quarto undated; (7) *The True Tragedy of Richard Duke of York*, Pembroke's Men, Q1595.

38 I base these numbers on items that are documented in the *Short-Title Catalogue.*

39 Following Greg's lead, Pollard imagined a scenario by which a "treacherous 'hired man' lighted on a printer such as John Danter when the latter was in his worst straits," and sold him a pirated copy of *The Merry Wives of Windsor.* Pollard continued: "Danter could hawk the edition among the booksellers without employing a publisher, and as soon as the copies were off his hands his known poverty would make it useless to take action against him. . . . Danter saved the sixpence registration fee, sacrificed the hope of future profit, and was content with his gains on a single edition. Had he flown at the higher game, he might have found himself cross-examined as to the provenance of his copy, and finally have been fobbed off with a conditional entry" (*Shakespeare's Fight with the Pirates and the Problems of the Transmission of his Text,* p. 40).

40 Blayney, "The Publication of Playbooks," p. 386. McMillin and MacLean point out the likelihood that playbooks became available as groups of players reorganized into different companies (pp. 84–5).

41 Pollard, *Shakespeare's Fight with the Pirates and the Problems of the Transmission of his Text,* p. 42.

42 Blayney, "The Publication of Playbooks," p. 386. Blayney suggests that stationers paid 40s. to acquire a playbook (p. 396).

43 Gurr, *The Shakespearian Playing Companies,* p. 272.

44 See McMillin and MacLean, *The Queen's Men and their Plays,* pp. 156–60, for a discussion of the competition for readers and playgoers by the Queen's Men, 1590–4.

45 Pinciss, "Thomas Creede and the Repertory of the Queen's Men."

46 In *The Shakespearian Playing Companies,* Gurr appropriates the word "brocke" to describe Pembroke's Men in 1593 (p. 272); but as Gurr himself suggests, "broke" could mean "bankrupt" (p. 272) or "divided [into] fragments of former groupings" (p. 23).

47 The inference that White obtained all five from Queen's players is to me irresistible. Two of the remaining four – *David and Bethsabe* (Q1599) and *King Leir* (1605) – were printed without a company advertisement on the title page. Another two – "John of Gaunt" and "Robin Hood and Little John" – were not printed, as far as is known.

48 The publication of *The Massacre at Paris* in 1594, with a title-page advertisement that includes the name of Christopher Marlowe, raises the possibility that his death prompted some publications. *Edward II* also came out in 1594, as did *Dido, Queen of Carthage,* both advertising Marlowe. Yet the stationers who owned *Tamburlaine* and *The Jew of Malta* did not bring out editions at this time, as far as is known.

49 Jones obviously knew the commercial value of theatrical information; on the title page of the 1594 quarto, he advertised the gambit of "*KEMPS applauded* Merrimentes."

50 For clarity, I list here Blayney's twenty-seven, with dates of initial publication as applicable: (1) "Cloth Breeches and Velvet Hose"; (2) *A Larum for London*, Q1602; (3) *The Maid's Metamorphosis*, Q1600; (4) "Give a Man Luck and Throw Him into the Sea"; (5) *As You Like It*, F1623; (6) *Henry V*, Q1600; (7) *Every Man In his Humour*, Q1601; (8) *Much Ado About Nothing*, Q1600; (9) *1 John Oldcastle*, Q1600; (10) "*2* John Oldcastle"; (11) *Captain Thomas Stukeley*, Q1605; (12) "The Tartarian Cripple"; (13) *2 Henry 4*, Q1600; (14) *Jack Drum's Entertainment*, Q1601; (15) *The Wisdom of Doctor Dodypoll*, Q1600; (16) *A Midsummer Night's Dream*, Q1600; (17) *The Weakest Goeth to the Wall*, Q1600; (18) *Doctor Faustus*, Q1604; (19) *Summer's Last Will and Testament*, Q1600; (20) *Love's Metamorphosis*, Q1601; (21) *The Downfall of Robert, Earl of Huntingdon*, Q1601; (22) *The Death of Robert, Earl of Huntingdon*, Q1601; (23) *Cynthia's Revels*, Q1601; (24) "George Scanderbeg"; (25) *A Woman Will Have Her Will* [*Englishmen for my Money*], Q1616; (26) *Antonio and Mellida*, Q1602; (27) *Antonio's Revenge*, Q1602.

51 Among those published in 1594–5, five carry the authors' names or initials; one of those carries the company's name as well (*Friar Bacon and Friar Bungay*).

52 Andrew Gurr points to the sale of Shakespeare's plays in 1597–8 as a sign that the Chamberlain's Men were financially strapped during the time that they were shut out of the Theatre but had not yet built the Globe. However, he does not connect these sales with those in 1600–1, for he says that the strategy of selling repertory pieces in 1597–8 was "a cash-raising device they [the Chamberlain's Men] had never used before and never used again" ("Money or Audiences," p. 7). A title-page advertisement of the Globe did not appear until the 1608 quarto of *Richard II*; one of the Fortune did not appear until the 1611 printing of *The Roaring Girl*.

53 This Privy Council order authorized two playhouses (the Fortune and Globe), two companies (the Admiral's Men and Chamberlain's Men), and two performances only per week (Malone Society *Collections*, I.i., item no. xxvi, pp. 81–83).

54 As Blayney makes clear, the clerk of the Stationers' Company expected more entries to come from the Chamberlain's Men, and he used the flyleaf of Register C to start a list ("The Publication of Playbooks," p. 387).

55 *Look About You* and *The Shoemakers' Holiday* were not registered at Stationers' Hall; thus their publication in quarto in 1600 is the only clue to the timing of their sales. However, *The Shoemakers' Holiday* could not have been sold much before 1 January because its title page advertises a performance before the queen on New Year's night (presumably 1600). It is possible that *Two Lamentable Tragedies*, Q1601, also belonged to the Admiral's Men. One of the stories dramatizes the murder of Thomas Merry, and they had such a play in November 1599.

56 Dutton, *Licensing, Censorship, and Authorship*, pp. 28–40.

4 "HISTRIO-MASTIX" AND COMPANY COMMERCE

1 Chambers and Frost, ed., *The Works of John Dryden*, "Discourse concerning the Original and Progress of Satire," vol. IV, p. 10.
2 Simpson, ed., *The School of Shakspere*, vol. II, pp. 3–15.
3 For example, W. David Kay describes the beginning of the Jonson-Marston argument "as a quarrel among two private theatre playwrights as to which one most fitly addressed the ethos of the private theatre audience" (*Ben Jonson*, p. 56).
4 Simpson, ed., *The School of Shakspere*, vol. II, p. 4.
5 Small, *The Stage Quarrel*, p. 72; Kernan, "John Marston's Play *Histrio-mastix*," p. 134.
6 Lake looked for occurrences of sets of word variants, and he did find several correspondences; however, because there were also non-Marstonian preferences in allegedly Marstonian passages, Lake had to hypothesize a non-Marstonian collaborator in addition to the original author ("*Histriomastix*: Linguistic Evidence for Authorship").
7 I treat the issue of authorship on the basis of style, vocabulary, and topical references more fully in "*Histrio-Mastix*: Not by John Marston."
8 One of many problems in ascribing *Histrio-Mastix* has been that Marston was busy with other projects in 1599, especially after July: he worked for Henslowe at the Rose in September, and he started writing for Paul's as soon as an opportunity arose. Thus, if any work in Marston's canon is contemporaneous with the putative date when *Histrio-Mastix* was written or revised, it is *The Scourge of Villanie*, 1598–9.
9 Farmer, ed. *Histrio-Mastix*; all quotations are taken from this edition.
10 Davenport, ed., *The Poems of John Marston*; I use here the 1599 text and its numbering of poems.
11 Leishman, ed., *The Three Parnassus Plays*, 1.2.267–8; see also 5.4.2191–5.
12 There is influence here: Herford was the editor of the Mermaid Series to which Nicholson's 1894 edition belongs, and he wrote the introduction to Nicholson's edition.
13 Schoenbaum, *Internal Evidence and Elizabethan Dramatic Authorship*, p. 189. M. St. Clare Byrne's observations occur in "Bibliographic Clues in Collaborate Plays," *The Library*, 4th Ser., XIII (1932), 21–48.
14 Gifford, ed., *The Works of Ben Jonson*, vol. II, note to Clove's speech, p. 99; Kay, *Ben Jonson*, p. 55.
15 Proponents of Marston's authorship of *Histrio-Mastix* have cited the treatment of the playing company, Oliver Owlet's Men, as satire of contemporary companies, but Owlet's Men are a dystopian caricature of a bad company: old-fashioned in repertory, dramaturgy, and playing venues.
16 William Shakespeare likewise does not refer to tobacco (but I do not therefore make a case for his authorship of *Histrio-Mastix*). For ref-

erences to tobacco in Elizabethan literature, see Dickson, *Panacea or Precious Bane*, and Knapp, "Elizabethan Tobacco."

17 Hunter, ed., *Antonio and Mellida*.

18 Wood, ed., *The Plays of John Marston*, vol. ii, pp. 246, 270.

19 Finkelpearl, "John Marston's *Histrio-Mastix* as an Inns of Court Play," p. 226.

20 F. G. Fleay gives *Histrio-Mastix* to Derby's Men at the Curtain (*A Biographical Chronicle of the English Drama*, vol. ii, p. 70.)

21 Finkelpearl, "John Marston's *Histrio-Mastix* as an Inns of Court Play," p. 228.

22 I do not include *What You Will* here because it was published in 1607 with a title-page advertisement of Marston's authorship but without the specification of a playhouse.

23 See Bevington, *From Mankind to Marlowe*; Ringler, "The Number of Actors in Shakespeare's Early Plays"; King, *Casting Shakespeare's Plays*; Bradley, *From Text to Performance*; McMillin, "Casting for Pembroke's Men," *The Elizabethan Theatre and The Book of Sir Thomas More*, and "Casting the *Hamlet* Quartos"; and McMillin and MacLean, *The Queen's Men and their Plays*. "Immediate juxtaposition" is McMillin and Mac-Lean's term, p. 99. Obviously, I ignore the rule by which boys are not cast in men's roles.

24 Hillebrand, *The Child Actors*, pp. 110–12; the lists name also six vicars choral. Finkelpearl, who counts 120 parts in *Histrio-Mastix*, asserts that staging might have been handled by the Children of Paul's "with a prodigious amount of 'doubling,'" but that the membership of Middle Temple was sufficient to handle the parts with no doubling at all ("John Marston's *Histrio-Mastix* as an Inns of Court Play," p. 228).

25 Gair provides partial lists in nine years, 1582–1607, none with more than eleven names (*The Children of Paul's*, p. 184).

26 Lennam, "The Children of Paul's, 1551–1582," p. 26.

27 Gair, *The Children of Paul's*, p. 120. Part of Gair's argument (and mine) is that Marston knew the size of the company available to him at Paul's. In *What You Will*, which is usually assigned to Paul's in 1600–1, he wrote one permissive stage direction, which could be interpreted as his not knowing the cast available: "Enter as many Pages with Torches as you can . . ." (Wood, ed., *The Plays of John Marston*, vol. ii, p. 290).

28 Scott McMillin points out that scenes with the largest number of speaking parts are keys to a company's doubling capabilities ("Casting for Pembroke's Men," pp. 150 and 153).

29 Bullen, ed. *A Collection of Old English Plays*, vol. i. I take the specific call for three charities in the third act of *The Maid's Metamorphosis* as a sign that clusters of singers (e.g., shepherds, woodmen, and fairies) are also in threes. In the fifth act, a stage direction calls for "three or foure Muses" (p. 158), one of whom has a substantial speaking part (36 lines); therefore I double that part (Muse 1) with another speaking part

(Iris) and cast the three extras as the additional muses. With more rigorous doubling, *The Maid's Metamorphosis* could be played with fifteen boys.

30 In *The Children of Paul's*, Gair suggests that the parts of Mellida and Andrugio's Ghost were doubled (p. 131), and he points out that Alberto says in the Induction he will play Andrugio (p. 119).

31 According to King, Shakespeare had found that many for *Troilus and Cressida*, an offering contemporary with *Satiromastix* (*Casting Shakespeare's Plays*, pp. 215–16).

32 I assume that the "gentlewomen" who open the play with Fescennine joking are two of the threesome of Dicache, Philocalia, and Petula, the women who keep Blunt, Crispinus, and Demetrius company through much of the play. I interpret the stage direction at 1.1.138 ("*. . . and others with Ladies, lights before them*") to describe two unnamed couples, with the ladies carrying their own lights. I interpret the stage direction at 1.1.144 ("*. . .and other Ladies and attendants with lights*") to indicate that Dicache, Philocalia, and Petula (i.e., the "*other Ladies*") have attendants who bear lights. At 5.1.161–162, however, I assume that Dicache, Philocalia, and Petula carry their own lights ("*. . . Dicache, Philocalia, Petula, lights before them.*").

33 Bullen, ed., *The Works of Thomas Middleton*, vol. 1, p. 76.

34 In *The Elizabethan Theatre and The Book of Sir Thomas More*, McMillin surveys the requirement for characters in "the first 500 lines of every extant play assigned to a public-theatre company for the years 1580 to 1610," and he finds that only twelve texts require as many as twenty-three speaking parts (p. 55). *Histrio-Mastix*, by contrast, has forty speaking parts in the first 500 lines.

35 Finkelpearl argues that the reference to "Proud Statute Rogues" (D4ᵛ) harkens back to the vagrancy act of 9 February 1598, but there were similar acts in 1572, 1576, and 1584–5 ("John Marston's *Histrio-Mastix* as an Inns of Court Play," p. 227).

36 Simpson, ed., *The School of Shakspere*, vol. II, pp. 9 and 14.

37 Small, *The Stage Quarrel*, pp. 77–8.

38 Chambers, *The Elizabethan Stage*, vol. IV, p. 18.

39 Shaaber, *Some Forerunners of the Newspaper in England*," p. 266.

40 Duncan-Jones, "Was the 1609 *Shake-speares Sonnets* Really Unauthorized?" pp. 154–5. Leona Rostenberg provides an account of the career of Thorpe that puts the publication of *Shake-speares Sonnets* into the context of his other work (*Literary, Political, Scientific, Religious & Legal Publishing, Printing & Bookselling in England, 1551–1700*).

41 Foster suggests that the elegy for William Peter was "printed at a customer's expense," a possibility worth considering also for *Histrio-Mastix*, which seems to have no constituency in 1610 except its author or his friends, the former apparently desiring to remain anonymous (*Elegy By W. S.*, pp. 73–4).

42 Parkes, "The Epistle Dedicatorie" to "An Apologie: of Three Testimonies of Holy Scripture," STC 19295, [6ᵛ].
43 Willet, "Loidoromastix," STC 25693, D4ᵛ. Other contemporary instances of "mastix" words are *Papisto-Mastix*, a pamphlet by William Middleton in 1606 (STC 17913); *Atheomastix*, by Martin Fotherby, 1622 (STC 11205); *Arktomastix*, 1633 (STC 12808); and *Profano-mastix*, John Swan, 1639 (STC 23513). There is, in addition, Shakespeare's anglicized "mastic jaws" in *Troilus and Cressida*, 1.3.73, which fuses the whip and dog metaphors so loved by Marston.
44 Herford and Simpson, ed., *Ben Jonson*, vol. x, p. 654.
45 Moore Smith, ed., *Fucus Histriomastix*, pp. 84–85. In conversation in 1996, J. W. Binns, author of *Intellectual Culture in Elizabethan and Jacobean England*, expressed the opinion that words fabricated with the suffix of "mastix" were common, and no particular knowledge was needed to make this compound.
46 Simpson, ed., *The School of Shakspere*, vol. ii, p. 9. The banishment in *Histrio-Mastix* of common players from a redeemed state as in Plato's *Republic* may, indeed, have been all that Jonson meant to evoke when he gave Clove the phrase, "PLATO's *Histriomastix*."
47 Kernan, "John Marston's Play *Histriomastix*," p. 135.
48 Finkelpearl, "John Marston's *Histrio-Mastix* as an Inns of Court Play," p. 230.
49 McMillin and MacLean, *The Queen's Men and their Plays*, pp. 121–24 and 155.
50 The titles of lost plays are indicated by quotation marks; titles of surviving plays are indicated by italics.

5   "HAMLET" AND COMPANY COMMERCE

1 Chedworth, *Notes Upon Some of the Obscure Passages in Shakespeare's Plays*, p. 350; Dover Wilson, ed., *Hamlet*, p. viii.
2 For a modern text, I use the Arden edition of *Hamlet* edited by Jenkins; the "little eyases" passage is 2.2.328–58.
3 So claims the preface to the 1825 edition of the 1603 *Hamlet* (Q1); see Duthie, *The 'Bad' Quarto of Hamlet*, p. 85.
4 Collier, ed., *The Works of William Shakespeare*, vol. vii, pp. 190–92.
5 According to Duthie, respected critics such as Samuel W. Singer, Thomas Caldecott, Charles Knight, F. J. Furnivall, Edward Dowden, and the Rev. Alexander Dyce held the view that Q1 was Shakespeare's first draft; others such as W. G. Clark and W. A. Wright thought Q1 was at best merely revised by Shakespeare (*The 'Bad' Quarto of Hamlet*, pp. 85–6).
6 Rowe, ed., *The Works of Mr. William Shakespear*, vol. v. For a text of F and the through-line numbering system, I use Hinman, ed., *The Norton*

Facsimile: The First Folio of Shakespeare; for a text of Q1 and Q2, I use Allen and Muir, eds., *Shakespeare's Plays in Quarto.*

7 Mowat, "The Form of *Hamlet*'s Fortunes," p. 100.
8 Dover Wilson, ed., *Hamlet*, p. xxvii.
9 *Ibid.*, pp. xxii, xxvii, and 178n.
10 For the New Cambridge edition of *Hamlet*, Philip Edwards made "an eclectic text" of Q2 and F, marking Q2-only passages with brackets. Bernice W. Kliman and Paul Bertram resolved textual choice by printing a parallel-text edition in *The Three-Text Hamlet* (1991).
11 Wells and Taylor, *William Shakespeare: A Textual Companion*, p. 399.
12 Furness, ed., *Hamlet*, vol. II, p. 13.
13 Quoted by Duthie, *The 'Bad' Quarto of Hamlet*, p. 85.
14 Halliwell[-Phillipps], ed., *The Works of William Shakespeare*. vol. XIV, p. 130.
15 Duthie, *The 'Bad' Quarto of Hamlet*, p. 273.
16 Hibbard, ed., *Hamlet*, p. 5.
17 Honigmann, "The Date of *Hamlet*," p. 27.
18 Edwards, ed., *Hamlet, Prince of Denmark*, p. 19.
19 Honigmann, "The Date of *Hamlet*," p. 29.
20 Ioppolo, *Revising Shakespeare*, p. 145. Ioppolo gives the "humour of children" passage a short life, claiming that by the end of 1602 it was revised into the "little eyases" passage (p. 144).
21 Dessen, "Weighing the Options in *Hamlet* Q1," p. 66.
22 *Ibid.*, p. 66.
23 Hibbard, "The Chronology of the Three Substantive Texts of Shakespeare's *Hamlet*," p. 79.
24 Dessen, "Weighing the Options in *Hamlet* Q1," p. 76.
25 Weiner, ed., *Hamlet: The First Quarto 1603*, p. 58. Weiner does not mention the "humour of children" passage specifically.
26 Jenkins dates "the essential *Hamlet*" in 1599–1600; he believes that the "little eyases" passage was added by 1601, then cut; see the Arden *Hamlet*, pp. 2–3, 13, and 472.
27 See Jenkins, ed., *Hamlet*, p. 13, and Hibbard, ed., *Hamlet*, p. 5.
28 See Weiner, ed. *Hamlet: The First Quarto 1603*, pp. 7–45; Maguire, *Shakespearean Suspect Texts*; Urkowitz, "Good News about 'Bad' Quartos"; and Werstine, "Narratives About Printed Shakespeare Texts."
29 See Blayney, "The Publication of Playbooks."
30 Gerald Johnson, "Nicholas Ling, Publisher 1580–1607," p. 211.
31 *Ibid.*, p. 212; Weiner, ed., *Hamlet: The First Quarto 1603*, pp. 59–60.
32 Greg, *Two Elizabethan Stage Abridgements*, pp. 15–16, 133–4, and 352–6.
33 In a letter putatively dated 1 August 1593, Edward Alleyn said that his company was getting ready to play "Harry of Cornwall," but no copy of the text survives (Foakes and Rickert, eds., *Henslowe's Diary*, p. 276; cited in the text as *HD*). Charles Sisson assumed that Cholmeley's Men

used published quartos of Shakespeare's *Pericles* and *King Lear* in performances in Yorkshire on Candlemas, 1609–10 ("Shakespeare Quartos as Prompt-Copies").

34 McMillin, "Casting for Pembroke's Men," p. 154.

35 McMillin, "Casting the *Hamlet* Quartos." Maguire considers Q1 of *Hamlet* to be "possibly" a memorially reconstructed text, but if it is, she says, it is "a very good one" (*Shakespearean Suspect Texts*, p. 256).

36 Jenkins, ed., *Hamlet*, p. 5.

37 Pope, ed., *The Works of Mr. William Shakespear*, vol. VI, pp. 389–90; Pope's "his" should of course be "her."

38 Steevens, ed., *The Plays of William Shakespeare*, vol. X, pp. 254–7, esp. p. 254.

39 Malone, ed., *The Plays and Poems of William Shakespeare*, vol. IX, pp. 264–67; Malone and Boswell, eds., *The Plays and Poems of William Shakespeare*, vol. VII, pp. 288–94, esp. p. 291.

40 Chambers, *The Elizabethan Stage*, vol. II, p. 206.

41 Harbage, *Shakespeare and the Rival Traditions*, p. 29.

42 Smith, *Shakespeare's Blackfriars Playhouse*, pp. 177–209.

43 *Ibid.*, p. 176.

44 Cuthbert Burbage was also a Blackfriars householder; Will Kempe sold out of the Globe on leaving the company, possibly in 1600.

45 That members of a company noticed and envied the financial successes of their fellows is suggested by the Sharers Papers in 1635, in which three players with the King's Men who did not own shares in the playhouses petitioned to be granted such shares (Malone Society *Collections*, vol. II.3, pp. 362–73).

46 Bevington, ed., *The Complete Works of Shakespeare*, p. 1083n.

47 As quoted by Chambers, *The Elizabethan Stage*, vol. IV, p. 333.

48 Rann, ed., *The Dramatic Works of Shakspeare*, vol. VI, p. 302.

49 Singer, ed., *The Dramatic Works of Shakspeare*, vol. X, p. 222.

50 Honigmann, "The Date of *Hamlet*," p. 29; Bevington, ed., *The Complete Works of Shakespeare*, p. 1083n.

51 Dover Wilson, ed., *Hamlet*, p. 177.

52 Jenkins, ed., *Hamlet*, p. 472.

53 Dutton, *Mastering the Revels*, pp. 165–70.

54 Mason, *Comments on the Last Edition of Shakespeare's Plays*, p. 381. According to the *OED*, a meaning for "innovation" specific to Scottish law is "the substitution of a new obligation for the old" (dated 1861).

55 In *A London Life in the Brazen Age*, William Ingram suggests that performances of "The Isle of Dogs," traditionally believed to be the cause of the order by the Privy Council to close the playhouses in July 1597, were merely coincident with that order (pp. 176–84).

56 Barroll, *Politics, Plague, and Shakespeare's Theater*, pp. 15, 71–2, 217–26, and 173.

57 Somerset, " 'How chances it they travel?' " p. 54.

58 See *Hamlet*, in Malone's 1821 edition, *The Plays and Poems of William Shakespeare*, vol. vii, pp. 288–92.

59 Fleay, *A Chronicle History of the London Stage*, pp. 227–8.

60 Heywood, "An Apology for Actors," G3^v. Dutton argues "that the whole system of a factional court, supported by a complex interweaving of patronage, conspired in most circumstances to 'allow' a wide range of comment on contemporary affairs, so long as this was properly licensed, suitably veiled and not slanted with offensive particularity at a powerful constituency" (*Mastering the Revels*, p. 178). This thesis is significant in describing the line over which the Blackfriars company repeatedly stepped and (according to my argument) provoked the King's Men into adding the "little eyases" passage to the script for a revival of *Hamlet*.

61 Dutton suggests that Jonson's *Sejanus* seems to be "the first occasion on which any dramatist was made to answer *by the government* for his text"; further, he thinks it possible that the objection "followed the *publication* of the play in 1605 rather than its 1603 *performance*" (*Mastering the Revels*, p. 164). *Sejanus* was performed by Shakespeare's company; in 1605, however, Jonson was writing for the Blackfriars company.

62 As paraphrased by Hillebrand, *The Child Actors*, p. 199.

63 Theobald, *Shakespeare Restored*, p. 66. John Hughes had made the emendation of "faction" that Theobald here accepted. Hughes made it for an acting edition of *Hamlet* prepared for Robert Wilks at Drury Lane in 1718 (also in 1723). Theobald made the emendation of "stagers." He conjectured that Shakespeare was making a joke about his own players, who resented the behavior of the children players toward their elders in the profession: "The Poet certainly cannot intend . . . that Gentlemen-Spectators were afraid to go to the common Theatres, for Fear of the Resentment of these Children . . . What greater Affront could SHAKE-SPEARE put upon his Audience, than to suppose any of them were of such tame and cowardly Spirits? No, if I understand him, he seems to me to hint, that this young Fry were so pert upon the profest *Actors*, that even they, tho' they wore Swords, were afraid of going near them, least they should be *banter'd*, or *insulted*, past Sufferance" (p. 67).

64 *Ibid.*, p. 67.

65 Theobald, *The Works of Shakespeare*, vol. vii, p. 275.

66 Malone and Boswell, eds., *Plays and Poems of William Shakespeare*, vol. vii, p. 294, n. 7.

67 Steevens, ed., *The Plays of William Shakespeare*, vol. x, p. 256.

68 Jenkins, ed., *Hamlet*, p. 473.

69 Loewenstein, "Plays Agonistic and Competitive," p. 73.

70 *Philotas* was registered at Stationers' Hall on 29 November 1604; for a full discussion of the issues of contemporary pointing and governmental reaction, see Dutton, *Mastering the Revels*, pp. 164–93.

71 In *Mastering the Revels* Dutton makes the point that new favorites at

Court in 1603–4 were unusually sensitive to implications that they had benefited from the downfall of former favorites such as Essex, Ralegh, and Cobham (pp. 170–71). Barroll, in explaining how little the players mattered to King James personally, also conveys the sense of a Court absorbed in the redistribution of power as courtiers jockeyed for position with the new monarch (*Politics, Plague, and Shakespeare's Theater*, pp. 35–42).

72 Dutton, *Mastering the Revels*, p. 179.

73 Players in the King's Men – William Sly, John Sinklo, Richard Burbage, Henry Condell, and John Lowin – appear in the Induction as themselves, thus making an unequivocal statement as "company" men. When Sly asks Condell how he "come by" the play to be performed that day, Condell answers, "Faith, sir, the book was lost, and because 'twas pity so good a play should be lost, we found it and play it" (Harris, ed., *The Malcontent*, lines 70 and 71–2). Sly then asks if the play had belonged first to another company, and Condell explains the nature of the tit-for-tat: "Why not Malvole in folio with us, as Jeronimo in decimo sexto with them: they taught us a name for our play, we call it *One for another*" (lines 75–7). A quarto of *The Malcontent* with this Induction was published in 1604.

74 These are the words of John Chamberlain in a letter to Ralph Winwood, 18 December 1604 (Sawyer, ed., *Memorials of Affairs of State* . . . , vol. II, p. 41).

75 I construct a maiden run for *Hamlet* based on that of *The Blind Beggar of Alexandria*, which was first played by the Admiral's Men on 12 February 1596 and enjoyed twenty-two performances through 1 April 1597, by which time it was being offered about once a month. It may be inappropriate to model the initial stage run of *Hamlet* on that of a comedy, but there is not a long-running new tragedy in the playlists of Henslowe's diary from which to choose.

76 Barroll notices an entry in Henslowe's diary for 5 May 1603 that implies an inhibition literally caused by the innovation: "we leafte of playe *now* at the kynges cominge" (Barroll, *Politics, Plague, and Shakespeare's Theater*, p. 102; *HD 209*).

77 On 19 November 1607, John Smethwick bought the text of *Hamlet* from Nicholas Ling in a mass purchase, but he did not reprint it until 1611.

78 I do not attribute the "little eyases" addition to Shakespeare. In my opinion, the passage is awkward and unclear. Indeed, its very obtuseness is responsible for the welter of critical opinions about its textual provenance and theatre history.

6   "POETASTER," "SATIROMASTIX," AND COMPANY COMMERCE

1 Edward Pudsey's Commonplace Book, f 42.

2 Palmer and Wasson, Derbyshire volume, H MS 10a, f 144^{v}, to be

published in the series, Records of Early English Drama. Cavendish, created first Earl of Devonshire in 1618, was the uncle of William Cavendish, Duke of Newcastle (to and for whom Jonson wrote the occasional poem).

3 David Kay observes that "recent scholarship has been rightly skeptical of . . . [the] reckless identifications" by Victorian scholars (*Ben Jonson*, p. 55).

4 *Ibid.*, p. 43. James Bednarz puts the issue this way: "the literary combat of the Poets' War involved a basic philosophical issue – a debate on the theory of literature that came into being as a result of Jonson's insistence on a new and dignified status for the poet, based on principles of academic humanism" ("Representing Jonson," p. 23).

5 Palmer and Wasson, Derbyshire volume, H MS 10a, f 206ᵛ.

6 Kay, *Ben Jonson*, p. 56. For the basis of dating *Poetaster* and *Satiromastix*, see Hoy, *Introductions, Notes, and Commentaries . . . Thomas Dekker . . .*, vol. I, p. 181, notes 4 and 5.

7 Cain, ed., *Poetaster*, p. 28.

8 Tricomi assigns *All Fools* to Blackfriars, possibly in 1600–1 ("The Dates of the Plays of George Chapman," pp. 243–5). Hillebrand assigned *Sir Giles Goosecap* and *May Day* to 1601–2 (*The Child Actors*, p. 172, n. 3); Chambers assigned *The Gentleman Usher* to 1602 (*The Elizabethan Stage*, vol. III, p. 251). The basis for the chronology of Chapman's comedies is *The Plays and Poems of George Chapman*, vol. II, ed. T. M. Parrott (London, Routledge, 1914).

9 The relevant line is "Why not Malevole in folio with us, as Jeronimo in decimo-sexto with them?" (Harris, ed., *The Malcontent*, Induction 75–6). Reibetanz discusses the possibility that the "Hieronimo" play was *1 Jeronimo*, Q1605 ("Hieronimo in Decimosexto"). The playlists of Richard Rogers and William Ley (1656), Edward Archer (1656), and Francis Kirkman (1661) include an item entitled "Hieronimo, both parts."

10 In 1943 Berringer delivered a disabling blow by debunking the claim that Jonson pointed to Marston satirically in the character of Hedon in *Cynthia's Revels* ("Jonson's *Cynthia's Revels* and the War of the Theatres"). Kay truncates the narrative to four plays: *Cynthia's Revels*, *What You Will*, *Poetaster*, and *Satiromastix* (*Ben Jonson*, pp. 55–6). Gair, among others, revises the motive of the satirical pointing from personal and literary attacks to commercial advertising (*The Children of Paul's*, p. 134).

11 See Cain, ed., *Poetaster*, pp. 40–47; Robert C. Evans, *Ben Jonson and the Poetics of Patronage*, pp. 146–48; Dutton, *Mastering the Revels*, pp. 136–41; and Haynes, *The Social Relations of Jonson's Theater*, pp. 76–90.

12 See Maus, *Ben Jonson and the Roman Frame of Mind*, pp. 22–35, George Rowe, *Distinguishing Jonson*, pp. 68–89, and Sweeney, *Jonson and the Psychology of Public Theater*, pp. 35–46. Pearlman succinctly itemizes issues that provide context for *Poetaster*: "I have treated . . . *Poetaster* as

an expression of inner psychological needs, . . . [but] a full understanding of the play requires knowledge of Jonson's classical indebtedness, of the traditional subjects of satire and the postures of satirists, of the constraints and conventions of the boys' theatrical troupes, of fashionable attitudes among the patrons of the private theatres, of comic theory, of the tensions between humanist and courtier, Shakespeare, of the influence of the court, and of many other factors which I have omitted or which are not yet known" ("Ben Jonson: An Anatomy," p. 394, n. 27).

13 George Rowe crystallizes the issue of making distinctions between classes and poets, distinctions applicable in Jonson's mind to audiences and playhouses (*Distinguishing Jonson*, pp. 68–89, especially p. 82).

14 Sinfield, "*Poetaster*, the Author, and the Perils of Cultural Production," p. 12.

15 For this passage, Jonson lifted a line from the players' song in *Histrio-Mastix*, to which, in the Folio edition, he added "and stalke vpon boords, and barrell heads, to an old crackt trumpet."

16 Sinfield, "*Poetaster*, the Author, and the Perils of Cultural Production," p. 12.

17 *Ibid.*, p. 13.

18 Kay, *Ben Jonson*, p. 58. Two of the pages' scraps have not been identified. One contains the line, ". . . *A* roman *spirit scornes to beare a braine* . . ." (3.4.225). Neither Cain nor Herford and Simpson note that the Admiral's Men paid Dekker 40s. for "Bear a Brain" in August 1599, when Dekker was working on other scripts with Jonson. (The titles of surviving plays are indicated by italics; the titles of lost plays are indicated by quotation marks.)

19 All citations from Henslowe's diary are taken from the edition by Foakes and Rickert unless otherwise noted; I designate these in the text by the abbreviation, *HD*.

20 No one knows how many discrete plays are represented by the titles "Mahomet," *The Battle of Alcazar*, "Muly Mollocco" (*HD* 16–19), and "The Turkish Mahomet and Hiren the Fair Greek."

21 Henslowe recorded a payment of 60s. for the book of "The Spanish Moor's Tragedy" in February 1600 (*HD* 131); 39s. toward the book of "The Conquest of Spain" in the spring of 1601 (*HD* 167–68), and £6 for "King Sebastian of Portugal" (*HD* 168). Shakespeare also used the name "Calipolis" to evoke *The Battle of Alcazar* (*2 Henry IV*, 2.4.179).

22 Jonson was paid 40s. on 25 September 1601 for additions to Kyd's play and some part of 200s. on 22 June 1602 (*HD* 182, 203). *The Spanish Tragedy* was an old target for Jonson; Matheo in *Every Man In his Humour* reads "Goe by HIERONIMO" (1.5.47) and, at 1.5.57–61, quotes rather accurately from the speech beginning "O eyes, no eyes."

23 Harbage, *Shakespeare and the Rival Traditions*, p. 105.

24 Shapiro, *Rival Playwrights*, pp. 42, 44, 59–61, and 65–6.

25 Henslowe entered payments toward revivals of *The Jew of Malta* in May 1601, *The Massacre at Paris* in November and January, 1601–2, and *Doctor Faustus* in November 1602, but there is no similar evidence for a revival of the two-part *Tamburlaine*. Yet it would be surprising if no revival took place. The plays had been in retirement since November 1596, and the Admiral's Men kept Tamburlaine's apparel and properties in inventory. Edward Alleyn, who left playing in 1597, returned at the opening of the Fortune where – among other old favorites – he reprised his Marlovian parts. Another clue to a revival in 1600–1 is the subsequent revival in October 1602 of "Tamar Cham," which had once been the sequel of *Tamburlaine* in performance.

26 A quarto of *A Midsummer Night's Dream* was published in 1600.

27 Mann, "Sir Oliver Owlet's Men," p. 302. See Cain, ed., *Poetaster*, for the gymnastics required to turn Tucca's catalogue of potential supper guests into specific satirical portraits (note to 3.4.280–307).

28 Sinfield, "*Poetaster*, the Author, and the Perils of Cultural Production," p. 13.

29 Dutton, "The Revels Office and the Boy Companies, 1600–1613," forthcoming in *English Literary Renaissance*.

30 In "How Often Did the Eyases Fly?" Farley-Hills decides that there must have been not one performance (orthodox position) or three (Eccles's opinion in "Martin Peerson and the Blackfriars," p. 104) but six per week in order for the boys' companies to be "a serious threat" the men's companies (p. 466).

31 Palmer and Wasson, Derbyshire volume, H MS 10a. f 206^v.

32 Harbage, *Shakespeare and the Rival Traditions*, p. 102; Campbell, *Comicall Satyre and Shakespeare's Troilus and Cressida*, p. 109; Hoy, *Introductions, Notes, and Commentaries . . . Thomas Dekker . . .*, vol. I, p. 191.

33 Bednarz implies the significance of this time for later hostilities in "Marston's Subversion of Shakespeare and Jonson," p. 127, n. 26.

34 Hoy, *Introductions, Notes, and Commentaries . . . Thomas Dekker . . .*, vol. I, p. 180.

35 *Ibid.*, p. 180. However, *Every Man Out of his Humour* was not a failure; in "The Shaping of Ben Jonson's Career" Kay claims for it "at least a moderate reception in the theater" (p. 230).

36 Harbage, *Shakespeare and the Rival Traditions*, p. 102.

37 Langbaine, *An Account of the English Dramatick Poets*, p. 123.

38 Shepherd, ed., *The Dramatic Works of Thomas Dekker*, vol. I, p. vii.

39 *Ibid.*, pp. xv and xvii (the latter quoting Disraeli).

40 See Hoy's notes on the play in *Introductions, Notes, and Commentaries . . . Thomas Dekker . . .* for an exhaustive treatment of Dekker's charges.

41 *Ibid.*, p. 180.

42 Champion, *Thomas Dekker and the Traditions of English Drama*, p. 28

43 Robert C. Evans, "Jonson, *Satiromastix*, and the Poetomachia," p. 375.

44 However *Poetaster* and *Satiromastix* might have been cobbled together to

respond to one another's satire, Tucca and Crispinus are ubiquitous in both plays, and neither part can be doubled.

45 Hoy documents the allusions scrupulously in *Introductions, Notes, and Commentaries . . . Thomas Dekker . . .*, and I am therefore much in his debt; but he has little to say about Dekker's agenda with these references.

46 Trademark stage business of Edward Alleyn as Tamburlaine (stamping) and stage action (unfurled colored flags) appears to be captured in these allusions as well.

47 In *Introductions, Notes, and Commentaries . . . Thomas Dekker . . .*, Hoy notes Dekker's many allusions to ballad and romance materials: Amadis of Gaul, Dives, the Mirror of Knighthood, Susanna, the Devil of Dowgate, Mary Ambree, Annis a Cleere, Guy of Warwick, Sir Eglamour, and Adam Bell. It is tempting to conjecture that one or more of these references would have been recognized by audiences as the subjects of plays.

48 In Travice's records for his master's playgoing, there are five entries for which no playhouse is specified (in addition to the entry for Hallam). The expense entered ranges from 3s. to 11d., a sum that includes 2d. for "a stoole to sit downe on" (Palmer and Wasson, Derbyshire volume, H MS 10a, f 229).

49 The demands of *Cynthia's Revels* and *Poetaster* on the resources of a company suggest that the Children of the Chapel had more players, and more accomplished ones, at their disposal in 1601 than did the Children of Paul's. Nine players in *Cynthia's Revels* have parts of 150 lines or more; four have parts of one hundred lines or more (according to the text in Herford and Simpson's edition, *Ben Jonson*). *Poetaster* requires at least twenty players (Cain, *Poetaster*, p. 40); seven of those players have parts of 150 lines or more, and four have one hundred lines or more.

50 Leishman, ed., *The Three Parnassus Plays*, pp. 24–26; Nelson, ed., *Cambridge*, vol. II, Appendices 6 (p. 914) and 8 (p. 974).

51 Leishman, ed., *The Three Parnassus Plays*, 4.3.1769–73.

52 For *Troilus and Cressida* as Shakespeare's purge, see Bednarz, "Shakespeare's Purge of Jonson"; for *Twelfth Night*, see Riggs, *Ben Jonson: A Life*, pp. 84–85 and Cain, ed., *Poetaster*, pp. 36–38.

53 Savage thought Pudsey lived near the home of the Ardens at Park Hall (*Shakespearean Extracts from "Edward Pudsey's Booke,"* pp. vi–viii). Gowan establishes that Pudsey lived as a youth at Ardesley farm, Longford, Derbyshire ("An Edition of Edward Pudsey's Commonplace Book . . .," p. 8). David Kathman establishes that Pudsey married in London in 1605 before moving by 1610 to Tewkesbury, Gloucestershire ("Edward Pudsey").

54 Quoted by Hoy, *Introductions, Notes, and Commentaries . . . Thomas Dekker . . .*, vol. I, p. 197.

55 Gurr, *Playgoing in Shakespeare's London*, agrees with Halliwell-Phillipps

that Pudsey's source was playhouse jottings. Gowan ("An Edition of Edward Pudsey's Commonplace Book," p. 68), Kathman ("Edward Pudsey"), and I agree that Pudsey – though he was probably a playgoer – relied primarily on texts for the quotations in his commonplace book.

56 Pudsey's quotations from *Every Man Out of his Humour, Cynthia's Revels, Jack Drum's Entertainment,* and *What You Will* show no more interest in the satirical pointing of the Stage Quarrel than do the extracts from *Poetaster* and *Satiromastix*. Gowan observes that a number of plays quoted by Pudsey belong to the Stage Quarrel ("An Edition of Edward Pudsey's Commonplace Book," pp. 11, 69), but she does not pursue the implications of his choice of passages beyond their appeal as wit.

57 Seven leaves were separated from the commonplace book while Savage and Halliwell-Phillipps were working with it. Three were soon found and bound at the end of the book (ff. 86–88). One (f 86) has play-scraps, and Gowan determines that its proper place is as follows: f 42–f 86–f 43 ("An Edition of Edward Pudsey's Commonplace Book," pp. 28–30). The remaining four have subsequently been found at the Shakespeare Birthplace Trust (for which location, the pages are designated SBT1–4). Two – SBT1 and SBT2 – have play extracts, and Kathman puts them in the following order: f 42–f 86–SBT1–f 43; and f 79–SBT2–f 80–f 81 (personal e-mail, 21 May 2000).

The proper location of the seven leaves creates two sections of play extracts in the commonplace book. The first (f 39^v – SBT1^v) has extracts from plays published in 1602 or earlier (except for *Othello*): *Every Man Out of his Humour* (f 39^v), *Cynthia's Revels* (f 40, f 40^v), *Jack Drum's Entertainment* (f 40^v), *The Merchant of Venice* (f 41), "Irus," i.e., *The Blind Beggar of Alexandria* (f 41), *Every Man In his Humour* (but labeled "Eu^{r}y ma*n* out of his humo^r, f 41), *Antonio and Mellida* (f 41^v), *Antonio's Revenge* (f 41^v), *Poetaster* (f 41^v, f 42), *Satiromastix* (f 42^v), *How a Man may Choose a Good Wife from a Bad* (f 86), *Blurt, Master Constable* (f 86), *Love's Metamorphosis* (f 86^v), *Campaspe* (f 86^v), *Titus Andronicus* (f 86^v), *Romeo and Juliet* (f 86^v, SBT1), *Richard II* (SBT1), *Richard III* (SBT1), *Othello* (SBT1), and *Much Ado About Nothing* (SBT1^v). The extracts from *Othello* appear to have been added at a later date (Kathman, electronic communication).

The second section (SBT2 – f 81) has extracts from plays published after 1602: *Hamlet* (SBT2, SBT2^v), *The Honest Whore*, part one (SBT2^v, f 80), *The Case is Altered* (f 80, labeled "Tis a mad world"), *The Atheist's Tragedy* (f 80^v-f 81), *What You Will* (f 81), and *The White Devil* (f 81). Quotations from one play occur outside of these sections. Pudsey copied play-scraps from *Summer's Last Will and Testament* (f 21^v) with other extracts from Nashe's work (f 21–f 21^v).

58 If he bought these plays in quarto, Pudsey was as good a customer of booksellers as playhouses. He could have bought one or more of his play-quartos at the following locations: the sign of the Gun near Holborn Conduit; Cuthbert Burby's shop near the Royal Exchange;

shops in St. Paul's Churchyard including the Green Dragon, Fleur-de-lis and Crown, Angel, Tiger's Head, and Gun; William Holme's shop in Fleet Street at Serjeants Inn Gate; Matthew Lownes's shop in St. Dunstan's Churchyard; Richard Oliffe's shop in Long Lane; and the Long Shop in St. Mildred Poultry.

59 Which of the old plays by Shakespeare might Pudsey have seen in revival *circa* 1600–1? *Richard II* played once in February 1601 at the request of Essex's supporters. I have posited a revival *circa* 1600 for *The Merchant of Venice* and *Titus Andronicus* on the evidence of their publication in 1600, and one for *Richard III* in 1602 (*The Repertory of Shakespeare's Company*, pp. 81, 168–9). *Romeo and Juliet*, which was perennially popular, might have been an attractive revival at any time; quartos came out in 1597 and 1599.

60 Gurr, *The Shakespearian Playing Companies*, pp. 116–17. According to Wells and Taylor (*William Shakespeare: A Textual Companion*, p. 90), James Wright is responsible for the belief that the King's Men split the playing year between the two playhouses (*Historia Histrionica*, 1699).

61 Bentley, "Shakespeare and the Blackfriars Theatre."

7 CONCLUSION

1 Donaldson, "Jonson and Anger," p. 57. For the creativity of Jonson's anger, see also Rollin, "The Anxiety of Identification."

2 Donaldson, "Jonson and Anger," p. 66.

3 Gurr, *The Shakespearian Playing Companies*, pp. 319–26. Beeston's stewardship of the company was legally challenged in 1623 by the widow of Thomas Greene, who sued the company for payment of previous loans and debts.

4 In *The Shakespearian Playing Companies*, Gurr attempts to explain the decision of the King's Men to alternate between the Globe and Black-friars (pp. 116–18 and 296–8), as he believes they did, and elsewhere terms their decision a sign that they were "affluent and easygoing" (p. 325).

Bibliography

Bibliographic information on manuscript sources and the Malone Society *Collections* are provided in the notes and not repeated here.

Allen, Michael J. B., and Kenneth Muir (eds.), *Shakespeare's Plays in Quarto*. Berkeley: University of California Press, 1981.

Anderson, J. J. (ed.), *Newcastle*, Records of Early English Drama. University of Toronto Press, 1982.

Archer, Ian. *The Pursuit of Stability: Social Relations in Elizabethan London*. Cambridge University Press, 1991.

Barroll, J. Leeds. *Politics, Plague, and Shakespeare's Theater*. Ithaca: Cornell University Press, 1991.

Bate, Walter Jackson, and A. B. Strauss (eds.), *The Yale Edition of the Works of Samuel Johnson*. 15 vols. New Haven, CN: Yale University Press, 1969.

Beckerman, Bernard. "Philip Henslowe" in *The Theatrical Manager in England and America: Player of a Perilous Game*, ed. Joseph W. Donohue, Jr. Princeton: Princeton University Press, 1971, 19–62.

Shakespeare at the Globe, 1599–1609. New York: Macmillan, 1962.

Bednarz, James P. "Marston's Subversion of Shakespeare and Jonson: *Histriomastix* and the War of the Theaters." *Medieval and Renaissance Drama in England* 6 (1993): 103–28.

"Representing Jonson: *Histriomastix* and the Origin of the Poets' War." *Huntington Library Quarterly* 54 (1991): 1–30.

"Shakespeare's Purge of Jonson: The Literary Context of *Troilus and Cressida*." *Shakespeare Studies* 21 (1993): 175–212.

Bennett, Paul E. "The Word 'Goths' in 'A Knack to Know a Knave'." *Notes and Queries* 200 (November 1955): 462–63.

Bentley, Gerald E. *The Profession of Dramatist in Shakespeare's Time, 1590–1642*. Princeton University Press, 1971.

"Records of Players in the Parish of St. Giles, Cripplegate." *PMLA* 44 (1929): 789–816.

"Shakespeare and the Blackfriars Theatre." *Shakespeare Survey* 1 (1948): 38–50.

Bergeron, David. "Thomas Middleton and Anthony Munday: Artistic Rivalry?" *Studies in English Literature* 36 (1996): 461–79.

Berringer, Ralph W. "Jonson's *Cynthia's Revels* and the War of the Theatres." *Philological Quarterly* 22 (1943): 1–22.

Berry, Herbert. *The Boar's Head Playhouse*, illus. C. Walter Hodges. Washington, DC: Folger Shakespeare Library, 1986.

"The First Public Playhouses, Especially the Red Lion." *Shakespeare Quarterly* 40 (1989): 133–45.

"The Player's Apprentice." *Essays in Theatre* (May 1983): 73–80.

Shakespeare's Playhouses. New York: AMS Press, 1987.

Bevington, David (ed.), *The Complete Works of Shakespeare*, 4th edn. New York: Harper-Collins, 1992.

From Mankind to Marlowe. Cambridge, MA: Harvard University Press, 1962.

Blayney, Peter W. M. *The Bookshops in St. Paul's Churchyard*. London: The Bibliographic Society, 1990.

"The Publication of Playbooks" in *A New History of Early English Drama*, eds. John D. Cox and David Scott Kastan. New York: Columbia University Press, 1997, 383–422.

Bowers, Fredson (ed.), *The Dramatic Works of Thomas Dekker*, 4 vols. Cambridge University Press, 1953. All quotations from *Satiromastix* are taken from this edition (vol. 1).

Bradley, David. *From Text to Performance in the Elizabethan Theatre: Preparing the Play for the Stage*. Cambridge University Press, 1992.

Bruster, Douglas. *Drama and the Market in the Age of Shakespeare*. Cambridge University Press, 1992.

Bullen, A. H. (ed.), *Blurt, Master Constable*, in *The Works of Thomas Middleton*, 8 vols. (1885). New York: AMS Press, 1964 (vol. 1).

The Maydes Metamorphosis, in *A Collection of Old English Plays*, 4 vols. London: Wyman Sons, 1882 (vol. 1).

Cain, Tom (ed.), *Poetaster*. The Revels Plays. Manchester University Press, 1995.

Campbell, Oscar J. *Comicall Satyre and Shakespeare's Troilus and Cressida*. San Marino, CA: Huntington Library Publications, 1959.

Carson, Neil. *A Companion to Henslowe's Diary*. Cambridge University Press, 1988.

"Literary Management in the Lord Admiral's Company, 1597–1603." *Theatre Research International* 2 (1977): 186–97.

Cartwright, Dr. Robert. *Shakspere and Jonson. Dramatic, versus Wit-combats*. London: John Russell Smith, 1864.

Cerasano, S. P. "Anthony Jeffes, Player and Brewer." *Notes and Queries* 31 (1984): 221–25.

"'Borrowed Robes,' Costume Prices, and the Drawing of *Titus Andronicus*." *Shakespeare Studies* 22 (1994): 45–57.

"Edward Alleyn's Early Years: His Life and Family." *Notes and Queries* c. s. 232 (June 1987): 237–43.

"Edward Alleyn: 1566–1626" in *Edward Alleyn: Elizabethan Actor, Jacobean Gentleman*, ed. Aileen Reid and Robert Maniura. London: Dulwich Picture Gallery, 1994, 11–31.

"New Renaissance Players' Wills." *Modern Philology* 82 (1985): 299–304.

Chambers, A. B., and William Frost (eds.), *The Works of John Dryden.* vol. IV. Berkeley, CA: University of California Press, 1956.

Chambers, E. K. *The Elizabethan Stage,* 4 vols. Oxford: Clarendon Press, 1923.

Champion, Larry S. *Thomas Dekker and the Traditions of English Drama.* New York: Peter Lang, 1983.

Chedworth, John Lord. *Notes Upon Some of the Obscure Passages in Shakespeare's Plays.* London: Bulmer and Co., 1805.

Collier, John Payne (ed.), *The Diary of Philip Henslowe.* London: Shakespeare Society, 1845.

(ed.), *King Edward the Third: A Historical Play, attributed by Edward Capell to William Shakespeare and now proved to be his work.* London: T. Richards, 1874.

(ed.), *The Works of William Shakespeare,* 8 vols. London: Whitaker & Co., 1843.

Collins, Arthur (ed.), *Letters and Memorials of State,* 2 vols. London: T. Osborne, 1746.

Cook, Ann Jennalie. *The Privileged Playgoers of Shakespeare's London, 1597–1642.* Princeton University Press, 1981.

Davenport, Arnold (ed.), *The Collected Poems of Joseph Hall, Bishop of Exeter and Norwich.* Liverpool University Press, 1949.

(ed.), *The Poems of John Marston.* Liverpool University Press, 1961.

Denkinger, E. M. "Actors' Names in the Registers of St. Bodolph Aldgate." *PMLA* 41 (1926): 91–109.

Dessen, Alan C. "Weighing the Options in *Hamlet* Q1" in *The Hamlet First Published (Q1, 1603): Origins, Form, Intertextualities,* ed. Thomas Clayton. Newark: University of Delaware Press, 1992, 65–78.

Dessen, Alan C., and Leslie Thomson. *A Dictionary of Stage Directions in English Drama, 1580–1642.* Cambridge University Press, 1999.

Dickson, Sarah Augusta. *Panacea or Precious Bane: Tobacco in Sixteenth Century Literature.* The New York Public Library, 1954.

Donaldson, Ian. "Jonson and Anger" in *English Satire and the Satiric Tradition,* ed. Claude Rawson. Oxford: Basil Blackwell, 1984, 56–71.

Duncan-Jones, Katherine. "Was the 1609 *Shake-speares Sonnets* Really Unauthorized?" *Review of English Studies* n. s. 34 (1983): 151–71.

Duthie, George I. *The 'Bad' Quarto of Hamlet: A Critical Study.* Cambridge University Press, 1941.

Dutton, Richard. "The Birth of the Author" in *Elizabethan Theater: Essays in Honor of S. Schoenbaum,* ed. R. B. Parker and S. P. Zitner. Newark: University of Delaware Press, 1996, 71–92.

"*Hamlet, An Apology for Actors,* and the Sign of the Globe." *Shakespeare Survey* 41 (1988): 35–43.

"The Revels Office and the Boy Companies 1600–1613: New Perspectives." *English Literary Renaissance* (forthcoming).

Licensing, Censorship and Authorship in Early Modern England: Buggeswords. New York: Palgrave, 2000.

Mastering the Revels: The Regulation and Censorship of English Renaissance Drama. University of Iowa Press, 1991.

Eccles, Mark, "Elizabethan Actors I: A-D." *Notes and Queries* c. s. 236 (1991): 38–49.

"Elizabethan Actors II: E-J." *Notes and Queries* c. s. 236 (1991): 454–61.

"Elizabethan Actors III: K-R." *Notes and Queries* c. s. 237 (1992): 293–303.

"Elizabethan Actors IV: S to End." *Notes and Queries* c. s. 238 (1993): 165–76.

"Martin Peerson and the Blackfriars." *Shakespeare Survey* 11 (1958): 100–109.

Edmond, Mary, "Pembroke's Men." *Review of English Studies* n. s. 25 (1974): 129–36.

Edwards, Philip (ed.), *Hamlet, Prince of Denmark*, The New Cambridge Shakespeare. Cambridge University Press, 1985.

Evans, G. Blakemore, and others (eds.), *The Riverside Shakespeare*, 1st edn. Boston: Houghton-Mifflin, 1974. Quotations from Shakespeare's plays are from this edition unless otherwise noted.

Evans, Robert C. *Ben Jonson and the Poetics of Patronage*. Lewisburg, PA: Bucknell University Press, 1989.

"Jonson, *Satiromastix*, and the Poetomachia: A Patronage Perspective." *Iowa State Journal of Research* 60, no. 3 (1986): 369–83.

Farley-Hills, David. "How Often Did the Eyases Fly?" *Notes and Queries* c. s 235 (1991): 461–66.

Farmer, John S. (ed.), *Histrio-Mastix. Tudor Facsimile Texts*, 1912.

Finkelpearl, Philip J. *John Marston of the Middle Temple: An Elizabethan Dramatist in his Social Setting*. Cambridge, MA: Harvard University Press, 1969.

"John Marston's *Histrio-Mastix* as an Inns of Court Play: A Hypothesis." *Huntington Library Quarterly* 20 (1966): 223–34.

Fleay, Frederick G. *A Biographical Chronicle of the English Drama, 1559–1642*, 2 vols. (1891). New York: Burt Franklin, 1966.

A Chronicle History of the London Stage, 1559–1642 (1890). New York: Burt Franklin, 1964.

Foakes, R. A., and R. T. Rickert (eds.), *Henslowe's Diary*. Cambridge University Press, 1961.

Foard, James T. "The Dramatic Dissensions of Jonson, Marston, and Dekker." *The Manchester Quarterly* 51 (1897): Part I: 1–18; Part II: 175–92.

Foster, Donald. *Elegy By W. S.: A Study in Attribution*. Newark: University of Delaware Press, 1989.

Furness, Howard Horace (ed.), *Hamlet*, 2 vols., The New Variorum Shakespeare. Philadelphia: J. B. Lippincott, 1877.

Gair, W. Reavley. *The Children of Paul's: The Story of a Theatre Company, 1553–1608*. Cambridge University Press, 1982.

Gifford, William (ed.), *The Works of Ben Jonson, in nine volumes,* 9 vols. London: G. and W. Nicol and others, 1816.

Gilchrist, Octavius. *An Examination of the Charges Maintained by Messrs. Malone, Chalmers, and Others of Ben Jonson's Enmity, &c. towards Shakspeare.* London: Taylor and Hessey, 1808.

Gowan, Juliet Mary (ed.), "An Edition of Edward Pudsey's Commonplace Book (c.1600–1615) from the Manuscript in the Bodleian Library." University of London, 1967.

Greg, W. W. (ed.), *A Bibliography of the English Printed Drama,* 4 vols. London: Bibliographic Society, 1939.

Dramatic Documents from the Elizabethan Playhouses: Stage Plots: Actors' Parts: Prompt Books, 2 vols. Oxford: Clarendon Press, 1931.

(ed.), *Henslowe Papers: being documents supplementary to Henslowe's Diary* (1907). New York: AMS Press, 1975.

(ed.), *Henslowe's Diary,* 2 vols. London: A. H. Bullen, 1904.

Two Elizabethan Stage Abridgements. Oxford University Press, 1922.

Gurr, Andrew. "Intertextuality at Windsor." *Shakespeare Quarterly* 38 (1987): 189–200.

"Money or Audiences: The Impact of Shakespeare's Globe." *Theatre Notebook* 42 (1988): 3–13.

Playgoing in Shakespeare's London. Cambridge University Press, 1987.

The Shakespearian Playing Companies. Oxford: Clarendon Press, 1996.

Halliwell [-Phillipps], James O. (ed.), *The Works of William Shakespeare,* 16 vols. London: Adlard, 1853.

Harbage, Alfred. *Shakespeare and the Rival Traditions.* New York: Macmillan, 1952.

Harris, Bernard (ed.), *The Malcontent.* New Mermaids. London: Benn, 1976.

Haynes, Jonathan. *The Social Relations of Jonson's Theater.* Cambridge University Press, 1992.

Herford, C. H., and Percy and Evelyn Simpson (eds.), *Ben Jonson,* 11 vols. Oxford: Clarendon Press, 1925. Quotations from *Every Man Out of his Humour* (vol. III) and *Poetaster* (vol. IV) are taken from this edition unless otherwise noted.

Heywood, Thomas. *An Apology for Actors.* 1612. Introductory notes by J. W. Binns. New York: Johnson Reprint Company Ltd., 1972.

Hibbard, George R. "The Chronology of the Three Substantive Texts of Shakespeare's *Hamlet*" in *The Hamlet First Published (Q1, 1603): Origins, Form, Intertextualities,* ed. Thomas Clayton. Newark: University of Delaware Press, 1992, 79–89.

(ed.), *Hamlet,* The Oxford Shakespeare. Oxford University Press, 1987.

Hillebrand, H. N. *The Child Actors: A Chapter in Elizabethan Stage History.* Champagne, IL: University of Illinois Press, 1926.

Hinman, Charlton (ed.), *The Norton* Facsimile: *The First Folio of Shakespeare.* New York: W. W. Norton, 1968.

Honigmann, E. A. J. "The Date of *Hamlet*." *Shakespeare Survey* 9 (1955): 24–34.

Honigmann, E. A. J., and Susan Brock (eds.), *Playhouse Wills, 1558–1642: An Edition of Wills by Shakespeare and his Contemporaries in the London Theatre*, The Revels Plays Companion Library. Manchester University Press, 1993.

Hotson, Leslie. "The Adventure of the Single Rapier." *Atlantic Monthly* 148 (1931): 26–31.

Hoy, Cyrus. *Introductions, Notes, and Commentaries to Texts in 'The Dramatic Works of Thomas Dekker'* Edited by Fredson Bowers, 4 vols. Cambridge University Press, 1980. Notes on *Satiromastix* are in vol. 1.

Hunter, G. K. (ed.), *Antonio and Mellida*, Regents Renaissance Drama Series. Lincoln: University of Nebraska Press, 1965.

(ed.), *Antonio's Revenge*. Regents Renaissance Drama Series. Lincoln: University of Nebraska Press, 1965.

Ingram, William. *The Business of Playing*. Ithaca, NY: Cornell University Press, 1992.

"The Economics of Playing" in *A Companion to Shakespeare*, ed. David Scott Kastan. Oxford: Blackwell, 1999, 313–27.

"The Globe Playhouse and its Neighbors in 1600." *Essays in Theatre* 2 (1984): 63–72.

"Inside *and* Outside in Tudor London: How Useful a Category is 'Stage Player'?" Paper presented at the Midwest Conference on British Studies, Ann Arbor, MI, 1995.

A London Life in the Brazen Age: Francis Langley, 1548–1602. Cambridge, MA: Harvard University Press, 1978.

"'Neere the Playe Howse': The Swan Theater and Community Blight." *Renaissance Drama* n. s. 4 (1971): 53–72.

"What kind of future for the theatrical past: Or, What will count as theater history in the next millennium?" *Shakespeare Quarterly* 48 (1997): 215–25.

Ioppolo, Grace. *Revising Shakespeare*. Cambridge, MA: Harvard University Press, 1991.

Jenkins, Harold (ed.), *Hamlet*, The Arden Shakespeare. London: Methuen, 1982.

Johnson, Gerald. "Nicholas Ling, Publisher 1580–1607." *Studies in Bibliography* 38 (1985): 203–216.

Johnston, Alexandra F., and Margaret Rogerson (eds.), *York*, 2 vols., Records of Early English Drama. University of Toronto Press, 1979.

Kathman, David J. "Edward Pudsey," *Dictionary of National Biography*. *A Biographical Index to the Elizabethan Theater*. Available at http://www.clark.net/pub/tross/ws/bd/kathman.htm.

Kay, W. David. *Ben Jonson: A Literary Life*. Macmillan Literary Lives. Basingstoke, Hampshire: Macmillan, 1995.

"The Shaping of Ben Jonson's Career: A Reexamination of Facts and Problems." *Modern Philology* 67 (1969–70): 224–37.

Kernan, Alvin. "John Marston's Play *Histriomastix.*" *Modern Language Quarterly* 19 (1958): 134–40.

King, T. J. *Casting Shakespeare's Plays: London Actors and their Roles, 1590–1642.* Cambridge University Press, 1992.

Kliman, Bernice W., and Paul Bertram (eds.), *The Three-Text Hamlet*, AMS Studies in the Renaissance, no. 30. New York: AMS Press, 1991.

Knapp, Jeffrey. "Elizabethan Tobacco." *Representations* 21 (1988): 22–66.

Knutson, Roslyn L. "Evidence for the Assignment of Plays to the Repertory of Shakespeare's Company." *Medieval and Renaissance Drama in England* 4 (1989): 63–89.

"*Histrio-Mastix*: Not by John Marston." *Studies in Philology* (2001).

"Marlowe Reruns," in *Marlowe's* Empery, eds. Sara Munson Deats and Robert A. Logan. Newark, DE: University of Delaware, forthcoming.

The Repertory of Shakespeare's Company, 1594–1613. Fayetteville, AR: University of Arkansas Press, 1991.

Lake, D. J. "*Histriomastix*: Linguistic Evidence for Authorship." *Notes and Queries* c. s. 226 (1981): 148–52.

Langbaine, Gerard. *An Account of the English Dramatick Poets.* Oxford: Printed by L. L. for George West and Henry Clements, 1691.

Leishman, J. B. (ed.), *The Three Parnassus Plays (1598–1601).* London: Ivor Nicholson and Watson, Ltd, 1949.

Lennam, Trevor. "The Children of Paul's, 1551–1582" in *Elizabethan Theatre* ii, ed. David Galloway. Hamden, CN: Archon Books, 1980, 20–36.

Loewenstein, Joseph. "Plays Agonistic and Competitive: The Textual Approach to Elsinore." *Renaissance Drama* 19 (1988): 63–96.

Maguire, Laurie E. *Shakespearean Suspect Texts: The "Bad" Quartos and Their Contexts.* Cambridge and New York: Cambridge University Press, 1996.

Malone, Edmond (ed.), *The Plays and Poems of William Shakespeare*, 10 vols. London: Rivington, 1790.

Malone, Edmond, and James Boswell (eds.), *The Plays and Poems of William Shakespeare*, 21 vols. London: Rivington, 1821.

Mann, David. "Sir Oliver Owlet's Men: Fact or Fiction." *Huntington Library Quarterly* 54 (1991): 301–11.

Marsh, Bower (ed.), *Records of the Worshipful Company of Carpenters*, 7 vols. Oxford University Press, 1915. (vol. vii)

Martin, Peter. *Edmond Malone, Shakespearean Scholar.* Cambridge University Press, 1995.

Mason, John Monck. *Comments on the Last Edition of Shakespeare's Plays.* London: C. Dilly, 1785.

Maus, Katharine Eisaman. *Ben Jonson and the Roman Frame of Mind.* Princeton University Press, 1984.

McLuskie, Kathleen E., and Felicity Dunsworth. "Patronage and the Economics of Theater," in *A New History of Early English Drama*, eds. John D. Cox and David Scott Kastan. New York: Columbia University Press, 1997, 423–40.

McMillin, Scott. "Building Stories: Greg, Fleay, and the Plot of *2 Seven Deadly Sins.*" *Medieval and Renaissance Drama in England* 4 (1989): 53–62.

"Casting for Pembroke's Men: The *Henry VI* Quartos and *The Taming of A Shrew.*" *Shakespeare Quarterly* 23 (1972): 141–59.

"Casting the *Hamlet* Quartos: The Limit of Eleven," in *The Hamlet First Published (Q1, 1603): Origins, Form, Intertextualities,* ed. Thomas Clayton. Newark: University of Delaware Press, 1992, 179–94.

The Elizabethan Theatre and The Book of Sir Thomas More. Ithaca: Cornell University Press, 1987.

"The Plots of *The Dead Man's Fortune* and *2 Seven Deadly Sins*: Inferences for Theatre Historians." *Studies in Bibliography* 26 (1973): 235–43.

"Simon Jewell and the Queen's Men." *Review of English Studies* n. s. 27 (1976): 174–77.

"Sussex's Men in 1594: The Evidence of *Titus Andronicus* and *The Jew of Malta.*" *Theatre Survey* 32 (1991): 214–23.

McMillin, Scott, and Sally-Beth MacLean. *The Queen's Men and their Plays.* Cambridge University Press, 1998.

Moore-Smith, George C. (ed.), *Fucus Histriomastix (by Robert Ward).* Cambridge University Press, 1909.

Morley, Henry (ed.), *Plays and Poems by Ben Jonson,* 3rd edn. London: George Routledge and Sons, Ltd., 1890.

Mowat, Barbara A. "The Form of *Hamlet*'s Fortunes." *Renaissance Drama* n. s. 19 (1988): 97–126.

Mullaney, Steven. *The Place of the Stage: License, Play, and Power in Renaissance England.* University of Chicago Press, 1988.

Nelson, Alan H. (ed.), *Cambridge,* 2 vols., Records of Early English Drama. University of Toronto Press, 1988.

Nungezer, Edwin. *A Dictionary of Actors* (1929). New York: Greenwood Press, 1968.

Parkes, Richard. "*An Apologie: of Three Testimonies of Holy Scripture.*" STC 19295, 1607.

Pearlman, E. "Ben Jonson: An Anatomy." *English Literary Renaissance* 9 (1979): 364–94.

Penniman, Josiah H. *The War of the Theatres* (1897). New York: AMS Press, 1970.

Pinciss, G. M. "Thomas Creede and the Repertory of the Queen's Men, 1583–1592." *Modern Philology* 67 (1970): 321–30.

Pollard, Alfred W. *Shakespeare Folios and Quartos: A Study in the Bibliography of Shakespeare's Plays 1594–1685* (1909). New York: Cooper Square Publishers, Inc., 1970.

Shakespeare's Fight with the Pirates and the Problems of the Transmission of his Text (1917). Haskell House, 1974.

Pope, Alexander (ed.), *The Works of Mr. William Shakespear,* 6 vols. London: Tonson, 1725.

Pudsey, Edward. "Commonplace Book." Bodleian Library. MS Eng. Poet. D. 3.

Rann, Joseph (ed.), *The Dramatic Works of Shakspeare*, 6 vols. Oxford: Clarendon Press, 1786.

Reibetanz, John. "Hieronimo in Decimosexto: A Private-Theater Burlesque." *Renaissance Drama* n. s. 5 (1972): 89–121.

Riggs, David. *Ben Jonson: A Life*. Cambridge, MA: Harvard University Press, 1989.

Ringler, William A. Jr. "The Number of Actors in Shakespeare's Early Plays" in *The Seventeenth-Century Stage: A Collection of Critical Essays*, ed. G. E. Bentley. University of Chicago Press, 1968, 110–34.

Robbins, Larry M. (ed.), *Thomas Dekker's* A Knights Conjuring *(1607): A Critical Edition*. The Hague: Mouton, 1974.

Rollin, Roger B. "The Anxiety of Identification: Jonson and the Rival Poets" in *Classic and Cavalier: Essays on Jonson and the Sons of Ben*, ed. Claude J. Summers and Ted-Larry Pebworth. University of Pittsburgh Press, 1982, 139–54.

Rostenberg, Leona. *Literary, Political, Scientific, Religious & Legal Publishing, Printing & Bookselling in England, 1551–1700: Twelve Studies*. New York: Burt Franklin, 1965.

Rowe, George E. *Distinguishing Jonson*. Lincoln, NB: University of Nebraska Press, 1988.

Rowe, Nicholas (ed.), *The Works of Mr. William Shakespear*, 6 vols. London: Tonson, 1709.

Rutter, Carol C. (ed.), *Documents of the Rose Playhouse*, The Revels Companion Library. Manchester University Press, 1984.

Savage, Richard. *Shakespearean Extracts from "Edward Pudsey's Booke."* London: Simpkin and Marshall, 1888.

Sawyer, E. (ed.), *Memorials of Affairs of State in the Reigns of Q. Elizabeth and K. James I*, 3 vols. London: T. Ward, 1725. (vol. II)

Schoenbaum, S. *Internal Evidence and Elizabethan Dramatic Authorship*. Evanston, IL: Northwestern University Press, 1966.

Shaaber, M. A. *Some Forerunners of the Newspaper in England, 1476–1622* (1929). New York: Octagon Books, 1966.

Shapiro, James. *Rival Playwrights: Marlowe, Jonson, Shakespeare*. New York: Columbia University Press, 1991.

"*The Scot's Tragedy* and the Politics of Popular Drama." *English Literary Renaissance* 23 (1993): 428–49.

Shapiro, Michael. *Children of the Revels: The Boy Companies of Shakespeare's Time and their Plays*. New York: Columbia University Press, 1977.

Sharpe, Robert B. *The Real War of the Theaters: Shakespeare's Fellows in Rivalry with the Admiral's Men, 1594–1603*. Boston: D. C. Heath, 1935.

Shepherd, R. H. (ed.), *The Dramatic Works of Thomas Dekker*, 4 vols. London: Pearson, 1873.

Simpson, Richard (ed.), *The School of Shakspere*, 2 vols. New York: J. W. Bouton, 1878.

Sinfield, Alan. "*Poetaster*, the Author, and the Perils of Cultural Production." *Renaissance Drama* 27 (1998): 3–18.

Singer, Samuel Weller (ed.), *The Dramatic Works of Shakspeare*, 6 vols. Chiswick: Charles Whittingham, 1826.

Sisson, Charles J. "Shakespeare Quartos as Prompt-Copies." *Review of English Studies* 18 (1942): 129–43.

Small, Roscoe A. *The Stage Quarrel Between Ben Jonson and the So-Called Poetasters* (1899). New York: AMS Press, 1966.

Smith, Irwin. *Shakespeare's Blackfriars Playhouse*. New York University Press, 1964.

Somerset, J. A. B. "'How chances it they travel?': Provincial Touring, Playing Places, and the King's Men." *Shakespeare Survey* 47 (1994): 45–60.

(ed.), *Shropshire*, 2 vols., Records of Early English Drama. University of Toronto Press, 1994.

Steevens, George (ed.), *The Plays of William Shakespeare*, 2nd edn., 10 vols. London: Bathurst, et al, 1778.

Stokes, James with Robert J. Alexander (eds.), *Somerset including Bath*, 2 vols., Records of Early English Drama. University of Toronto Press, 1996.

Sweeney, John Gordon III. *Jonson and the Psychology of Public Theater*. Princeton University Press, 1985.

Theobald, Lewis. *Shakespeare Restored*. London: R. Franklin, 1726.

(ed.), *The Works of Shakespeare*, 7 vols. London: A. Bettesworth and others, 1733.

Thomson, Peter. *Shakespeare's Professional Career*. Cambridge University Press, 1992.

Tricomi, Albert H. "The Dates of the Plays of George Chapman." *English Literary Renaissance* 12 (1982): 242–66.

Urkowitz, Stephen. "Good News about 'Bad' Quartos" in *"Bad" Shakespeare: Revaluations of the Shakespeare Canon*, ed. Maurice Charney. Rutherford, NJ: Fairleigh Dickinson University Press, 1988, 189–206.

Wallace, Charles W. *The First London Theatre: Materials for a History*. Lincoln, NB: University of Nebraska Press, 1913.

"The Swan Theatre and the Earl of Pembroke's Servants." *Englische Studien* 43 (1911): 430–95.

Weiner, Albert B. (ed.), *Hamlet: The First Quarto 1603*. Great Neck, NY: Barron's Educational Series, Inc., 1962.

Wells, Stanley, Gary Taylor, with John Jowell and William Montgomery. *William Shakespeare: A Textual Companion*. Oxford: Clarendon Press, 1988.

Werstine, Paul. "Narratives About Printed Shakespeare Texts: 'Foul Papers' and 'Bad' Quartos." *Shakespeare Quarterly* 41 (1990): 65–86.

Whalley, Peter (ed.), *The Works of Ben. Jonson*, 7 vols. London: D. Midwinter and others, 1756.

White, Hayden. "The Value of Narrativity in the Representation of Reality" in *The Content of the Form*, ed. Hayden White. Baltimore, MD: Johns Hopkins University Press, 1987, 1–25.

Willet, Andrew. "Limbo-mastix." STC 25692, 1604.

"Loidoromastix: that is, A Scovrge for a Rayler." STC 25693, 1607.

Wilson, John Dover (ed.), *Hamlet*. Cambridge University Press, 1936.

Wood, H. Harvey (ed.), *The Plays of John Marston*, 3 vols. Edinburgh: Oliver and Boyd, 1934.

Yachnin, Paul. *Stage-Wrights: Shakespeare, Jonson, Middleton, and the Making of Theatrical Value*, New Cultural Studies. Philadelphia: University of Pennsylvania Press, 1997.

Index

Adam Bell (possible play subject), 174 n.47
A Larum for London, 69, 70, 162 n.50
Admiral's Men, 2–3, 6, 10, 15, 22, 30, 32, 33, 34–5, 38, 110, 115, 135
  companies playing together, 39–41, 43–5
  competition, cross-company, 19, 36–7, 53–4, 61–3, 67, 101, 123–4
  repertory, 49–52, 52–3, 54, 56–63, 129, 131–3, 138–9, 145, 147
  sale of playbooks, 69–72
  see also rivalry, Admiral's Men vs. Chamberlain's Men
"Agamemnon," 54
"Albere Galles," 52
"Alexander and Lodowick," 45, 138
"Alice Pierce," 157 n.70
All Fools, 98, 129
"All is not Gold that Glisters," 54
All's Well That Ends Well, 71
Allen, Giles, 36
Alleyn, Edward (player), 1–3, 13, 14, 25, 27, 30, 34, 35, 36, 38, 39–40, 41, 65, 68, 154 n.4, 174 n.46
  wife, Joan Woodward Alleyn, 40
Alleyn, John, 1–3, 20, 21, 22, 32, 39, 46, 154 n.4
  see also quarrels, Alleyn–Burbage feud
Alleyn, Richard (player), 30
Alphonsus King of Aragon, 66, 73
Amadis of Gaul (possible play subject), 174 n.47
anger, *see* quarrels
annals, *see* War of the Theatres
Annis a Cleere (possible play subject), 174 n.47
Antonio and Mellida, 56, 81, 134, 145, 162 n.50, 175 n.57
  doubling, 83–96, 86 (chart)
  publication, 69, 70, 72, 162 n.50
Antonio's Revenge, 56, 82, 132, 134, 145, 162 n.50, 175 n.57

doubling, 83–96, 88 (chart), 141
publication, 69, 70, 72, 162 n.50
Apologetical Dialogue, *see Poetaster*
Apology for Actors, 119
"Arcadian Virgin," 54
Archer, Francis (playlist), 76, 171 n.9
Archer, Ian W., 42–3, 47
Armin, Robert (player), 22, 26, 32, 71
"Arraignment of London," *see* "Bellman of London"
"As Merry as May Be," 52
As You Like It, 56, 71, 162 n.50
Atheist's Tragedy, 175 n.57
Attewell, George (player), 30, 61
audiences, 9, 11, 18–9, 55–6, 63, 99–100, 101, 129–30, 140–1, 169 n.63
Augustine, William (player), 27, 32

"bad" quartos, 15, 106–7, 110, 111–12
Barley, William (stationer), 64–5
Barnes, Barnabe, 80
Barroll, J. Leeds, 117, 170 n.76
Bartholomew Fair, 148
Bastard, Thomas, 19, 81
Battle of Alcazar, 68, 100, 102, 132, 138, 160 n.37, 172 n.20, 172 n.21
Beaumont, Francis (playwright), 59, 117, 145
"Bear a Brain," 172 n.18
Beckerman, Bernard, 14, 49, 158 n.6
Bednarz, James P., 17, 171 n.4, 173 n.33, 174 n.52
Beeston, Christopher (player), 3, 14, 25, 26–7, 149, 155 n.24, 176 n.3
Bell Inn (playing place), 31
"Bellendon," 57
"Bellman of London," *also* "Arraignment of London," 55
Belt, T. (player), 25
Bennett, Paul E., 39
Bentley, G. E., 50, 53, 55, 145
Bergeron, David, 153 n.60

188